# Clojure Data Analysis Cookbook

Over 110 recipes to help you dive into the world of practical data analysis using Clojure

Eric Rochester

BIRMINGHAM - MUMBAI

# Clojure Data Analysis Cookbook

Copyright © 2013 Packt Publishing

All rights reserved. No part of this book may be reproduced, stored in a retrieval system, or transmitted in any form or by any means, without the prior written permission of the publisher, except in the case of brief quotations embedded in critical articles or reviews.

Every effort has been made in the preparation of this book to ensure the accuracy of the information presented. However, the information contained in this book is sold without warranty, either express or implied. Neither the author, nor Packt Publishing, and its dealers and distributors will be held liable for any damages caused or alleged to be caused directly or indirectly by this book.

Packt Publishing has endeavored to provide trademark information about all of the companies and products mentioned in this book by the appropriate use of capitals. However, Packt Publishing cannot guarantee the accuracy of this information.

First published: March 2013

Production Reference: 1130313

Published by Packt Publishing Ltd.
Livery Place
35 Livery Street
Birmingham B3 2PB, UK.

ISBN 978-1-78216-264-3

www.packtpub.com

Cover Image by J.Blaminsky (milak6@wp.pl)

# Credits

**Author**
Eric Rochester

**Reviewers**
Jan Borgelin
Thomas A. Faulhaber, Jr.
Charles M. Norton
Miki Tebeka

**Acquisition Editor**
Erol Staveley

**Lead Technical Editor**
Dayan Hyames

**Technical Editors**
Nitee Shetty
Dennis John

**Project Coordinator**
Anugya Khurana

**Proofreaders**
Mario Cecere
Sandra Hopper

**Indexer**
Monica Ajmera Mehta

**Graphics**
Aditi Gajjar

**Production Coordinator**
Nilesh R. Mohite

**Cover Work**
Nilesh R. Mohite

# About the Author

**Eric Rochester** enjoys reading, writing, and spending time with his wife and kids. When he's not doing those things, he programs in a variety of languages and platforms, including websites and systems in Python and libraries for linguistics and statistics in C#. Currently, he's exploring functional programming languages, including Clojure and Haskell. He works at the Scholars' Lab in the library at the University of Virginia, helping humanities professors and graduate students realize their digitally informed research agendas.

> I'd like to thank everyone. My technical reviewers—Jan Borgelin, Tom Faulhaber, Charles Norton, and Miki Tebeka—proved invaluable. Also, thank you to the editorial staff at Packt Publishing. This book is much stronger for all of their feedbacks, and any remaining deficiencies are mine alone.
>
> Thank you to Bethany Nowviskie and Wayne Graham. They've made the Scholars' Lab a great place to work, with interesting projects, as well as space to explore our own interests.
>
> And especially I would like to thank Jackie and Melina. They've been exceptionally patient and supportive while I worked on this project. Without them, it wouldn't be worth it.

# About the Reviewers

**Jan Borgelin** is a technology geek with over 10 years of professional software development experience. Having worked in diverse positions in the field of enterprise software, he currently works as a CEO and Senior Consultant for BA Group Ltd., an IT consultancy based in Finland. For the past 2 years, he has been more actively involved in functional programming and as part of that has become interested in Clojure among other things.

> I would like to thank my family and our employees for tolerating my excitement about the book throughout the review process.

**Thomas A. Faulhaber, Jr.**, is principal of Infolace (www.infolace.com), a San Francisco-based consultancy. Infolace helps clients from startups to global brands turn raw data into information and information into action. Throughout his career, he has developed systems for high-performance TCP/IP, large-scale scientific visualization, energy trading, and many more.

He has been a contributor to, and user of, Clojure and Incanter since their earliest days. The power of Clojure and its ecosystem (of both code and people) is an important "magic bullet" in Tom's practice.

**Charles Norton** has over 25 years of programming experience, ranging from factory automation applications and firmware to network middleware, and is currently a programmer and application specialist for a Greater Boston municipality. He maintains and develops a collection of software applications that support finances, health insurance, and water utility administration. These systems are implemented in several languages, including Clojure.

**Miki Tebeka** has been shipping software for more than 10 years. He has developed a wide variety of products from assemblers and linkers to news trading systems to cloud infrastructures. He currently works at Adconion where he shuffles through more than 6 billion monthly events. In his free time, he is active in several open source communities.

# www.PacktPub.com

## Support files, eBooks, discount offers and more

You might want to visit www.PacktPub.com for support files and downloads related to your book.

Did you know that Packt offers eBook versions of every book published, with PDF and ePub files available? You can upgrade to the eBook version at www.PacktPub.com and as a print book customer, you are entitled to a discount on the eBook copy. Get in touch with us at service@packtpub.com for more details.

At www.PacktPub.com, you can also read a collection of free technical articles, sign up for a range of free newsletters and receive exclusive discounts and offers on Packt books and eBooks.

http://PacktLib.PacktPub.com

Do you need instant solutions to your IT questions? PacktLib is Packt's online digital book library. Here, you can access, read and search across Packt's entire library of books.

### Why Subscribe?

- Fully searchable across every book published by Packt
- Copy and paste, print and bookmark content
- On demand and accessible via web browser

### Free Access for Packt account holders

If you have an account with Packt at www.PacktPub.com, you can use this to access PacktLib today and view nine entirely free books. Simply use your login credentials for immediate access.

# Table of Contents

| | |
|---|---|
| **Preface** | **1** |
| **Chapter 1: Importing Data for Analysis** | **7** |
| Introduction | 7 |
| Creating a new project | 8 |
| Reading CSV data into Incanter datasets | 9 |
| Reading JSON data into Incanter datasets | 11 |
| Reading data from Excel with Incanter | 12 |
| Reading data from JDBC databases | 13 |
| Reading XML data into Incanter datasets | 16 |
| Scraping data from tables in web pages | 19 |
| Scraping textual data from web pages | 23 |
| Reading RDF data | 26 |
| Reading RDF data with SPARQL | 29 |
| Aggregating data from different formats | 34 |
| **Chapter 2: Cleaning and Validating Data** | **41** |
| Introduction | 41 |
| Cleaning data with regular expressions | 42 |
| Maintaining consistency with synonym maps | 44 |
| Identifying and removing duplicate data | 45 |
| Normalizing numbers | 48 |
| Rescaling values | 50 |
| Normalizing dates and times | 51 |
| Lazily processing very large data sets | 54 |
| Sampling from very large data sets | 56 |
| Fixing spelling errors | 57 |
| Parsing custom data formats | 61 |
| Validating data with Valip | 64 |

*Table of Contents*

## Chapter 3: Managing Complexity with Concurrent Programming — 67
  Introduction — 68
  Managing program complexity with STM — 69
  Managing program complexity with agents — 73
  Getting better performance with commute — 75
  Combining agents and STM — 77
  Maintaining consistency with ensure — 79
  Introducing safe side effects into the STM — 82
  Maintaining data consistency with validators — 84
  Tracking processing with watchers — 87
  Debugging concurrent programs with watchers — 90
  Recovering from errors in agents — 91
  Managing input with sized queues — 93

## Chapter 4: Improving Performance with Parallel Programming — 95
  Introduction — 95
  Parallelizing processing with pmap — 96
  Parallelizing processing with Incanter — 100
  Partitioning Monte Carlo simulations for better pmap performance — 102
  Finding the optimal partition size with simulated annealing — 106
  Parallelizing with reducers — 110
  Generating online summary statistics with reducers — 114
  Harnessing your GPU with OpenCL and Calx — 116
  Using type hints — 120
  Benchmarking with Criterium — 123

## Chapter 5: Distributed Data Processing with Cascalog — 127
  Introduction — 128
  Distributed processing with Cascalog and Hadoop — 129
  Querying data with Cascalog — 132
  Distributing data with Apache HDFS — 134
  Parsing CSV files with Cascalog — 137
  Complex queries with Cascalog — 139
  Aggregating data with Cascalog — 142
  Defining new Cascalog operators — 143
  Composing Cascalog queries — 146
  Handling errors in Cascalog workflows — 149
  Transforming data with Cascalog — 151
  Executing Cascalog queries in the Cloud with Pallet — 152

## Chapter 6: Working with Incanter Datasets — 159
  Introduction — 159
  Loading Incanter's sample datasets — 160

| | |
|---|---|
| Loading Clojure data structures into datasets | 161 |
| Viewing datasets interactively with view | 163 |
| Converting datasets to matrices | 164 |
| Using infix formulas in Incanter | 166 |
| Selecting columns with $ | 168 |
| Selecting rows with $ | 170 |
| Filtering datasets with $where | 171 |
| Grouping data with $group-by | 174 |
| Saving datasets to CSV and JSON | 175 |
| Projecting from multiple datasets with $join | 177 |

## Chapter 7: Preparing for and Performing Statistical Data Analysis with Incanter — 181

| | |
|---|---|
| Introduction | 182 |
| Generating summary statistics with $rollup | 182 |
| Differencing variables to show changes | 185 |
| Scaling variables to simplify variable relationships | 186 |
| Working with time series data with Incanter Zoo | 189 |
| Smoothing variables to decrease noise | 192 |
| Validating sample statistics with bootstrapping | 194 |
| Modeling linear relationships | 197 |
| Modeling non-linear relationships | 200 |
| Modeling multimodal Bayesian distributions | 204 |
| Finding data errors with Benford's law | 207 |

## Chapter 8: Working with Mathematica and R — 211

| | |
|---|---|
| Introduction | 212 |
| Setting up Mathematica to talk to Clojuratica for Mac OS X and Linux | 212 |
| Setting up Mathematica to talk to Clojuratica for Windows | 216 |
| Calling Mathematica functions from Clojuratica | 218 |
| Sending matrices to Mathematica from Clojuratica | 219 |
| Evaluating Mathematica scripts from Clojuratica | 220 |
| Creating functions from Mathematica | 221 |
| Processing functions in parallel in Mathematica | 222 |
| Setting up R to talk to Clojure | 224 |
| Calling R functions from Clojure | 226 |
| Passing vectors into R | 227 |
| Evaluating R files from Clojure | 228 |
| Plotting in R from Clojure | 230 |

## Chapter 9: Clustering, Classifying, and Working with Weka — 233
- Introduction — 233
- Loading CSV and ARFF files into Weka — 234
- Filtering and renaming columns in Weka datasets — 236
- Discovering groups of data using K-means clustering — 239
- Finding hierarchical clusters in Weka — 245
- Clustering with SOMs in Incanter — 248
- Classifying data with decision trees — 250
- Classifying data with the Naive Bayesian classifier — 253
- Classifying data with support vector machines — 255
- Finding associations in data with the Apriori algorithm — 258

## Chapter 10: Graphing in Incanter — 261
- Introduction — 261
- Creating scatter plots with Incanter — 262
- Creating bar charts with Incanter — 264
- Graphing non-numeric data in bar charts — 266
- Creating histograms with Incanter — 268
- Creating function plots with Incanter — 270
- Adding equations to Incanter charts — 272
- Adding lines to scatter charts — 273
- Customizing charts with JFreeChart — 276
- Saving Incanter graphs to PNG — 278
- Using PCA to graph multi-dimensional data — 279
- Creating dynamic charts with Incanter — 282

## Chapter 11: Creating Charts for the Web — 285
- Introduction — 285
- Serving data with Ring and Compojure — 286
- Creating HTML with Hiccup — 290
- Setting up to use ClojureScript — 293
- Creating scatter plots with NVD3 — 296
- Creating bar charts with NVD3 — 302
- Creating histograms with NVD3 — 305
- Visualizing graphs with force-directed layouts — 308
- Creating interactive visualizations with D3 — 313

## Index — 317

# Preface

Data's everywhere! And, as it has become more pervasive, our desire to use it has grown just as quickly. A lot hides in data: potential sales, users' browsing patterns, demographic information, and many, many more things. There are insights we could gain and decisions we could make better, if only we could find out what's in our data.

This book will help with that.

The programming language Clojure will help us. Clojure was first released in 2007 by Rich Hickey. It's a member of the lisp family of languages, and it has the strengths and flexibility that they provide. It's also functional, so Clojure programs are easy to reason with. And, it has amazing features for working concurrently and in parallel. All of these can help us as we analyze data while keeping things simple and fast.

Clojure's usefulness for data analysis is further improved by a number of strong libraries. Incanter provides a practical environment for working with data and performing statistical analysis. Cascalog is an easy-to-use wrapper over Hadoop and Cascading. Finally, when we're ready to publish our results, ClojureScript, an implementation of Clojure that generates JavaScript, can help us to visualize our data in an effective and persuasive way.

Moreover, Clojure runs on the **Java Virtual Machine** (**JVM**), so any libraries written for Java are available too. This gives Clojure an incredible amount of breadth and power.

I hope that this book will give you the tools and techniques you need to get answers from your data.

*Preface*

# What this book covers

*Chapter 1*, *Importing Data for Analysis*, will cover how to read data from a variety of sources, including CSV files, web pages, and linked semantic web data.

*Chapter 2*, *Cleaning and Validating Data*, will present strategies and implementations for normalizing dates, fixing spelling, and working with large datasets. Getting data into a useable shape is an important, but often overlooked, stage of data analysis.

*Chapter 3*, *Managing Complexity with Concurrent Programming*, will cover Clojure's concurrency features and how we can use them to simplify our programs.

*Chapter 4*, *Improving Performance with Parallel Programming*, will cover using Clojure's parallel processing capabilities to speed up processing data.

*Chapter 5*, *Distributed Data Processing with Cascalog*, will cover using Cascalog as a wrapper over Hadoop and the Cascading library to process large amounts of data distributed over multiple computers. The final recipe in this chapter will use Pallet to run a simple analysis on Amazon's EC2 service.

*Chapter 6*, *Working with Incanter Datasets*, will cover the basics of working with Incanter datasets. Datasets are the core data structure used by Incanter, and understanding them is necessary to use Incanter effectively.

*Chapter 7*, *Preparing for and Performing Statistical Data Analysis with Incanter*, will cover a variety of statistical processes and tests used in data analysis. Some of these are quite simple, such as generating summary statistics. Others are more complex, such as performing linear regressions and auditing data with Benford's Law.

*Chapter 8*, *Working with Mathematica and R*, will talk about setting up Clojure to talk to Mathematica or R. These are powerful data analysis systems, and sometimes we might want to use them. This chapter will show us how to get these systems to work together, as well as some tasks we can do once they are communicating.

*Chapter 9*, *Clustering, Classifying, and Working with Weka*, will cover more advanced machine learning techniques. In this chapter, we'll primarily use the Weka machine learning library, and some recipes will discuss how to use it and the data structures its built on, while other recipes will demonstrate machine learning algorithms.

*Chapter 10*, *Graphing in Incanter*, will show how to generate graphs and other visualizations in Incanter. These can be important for exploring and learning about your data and also for publishing and presenting your results.

*Chapter 11*, *Creating Charts for the Web*, will show how to set up a simple web application to present findings from data analysis. It will include a number of recipes that leverage the powerful D3 visualization library.

## What you need for this book

One piece of software required for this book is the **Java Development Kit** (**JDK**), which you can get from `http://www.oracle.com/technetwork/java/javase/downloads/index.html`. The JDK is necessary to run and develop on the Java platform.

The other major piece of software that you'll need is **Leiningen 2**, which you can download and install from `https://github.com/technomancy/leiningen`. Leiningen 2 is a tool for managing Clojure projects and their dependencies. It's quickly becoming the de facto standard project tool in the Clojure community.

Throughout this book, we'll use a number of other Clojure and Java libraries, including Clojure itself. Leiningen will take care of downloading these for us as we need them.

You'll also need a text editor or **integrated development environment** (**IDE**). If you already have a text editor that you like, you can probably use it. See `http://dev.clojure.org/display/doc/Getting+Started` for tips and plugins for using your particular favorite environment. If you don't have a preference, I'd suggest looking at using Eclipse with Counterclockwise. There are instructions for getting this set up at `http://dev.clojure.org/display/doc/Getting+Started+with+Eclipse+and+Counterclockwise`.

That is all that's required. However, at various places throughout the book, some recipes will access other software. The recipes in *Chapter 8, Working with Mathematica and R*, that relate to Mathematica will require Mathematica, obviously, and those that relate to R, will require that. However, these programs won't be used in the rest of the book, and whether you're interested in these recipes might depend on whether you already have this software available.

## Who this book is for

This book is for programmers or data scientists who are familiar with Clojure and want to use it in their data analysis processes. This isn't a tutorial on Clojure—there are already a number of excellent introductory books out there—so you'll need to be familiar with the language; however, you don't need to be an expert at it.

Likewise, you don't need to be an expert on data analysis, although you should probably be familiar with its tasks, processes, and techniques. While you might be able to glean enough from these recipes to get started, to be truly effective, you'll want to get a more thorough introduction to this field.

## Conventions

In this book, you will find a number of styles of text that distinguish between different kinds of information. Here are some examples of these styles, and an explanation of their meaning.

Code words in text are shown as follows: " We just need to make sure that the `clojure.string/upper-case` function is available."

A block of code is set as follows:

```
(defn fuzzy=
  "This returns a fuzzy match."
  [a b]
  (let [dist (fuzzy-dist a b)]
    (or (<= dist fuzzy-max-diff)
        (<= (/ dist (min (count a) (count b)))
            fuzzy-percent-diff))))
```

When we wish to draw your attention to a particular part of a code block, the relevant lines or items are set in bold:

```
[ring.middleware.file-info :only (wrap-file-info)]
[ring.middleware.stacktrace :only (wrap-stacktrace)]
[ring.util.response :only (redirect)]
[hiccup core element page]
[hiccup.middleware :only (wrap-base-url)]])
```

Any command-line input or output is written as follows:

```
$ lein cljsbuild auto
Compiling ClojureScript.
Compiling "resources/js/scripts.js" from "src-cljs"...
Successfully compiled "resources/js/script.js" in 4.707129 seconds.
```

**New terms** and **important words** are shown in bold. Words that you see on the screen, in menus or dialog boxes for example, appear in the text like this: "errors are found in the page **Agents and Asynchronous Actions** in the Clojure documentation ".

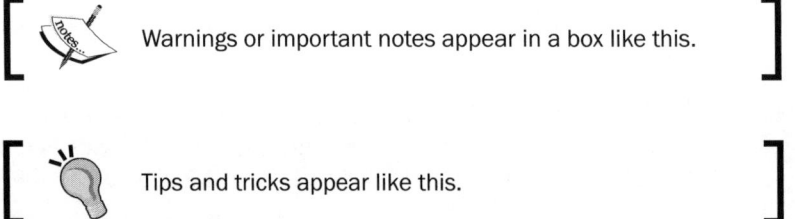

Warnings or important notes appear in a box like this.

Tips and tricks appear like this.

# Reader feedback

Feedback from our readers is always welcome. Let us know what you think about this book—what you liked or may have disliked. Reader feedback is important for us to develop titles that you really get the most out of.

To send us general feedback, simply send an e-mail to `feedback@packtpub.com`, and mention the book title via the subject of your message.

If there is a topic that you have expertise in and you are interested in either writing or contributing to a book, see our author guide on `www.packtpub.com/authors`.

## Customer support

Now that you are the proud owner of a Packt book, we have a number of things to help you to get the most from your purchase.

### Downloading the example code

You can download the example code files for all Packt books you have purchased from your account at `http://www.packtpub.com`. If you purchased this book elsewhere, you can visit `http://www.packtpub.com/support` and register to have the files e-mailed directly to you.

### Errata

Although we have taken every care to ensure the accuracy of our content, mistakes do happen. If you find a mistake in one of our books—maybe a mistake in the text or the code—we would be grateful if you would report this to us. By doing so, you can save other readers from frustration and help us improve subsequent versions of this book. If you find any errata, please report them by visiting `http://www.packtpub.com/submit-errata`, selecting your book, clicking on the **errata submission form** link, and entering the details of your errata. Once your errata are verified, your submission will be accepted and the errata will be uploaded on our website, or added to any list of existing errata, under the Errata section of that title. Any existing errata can be viewed by selecting your title from `http://www.packtpub.com/support`.

### Piracy

Piracy of copyright material on the Internet is an ongoing problem across all media. At Packt, we take the protection of our copyright and licenses very seriously. If you come across any illegal copies of our works, in any form, on the Internet, please provide us with the location address or website name immediately so that we can pursue a remedy.

Please contact us at `copyright@packtpub.com` with a link to the suspected pirated material.

We appreciate your help in protecting our authors, and our ability to bring you valuable content.

### Questions

You can contact us at `questions@packtpub.com` if you are having a problem with any aspect of the book, and we will do our best to address it.

# 1
# Importing Data for Analysis

In this chapter, we will cover:

- Creating a new project
- Reading CSV data into Incanter datasets
- Reading JSON data into Incanter datasets
- Reading data from Excel with Incanter
- Reading data from JDBC databases
- Reading XML data into Incanter datasets
- Scraping data from tables in web pages
- Scraping textual data from web pages
- Reading RDF data
- Reading RDF data with SPARQL
- Aggregating data from different formats

## Introduction

There's not a lot of data analysis that we can do without data, so the first step in any project is evaluating what data we have and what we need. And once we have some idea of what we'll need, we have to figure out how to get it.

Many of the recipes in this chapter and in this book use Incanter (http://incanter.org/) to import the data and target Incanter datasets. **Incanter** is a library for doing statistical analysis and graphics in Clojure, similar to R. Incanter may not be suitable for every task—later we'll use the Weka library for clustering and machine learning—but it is still an important part of our toolkit for doing data analysis in Clojure. This chapter has a collection of recipes for gathering data and making it accessible to Clojure. For the very first recipe, we'll look at how to start a new project. We'll start with very simple formats like comma-separated values (CSV) and move into reading data from relational databases using JDBC. Then we'll examine more complicated data sources, such as web scraping and linked data (RDF).

# Creating a new project

Over the course of this book, we're going to use a number of third-party libraries and external dependencies. We need a tool to download them and track them. We also need a tool to set up the environment and start a **read-eval-print-loop** (**REPL**, or interactive interpreter), which can access our code, or to execute our program.

We'll use **Leiningen** for that (http://leiningen.org/). This has become a standard package automation and management system.

## Getting ready

Visit the Leiningen site (http://leiningen.org/) and download the `lein` script. This will download the Leiningen JAR file. The instructions are clear, and it's a simple process.

## How to do it...

To generate a new project, use the `lein new` command, passing it the name of the project:

```
$ lein new getting-data
Generating a project called getting-data based on the 'default' template.
To see other templates (app, lein plugin, etc), try 'lein help new'.
```

Now, there will be a new subdirectory named `getting-data`. It will contain files with stubs for the `getting-data.core` namespace and for tests.

> **Downloading the example code**
> You can download the example code files for all Packt books you have purchased from your account at http://www.packtpub.com. If you purchased this book elsewhere, you can visit http://www.packtpub.com/support and register to have the files e-mailed directly to you.

## How it works...

The new project directory also contains a file named `project.clj`. This file contains metadata about the project: its name, version, and license. It also contains a list of dependencies that our code will use. The specifications it uses allows it to search Maven repositories and directories of Clojure libraries (Clojars, https://clojars.org/) to download the project's dependencies.

```
(defproject getting-data "0.1.0-SNAPSHOT"
  :description "FIXME: write description"
  :url "http://example.com/FIXME"
  :license {:name "Eclipse Public License"
            :url "http://www.eclipse.org/legal/epl-v10.html"}
  :dependencies [[org.clojure/clojure "1.4.0"]])
```

In the *Getting ready* section of each recipe, we'll see what libraries we need to list in the `:dependencies` section of this file.

# Reading CSV data into Incanter datasets

One of the simplest data formats is comma-separated values (CSV). And it's everywhere. Excel reads and writes CSV directly, as do most databases. And because it's really just plain text, it's easy to generate or access it using any programming language.

## Getting ready

First, let's make sure we have the correct libraries loaded. The project file of Leiningen (https://github.com/technomancy/leiningen), the `project.clj` file, should contain these dependencies (although you may be able to use more up-to-date versions):

```
:dependencies [[org.clojure/clojure "1.4.0"]
               [incanter/incanter-core "1.4.1"]
               [incanter/incanter-io "1.4.1"]]
```

Also, in your REPL or in your file, include these lines:

```
(use 'incanter.core
     'incanter.io)
```

Finally, I have a file named `data/small-sample.csv` that contains the following data:

```
Gomez,Addams,father
Morticia,Addams,mother
Pugsley,Addams,brother
Wednesday,Addams,sister
…
```

*Importing Data for Analysis*

You can download this file from `http://www.ericrochester.com/clj-data-analysis/data/small-sample.csv`. There's a version with a header row at `http://www.ericrochester.com/clj-data-analysis/data/small-sample-header.csv`.

## How to do it...

1. Use the `incanter.io/read-dataset` function:

   ```
   user=> (read-dataset "data/small-sample.csv")
   [:col0 :col1 :col2]
   ["Gomez" "Addams" "father"]
   ["Morticia" "Addams" "mother"]
   ["Pugsley" "Addams" "brother"]
   ["Wednesday" "Addams" "sister"]
   …
   ```

2. If we have a header row in the CSV file, then we include `:header true` in the call to `read-dataset`:

   ```
   user=> (read-dataset "data/small-sample-header.csv" :header true)
   [:given-name :surname :relation]
   ["Gomez" "Addams" "father"]
   ["Morticia" "Addams" "mother"]
   ["Pugsley" "Addams" "brother"]
   ```

## How it works...

Using Clojure and Incanter makes a lot of common tasks easy. This is a good example of that.

We've taken some external data, in this case from a CSV file, and loaded it into an Incanter dataset. In Incanter, a dataset is a table, similar to a sheet in a spreadsheet or a database table. Each column has one field of data, and each row has an observation of data. Some columns will contain string data (all of the columns in this example did), some will contain dates, some numeric data. Incanter tries to detect automatically when a column contains numeric data and coverts it to a Java `int` or `double`. Incanter takes away a lot of the pain of importing data.

## There's more...

If we don't want to involve Incanter—when you don't want the added dependency, for instance—`data.csv` is also simple (`https://github.com/clojure/data.csv`). We'll use this library in later chapters, for example, in the recipe *Lazily processing very large datasets* of *Chapter 2, Cleaning and Validating Data*.

## See also

▶ Chapter 6, *Working with Incanter Datasets*

## Reading JSON data into Incanter datasets

Another data format that's becoming increasingly popular is **JavaScript Object Notation** (**JSON**, http://json.org/). Like CSV, this is a plain-text format, so it's easy for programs to work with. It provides more information about the data than CSV does, but at the cost of being more verbose. It also allows the data to be structured in more complicated ways, such as hierarchies or sequences of hierarchies.

Because JSON is a much fuller data model than CSV, we may need to transform the data. In that case, we can pull out just the information we're interested in and flatten the nested maps before we pass it to Incanter. In this recipe, however, we'll just work with fairly simple data structures.

## Getting ready

First, include these dependencies in the Leiningen `project.clj` file:

```
:dependencies [[org.clojure/clojure "1.4.0"]
               [incanter/incanter-core "1.4.1"]
               [org.clojure/data.json "0.2.1"]]
```

Use these libraries in our REPL interpreter or in our program:

```
(use 'incanter.core
     'clojure.data.json)
```

And have some data. For this, I have a file named `data/small-sample.json` that looks like the following:

```
[{"given_name": "Gomez",
  "surname": "Addams",
  "relation": "father"},
 {"given_name": "Morticia",
  "surname": "Addams",
  "relation": "mother"}, ...
]
```

You can download this data file from http://www.ericrochester.com/clj-data-analysis/data/small-sample.json.

*Importing Data for Analysis*

## How to do it...

Once everything's in place, this is just a one-liner, which we can execute at the REPL interpreter:

```
user=> (to-dataset (read-json (slurp "data/small-sample.json")))
[:given_name :surname :relation]
["Gomez" "Addams" "father"]
["Morticia" "Addams" "mother"]
["Pugsley" "Addams" "brother"]
...
```

## How it works...

Like all Lisps, Clojure is usually read from inside out, from right to left. Let's break it down. `clojure.core/slurp` reads in the contents of the file and returns it as a string. This is obviously a bad idea for very large files, but for small ones it's handy. `clojure.data.json/read-json` takes the data from `slurp`, parses it as JSON, and returns native Clojure data structures. In this case, it returns a vector of maps. `maps.incanter.core/to-dataset` takes a sequence of maps and returns an Incanter dataset. This will use the keys in the maps as column names and will convert the data values into a matrix. Actually, `to-dataset` can accept many different data structures. Try `(doc to-dataset)` in the REPL interpreter or see the Incanter documentation at `http://data-sorcery.org/contents/` for more information.

# Reading data from Excel with Incanter

We've seen how Incanter makes a lot of common data-processing tasks very simple; reading an Excel spreadsheet is another example of this.

## Getting ready

First, make sure that our Leiningen `project.clj` file contains the right dependencies:

```
:dependencies [[org.clojure/clojure "1.4.0"]
               [incanter/incanter-core "1.4.1"]
               [incanter/incanter-excel "1.4.1"]]
```

Also, make sure that we've loaded those packages into the REPL interpreter or script:

```
(use 'incanter.core
     'incanter.excel)
```

And find the Excel spreadsheet we want to work on. I've named mine `data/small-sample-header.xls`. You can download this from `http://www.ericrochester.com/clj-data-analysis/data/small-sample-header.xls`.

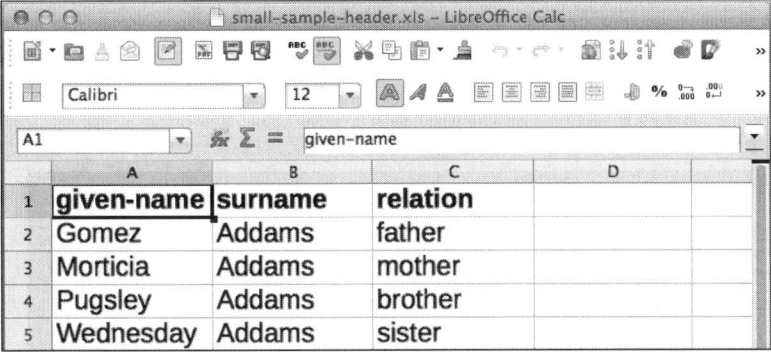

### How to do it...

Now, all we need to do is call `incanter.excel/read-xls`:

```
user=> (read-xls "data/small-sample-header.xls")
["given-name" "surname" "relation"]
["Gomez" "Addams" "father"]
["Morticia" "Addams" "mother"]
["Pugsley" "Addams" "brother"]
...
```

# Reading data from JDBC databases

Reading data from a relational database is only slightly more complicated than reading from Excel. And much of the extra complication is involved in connecting to the database.

Fortunately, there's a Clojure-contributed package that sits on top of JDBC and makes working with databases much easier. In this example, we'll load a table from an SQLite database (`http://www.sqlite.org/`).

### Getting ready

First, list the dependencies in our Leiningen `project.clj` file. We also need to include the database driver library. For this example that's `org.xerial/sqlite-jdbc`.

```
:dependencies [[org.clojure/clojure "1.4.0"]
               [incanter/incanter-core "1.4.1"]
```

*Importing Data for Analysis*

```
[org.clojure/java.jdbc "0.2.3"]
[org.xerial/sqlite-jdbc "3.7.2"]]
```

Then load the modules into our REPL interpreter or script file:

```
(use '[clojure.java.jdbc :exclude (resultset-seq)]
     'incanter.core)
```

Finally, get the database connection information. I have my data in a SQLite database file named `data/small-sample.sqlite`. You can download this from `http://www.ericrochester.com/clj-data-analysis/data/small-sample.sqlite`.

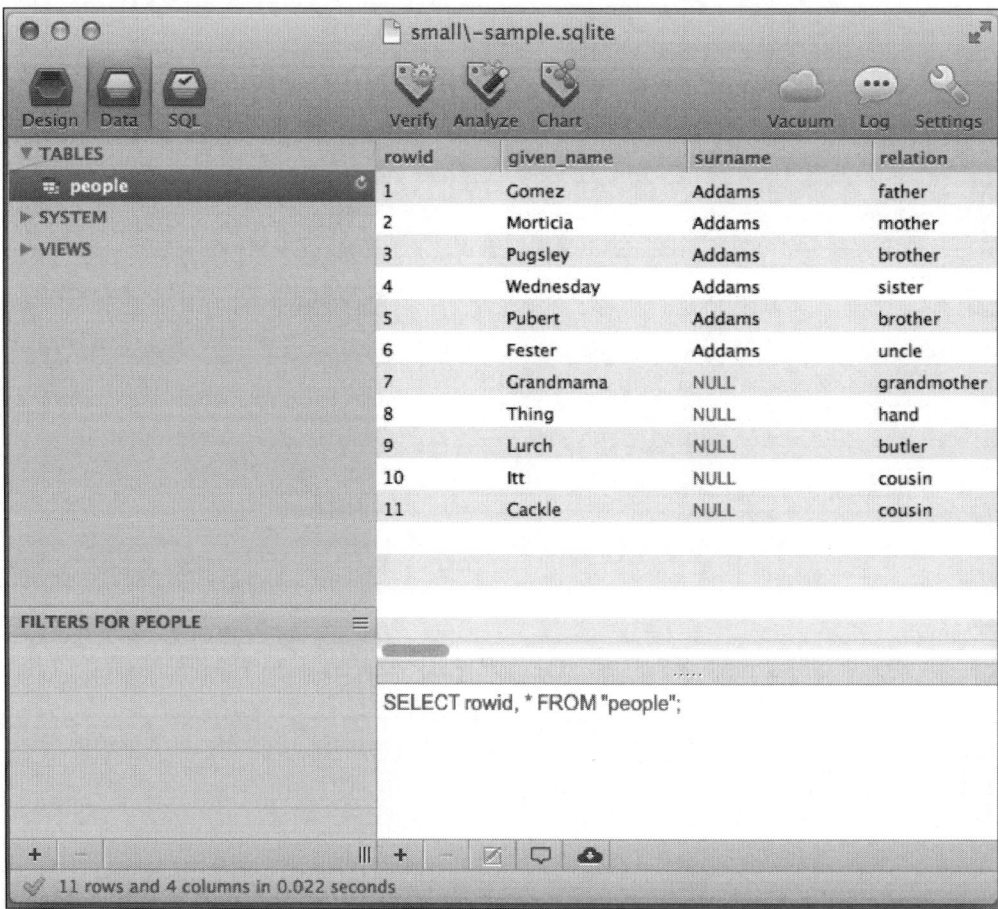

## How to do it...

Loading the data is not complicated, but we'll make it even easier with a wrapper function.

1. Create a function that takes a database connection map and a table name and returns a dataset created from that table:

   ```
   (defn load-table-data
     "This loads the data from a database table."
     [db table-name]
     (let [sql (str "SELECT * FROM "
                    table-name ";")]
       (with-connection db
         (with-query-results rs [sql]
           (to-dataset (doall rs))))))
   ```

2. Next, define a database map with the connection parameters suitable for our database:

   ```
   (def db {:subprotocol "sqlite"
            :subname "data/small-sample.sqlite"
            :classname "org.sqlite.JDBC"})
   ```

3. Finally, call `load-table-data` with `db` and a table name as a symbol or string:

   ```
   user=> (load-table-data db 'people)
   [:relation :surname :given_name]
   ["father" "Addams" "Gomez"]
   ["mother" "Addams" "Morticia"]
   ["brother" "Addams" "Pugsley"]
   ...
   ```

## How it works...

The `load-table-data` function sets up a database connection using `clojure.java.jdbc/with-connection`. It creates a SQL query that queries all the fields of the table passed in. It then retrieves the results using `clojure.java.jdbc/with-query-results`. Each result row is a sequence of maps of column names to values. This sequence is wrapped in a dataset by `incanter.core/to-dataset`.

*Importing Data for Analysis*

## See also

Connecting to different database systems using JDBC isn't necessarily a difficult task, but it's very dependent on what database we wish to connect to. Oracle has a tutorial for working with JDBC at `http://docs.oracle.com/javase/tutorial/jdbc/basics/`, and the documentation for the `clojure.java.jdbc` library has some good information also (`http://clojure.github.com/java.jdbc/`). If you're trying to find out what the connection string looks like for a database system, there are lists online. This one, `http://www.java2s.com/Tutorial/Java/0340__Database/AListofJDBCDriversconnectionstringdrivername.htm`, includes the major drivers.

# Reading XML data into Incanter datasets

One of the most popular formats for data is XML. Some people love it, some hate it. But almost everyone has to deal with it at some point. Clojure can use Java's XML libraries, but it also has its own package, which provides a more natural way of working with XML in Clojure.

## Getting ready

First, include these dependencies in our Leiningen `project.clj` file:

```
:dependencies [[org.clojure/clojure "1.4.0"]
               [incanter/incanter-core "1.4.1"]]
```

Use these libraries in our REPL interpreter or program:

```
(use 'incanter.core
     'clojure.xml
     '[clojure.zip :exclude [next replace remove]])
```

And find a data file. I have a file named `data/small-sample.xml` that looks like the following:

```
<?xml version="1.0" encoding="utf-8"?>
<data>
  <person>
    <given-name>Gomez</given-name>
    <surname>Addams</surname>
    <relation>father</relation>
  </person>
  ...
```

You can download this data file from `http://www.ericrochester.com/clj-data-analysis/data/small-sample.xml`.

## How to do it...

1. The solution for this recipe is a little more complicated, so we'll wrap it into a function:

   ```
   (defn load-xml-data [xml-file first-data next-data]
     (let [data-map (fn [node]
                      [(:tag node) (first (:content node))])]
       (->>
         ;; 1. Parse the XML data file;
         (parse xml-file)
         xml-zip
         ;; 2. Walk it to extract the data nodes;
         first-data
         (iterate next-data)
         (take-while #(not (nil? %)))
         (map children)
         ;; 3. Convert them into a sequence of maps; and
         (map #(mapcat data-map %))
         (map #(apply array-map %))
         ;; 4. Finally convert that into an Incanter dataset
         to-dataset)))
   ```

2. Which we call in the following manner:

   ```
   user=> (load-xml-data "data/small-sample.xml" down right)
   [:given-name :surname :relation]
   ["Gomez" "Addams" "father"]
   ["Morticia" "Addams" "mother"]
   ["Pugsley" "Addams" "brother"]
   ...
   ```

## How it works...

This recipe follows a typical pipeline for working with XML:

1. It parses an XML data file.
2. It walks it to extract the data nodes.
3. It converts them into a sequence of maps representing the data.
4. And finally, it converts that into an Incanter dataset.

`load-xml-data` implements this process. It takes three parameters. The input file name, a function that takes the root node of the parsed XML and returns the first data node, and a function that takes a data node and returns the next data node or `nil`, if there are no more nodes.

*Importing Data for Analysis*

First, the function parses the XML file and wraps it in a **zipper** (we'll discuss more about zippers in a later section). Then it uses the two functions passed in to extract all the data nodes as a sequence. For each data node, it gets its child nodes and converts them into a series of tag-name/content pairs. The pairs for each data node are converted into a map, and the sequence of maps is converted into an Incanter dataset.

## There's more...

We used a couple of interesting data structures or constructs in this recipe. Both are common in functional programming or Lisp, but neither has made their way into more mainstream programming. We should spend a minute with them.

### Navigating structures with zippers

The first thing that happens to the parsed XML file is it gets passed to `clojure.zip/xml-zip`. This takes Clojure's native XML data structure and turns it into something that can be navigated quickly using commands such as `clojure.zip/down` and `clojure.zip/right`. Being a functional programming language, Clojure prefers immutable data structures; and zippers provide an efficient, natural way to navigate and modify a tree-like structure, such as an XML document.

Zippers are very useful and interesting, and understanding them can help you understand how to work with immutable data structures. For more information on zippers, the Clojure-doc page for this is helpful (`http://clojure-doc.org/articles/tutorials/parsing_xml_with_zippers.html`). But if you rather like diving into the deep end, see Gerard Huet's paper, *The Zipper* (`http://www.st.cs.uni-saarland.de/edu/seminare/2005/advanced-fp/docs/huet-zipper.pdf`).

### Processing in a pipeline

Also, we've used the `->>` macro to express our process as a pipeline. For deeply nested function calls, this macro lets us read it from right to left, and this makes the process's data flow and series of transformations much more clear.

We can do this in Clojure because of its macro system. `->>` simply rewrites the calls into Clojure's native, nested format, as the form is read. The first parameter to the macro is inserted into the next expression as the last parameter. That structure is inserted into the third expression as the last parameter and so on, until the end of the form. Let's trace this through a few steps. Say we start off with the `(->> x first (map length) (apply +))` expression. The following is a list of each intermediate step that occurs as Clojure builds the final expression (the elements to be combined are highlighted at each stage):

1. `(->> x first (map length) (apply +))`
2. `(->> (first x) (map length) (apply +))`
3. `(->> (map length (first x)) (apply +))`
4. `(apply + (map length (first x)))`

## Comparing XML and JSON

XML and JSON (from the *Reading JSON data into Incanter datasets* recipe) are very similar. Arguably, much of the popularity of JSON is driven by disillusionment with XML's verboseness.

When we're dealing with these formats in Clojure, the biggest difference is that JSON is converted directly to native Clojure data structures that mirror the data, such as maps and vectors. XML, meanwhile, is read into record types that reflect the structure of XML, not the structure of the data.

In other words, the keys of the maps for JSON will come from the domain, `first_name` or `age`, for instance. However, the keys of the maps for XML will come from the data format, **tag**, **attribute**, or **children**, say, and the tag and attribute names will come from the domain. This extra level of abstraction makes XML more unwieldy.

# Scraping data from tables in web pages

There's data everywhere on the Internet. Unfortunately, a lot of it is difficult to get to. It's buried in tables, or articles, or deeply nested div tags. Web scraping is brittle and laborious, but it's often the only way to free this data so we can use it in our analyses. This recipe describes how to load a web page and dig down into its contents so you can pull the data out.

To do this, we're going to use the Enlive library (https://github.com/cgrand/enlive/wiki). This uses a **domain-specific language** (**DSL**) based on CSS selectors for locating elements within a web page. This library can also be used for templating. In this case, we'll just use it to get data back out of a web page.

## Getting ready

First we have to add Enlive to the dependencies of the project:

```
:dependencies [[org.clojure/clojure "1.4.0"]
               [incanter/incanter-core "1.4.1"]
               [enlive "1.0.1"]]
```

Next, we use those packages in our REPL interpreter or script:

```
(require '(clojure [string :as string]))
(require '(net.cgrand [enlive-html :as html]))
(use 'incanter.core)
(import [java.net URL])
```

*Importing Data for Analysis*

Finally, identify the file to scrape the data from. I've put up a file at `http://www.ericrochester.com/clj-data-analysis/data/small-sample-table.html`, which looks like the following:

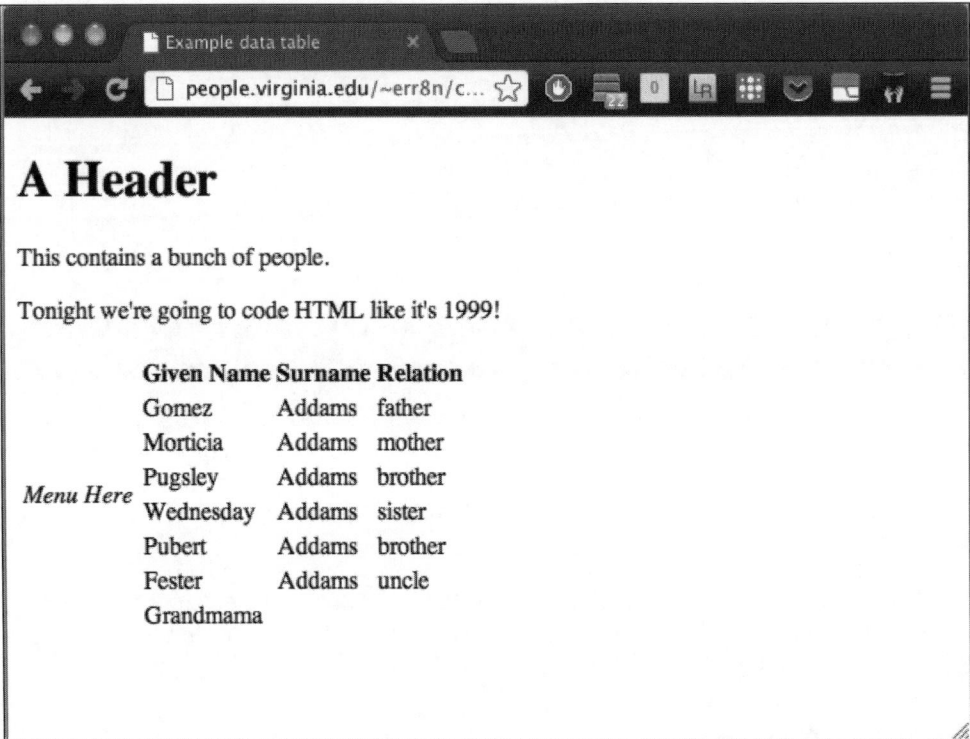

It's intentionally stripped down, and it makes use of tables for layout (hence the comment about 1999).

## How to do it...

1. Since this task is a little complicated, let's pull the steps out into several functions:

   ```
   (defn to-keyword
     "This takes a string and returns a normalized keyword."
     [input]
     (-> input
       string/lower-case
       (string/replace \space \-)
       keyword))

   (defn load-data
   ```

```
        "This loads the data from a table at a URL."
        [url]
        (let [html (html/html-resource (URL. url))
              table (html/select html [:table#data])
              headers (->>
                        (html/select table [:tr :th])
                        (map html/text)
                        (map to-keyword)
                        vec)
              rows (->> (html/select table [:tr])
                        (map #(html/select % [:td]))
                        (map #(map html/text %))
                        (filter seq))]
          (dataset headers rows)))
```

2. Now, call `load-data` with the URL you want to load data from:

```
user=> (load-data (str "http://www.ericrochester.com/"
  #_=>    "clj-data-analysis/data/small-sample-table.html "))
[:given-name :surname :relation]
["Gomez" "Addams" "father"]
["Morticia" "Addams" "mother"]
["Pugsley" "Addams" "brother"]
["Wednesday" "Addams" "sister"]
...
```

## How it works...

The `let` bindings in `load-data` tell the story here. Let's take them one by one.

The first binding has Enlive download the resource and parse it into its internal representation:

```
(let [html (html/html-resource (URL. url))
```

The next binding selects the table with the ID `data`:

```
        table (html/select html [:table#data])
```

Now, we select all header cells from the table, extract the text from them, convert each to a keyword, and then the whole sequence into a vector. This gives us our headers for the dataset:

```
        headers (->>
                  (html/select table [:tr :th])
                  (map html/text)
                  (map to-keyword)
                  vec)
```

*Importing Data for Analysis*

We first select each row individually. The next two steps are wrapped in `map` so that the cells in each row stay grouped together. In those steps, we select the data cells in each row and extract the text from each. And lastly, we filter using `seq`, which removes any rows with no data, such as the header row:

```
rows (->> (html/select table [:tr])
          (map #(html/select % [:td]))
          (map #(map html/text %))
          (filter seq))]
```

Here is another view of this data. In the following screenshot, we can see some of the code from this web page. The variable names and the select expressions are placed beside the HTML structures that they match. Hopefully, this makes it more clear how the select expressions correspond to the HTML elements.

```
<td><em>Menu Here</em></td>
<td>
  <!-- Here's the data. -->     table [:table#data]
  <table id="data" border="0">
    <tr><th>Given Name</th> <th>Surname</th> <th>Relation</th></tr>      headers [:tr :th]
    <tr><td>Gomez</td> <td>Addams</td> <td>father</td></tr>
    <tr><td>Morticia</td> <td>Addams</td> <td>mother</td></tr>           rows [:tr] > [:td]
    <tr><td>Pugsley</td> <td>Addams</td> <td>brother</td></tr>
    <tr><td>Wednesday</td> <td>Addams</td> <td>sister</td></tr>
    <tr><td>Pubert</td> <td>Addams</td> <td>brother</td></tr>
```

Finally, we convert everything to a dataset. `incanter.core/dataset` is a lower-level constructor than `incanter.core/to-dataset`. It requires us to pass in the column names and data matrix as separate sequences:

```
(dataset headers rows)))
```

It's important to realize that the code, as presented here, is the result of a lot of trial and error. Screen scraping usually is. Generally I download the page and save it, so I don't have to keep requesting it from the web server. Then I start REPL and parse the web page there. Then, I can look at the web page and HTML with the browser's "view source" functionality, and I can examine the data from the web page interactively in the REPL interpreter. While working, I copy and paste the code back and forth between the REPL interpreter and my text editor, as it's convenient. This workflow and environment makes screen scraping—a fiddly, difficult task even when all goes well—almost enjoyable.

### See also

- The *Scraping textual data from web pages* recipe
- The *Aggregating data from different formats* recipe

## Scraping textual data from web pages

Not all of the data in the web are in tables. In general, the process to access this non-tabular data may be more complicated, depending on how the page is structured.

### Getting ready

First, we'll use the same dependencies and `require` statements as we did in the last recipe.

Next, we'll identify the file to scrape the data from. I've put up a file at http://www.ericrochester.com/clj-data-analysis/data/small-sample-list.html.

This is a much more modern example of a web page. Instead of using tables, it marks up the text with the `section` and `article` tags and other features of HTML5.

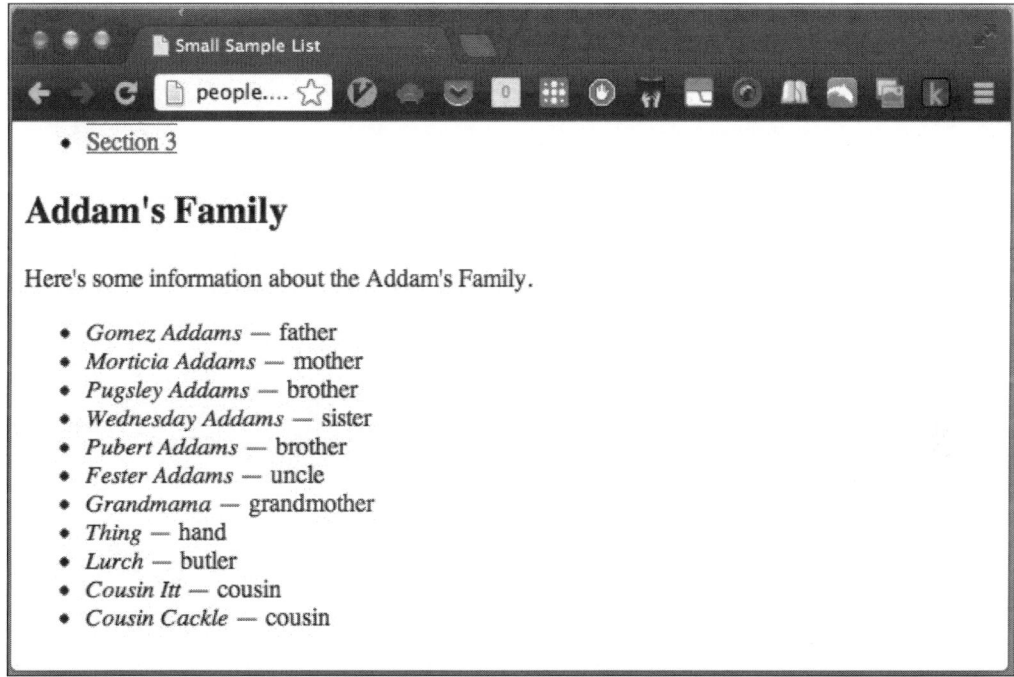

*Importing Data for Analysis*

## How to do it...

1. Since this is more complicated, we'll break the task down into a set of smaller functions.

   ```
   (defn get-family
     "This takes an article element and returns the family name."
     ([article]
      (string/join
        (map html/text (html/select article [:header :h2])))))

   (defn get-person
     "This takes a list item and returns a map of the persons' name
     and relationship."
     ([li]
      (let [[{pnames :content} rel] (:content li)]
        {:name (apply str pnames)
         :relationship (string/trim rel)})))

   (defn get-rows
     "This takes an article and returns the person mappings, with
     the family name added."
     ([article]
      (let [family (get-family article)]
        (map #(assoc % :family family)
             (map get-person
                  (html/select article [:ul :li]))))))

   (defn load-data
     "This downloads the HTML page and pulls the data out of it."
     [html-url]
     (let [html (html/html-resource (URL. html-url))
           articles (html/select html [:article])]
       (to-dataset (mapcat get-rows articles))))
   ```

2. Now that those are defined, we just call `load-data` with the URL that we want to scrape.

   ```
   user=> (load-data (str "http://www.ericrochester.com/"
     #_=>                 "clj-data-analysis/data/small-sample-list.html
   "))
   [:family :name :relationship]
   ["Addam's Family" "Gomez Addams" "— father"]
   ["Addam's Family" "Morticia Addams" "— mother"]
   ["Addam's Family" "Pugsley Addams" "— brother"]
   ["Addam's Family" "Wednesday Addams" "— sister"]
   ...
   ```

## How it works...

After examining the web page, we find that each family is wrapped in an `article` tag that contains a header with an `h2` tag. `get-family` pulls that tag out and returns its text.

`get-person` processes each person. The people in each family are in an unordered list (`ul`) and each person is in an `li` tag. The person's name itself is in an `em` tag. The `let` gets the contents of the `li` tag and decomposes it in order to pull out the name and relationship strings. `get-person` puts both pieces of information into a map and returns it.

`get-rows` processes each `article` tag. It calls `get-family` to get that information from the header, gets the list item for each person, calls `get-person` on that list item, and adds the family to each person's mapping.

Here's how the HTML structures correspond to the functions that process them. Each function name is beside the element it parses:

```
<article>
  <header>
    <h2 id='addams'>Addam's Family</h2>   get-family
  </header>
  <p>Here's some information about the Addam's Family.</p>
  <ul>
    <li><em>Gomez Addams</em> &mdash; father</li>
    <li><em>Morticia Addams</em> &mdash; mother</li>    get-rows
    <li><em>Pugsley Addams</em> &mdash; brother</li>
    <li><em>Wednesday Addams</em> &mdash; sister</li>
    <li><em>Pubert Addams</em> &mdash; brother</li>
    <li><em>Fester Addams</em> &mdash; uncle</li>
    <li><em>Grandmama</em> &mdash; grandmother</li>
    <li><em>Thing</em> &mdash; hand</li>
    <li><em>Lurch</em> &mdash; butler</li>
    <li><em>Cousin Itt</em> &mdash; cousin</li>
    <li><em>Cousin Cackle</em> &mdash; cousin</li>
  </ul>                         get-person
</article>
```

Finally, `load-data` ties the process together by downloading and parsing the HTML file and pulling the `article` tags from it. It then calls `get-rows` to create the data mappings, and converts the output to a dataset.

*Importing Data for Analysis*

# Reading RDF data

More and more data is going up on the Internet using linked data in a variety of formats: microformats, RDFa, and RDF/XML are a few common ones. Linked data adds a lot of flexibility and power, but it also introduces more complexity. Often, to work effectively with linked data, we'll need to start a triple store of some kind. In this recipe and the next three, we'll use Sesame (http://www.openrdf.org/) and the kr Clojure library (https://github.com/drlivingston/kr).

## Getting ready

First, we need to make sure the dependencies are listed in our `project.clj` file:

```
:dependencies [[org.clojure/clojure "1.4.0"]
               [incanter/incanter-core "1.4.1"]
               [edu.ucdenver.ccp/kr-sesame-core "1.4.5"]
               [org.clojure/tools.logging "0.2.4"]
               [org.slf4j/slf4j-simple "1.7.2"]]
```

And we'll execute this to have these loaded into our script or REPL:

```
(use 'incanter.core
     'edu.ucdenver.ccp.kr.kb
     'edu.ucdenver.ccp.kr.rdf
     'edu.ucdenver.ccp.kr.sparql
     'edu.ucdenver.ccp.kr.sesame.kb
     'clojure.set)
(import [java.io File])
```

For this example, we'll get data from the Telegraphis Linked Data assets. We'll pull down the database of currencies at http://telegraphis.net/data/currencies/currencies.ttl. Just to be safe, I've downloaded that file and saved it as `data/currencies.ttl`, and we'll access it from there.

## How to do it...

The longest part of this process will be defining the data. The libraries we're using do all the heavy lifting.

1. First, we will create the triple store and register the namespaces that the data uses. We'll bind that triple store to the name `tstore`.

   ```
   (defn kb-memstore
     "This creates a Sesame triple store in memory."
     []
   ```

```
      (kb :sesame-mem))
(def tele-ont "http://telegraphis.net/ontology/")
(defn init-kb
  "This creates an in-memory knowledge base and
  initializes it with a default set of namespaces."
  [kb-store]
  (register-namespaces
    kb-store
    '(("geographis" (str tele-ont
                         "geography/geography#"))
      ("code" (str tele-ont "measurement/code#"))
      ("money" (str tele-ont "money/money#"))
      ("owl" "http://www.w3.org/2002/07/owl#")
      ("rdf" (str "http://www.w3.org/"
                  "1999/02/22-rdf-syntax-ns#"))
      ("xsd" "http://www.w3.org/2001/XMLSchema#")
      ("currency" (str  "http://telegraphis.net/"
                        "data/currencies/"))
      ("dbpedia" "http://dbpedia.org/resource/")
      ("dbpedia-ont" "http://dbpedia.org/ontology/")
      ("dbpedia-prop" "http://dbpedia.org/property/")
      ("err" "http://ericrochester.com/"))))

(def tstore (init-kb (kb-memstore)))
```

2. After looking at some more data, we can identify what data we want to pull out and start to formulate a query. We'll use kr's query DSL and bind it to the name q:

```
(def q '((?/c rdf/type money/Currency)
         (?/c money/name ?/full_name)
         (?/c money/shortName ?/name)
         (?/c money/symbol ?/symbol)
         (?/c money/minorName ?/minor_name)
         (?/c money/minorExponent ?/minor_exp)
         (?/c money/isoAlpha ?/iso)
         (?/c money/currencyOf ?/country)))
```

3. Now we need a function that takes a result map and converts the variable names in the query into column names in the output dataset. The header-keyword and fix-headers functions will do that:

```
(defn header-keyword
  "This converts a query symbol to a keyword."
  [header-symbol]
  (keyword (.replace (name header-symbol) \_ \-)))
(defn fix-headers
```

*Importing Data for Analysis*

```
    "This changes all the keys in the map to make them
    valid header keywords."
    [coll]
    (into {}
        (map (fn [[k v]] [(header-keyword k) v])
             coll)))
```

4. As usual, once all the pieces are in place, the function that ties everything together is short:

```
(defn load-data
  [k rdf-file q]
  (load-rdf-file k rdf-file)
  (to-dataset (map fix-headers (query k q))))
```

5. And using this function is just as simple:

```
user=> (load-data t-store (File. "data/currencies.xml") q)
[:symbol :country :name :minor-exp :iso :minor-name :fullname]
["!.ع" http://telegraphis.net/data/countries/AE#AE "dirham" "2"
"AED" "fils" "United Arab Emirates dirham"]
["؋" http://telegraphis.net/data/countries/AF#AF "afghani" "2"
"AFN" "pul" "Afghan afghani"]
...
```

## How it works...

First, some background: **Resource Description Format** (**RDF**) isn't an XML format, although it's often written using XML (there are other formats as well, such as N3 and Turtle). RDF sees the world as a set of statements. Each statement has at least three parts (a triple): the **subject**, the **predicate**, and the **object**. The subject and the predicate have to be URIs. (URIs are like URLs, only more general. uri:7890 is a valid URI, for instance.) Objects can be a literal or a URI. The URIs form a graph. They link to each other and make statements about each other. This is where the linked-in linked data comes from.

If you want more information about linked data, `http://linkeddata.org/guides-and-tutorials` has some good recommendations.

Now about our recipe: From a high level, the process we used here is pretty simple:

1. Create the triple store (`kb-memstore` and `init-kb`).
2. Load the data (`load-data`).
3. Query it to pull out only what we want (`q` and `load-data`).
4. Transform it into a format Incanter can ingest easily (`rekey` and `col-map`).
5. Create the Incanter dataset (`load-data`).

The newest thing here is the query format. `kb` uses a nice SPARQL-like DSL to express the queries. In fact, it's so easy to use that we'll deal with it instead of working with raw RDF. The items starting with `?/` are variables; these will be used as keys for the result maps. The other items look like `rdf-namespace/value`. The namespace is taken from the registered namespaces defined in `init-kb`. These are different from Clojure's namespaces, although they serve a similar function for your data: to partition and provide context.

## See also

- The *Reading RDF data with SPARQL* recipe
- The *Aggregating data from different formats* recipe

## Reading RDF data with SPARQL

For the previous recipe, the **embedded domain-specific language** (**EDSL**) used for the query gets converted to SPARQL, the query language for many linked data systems. If you squint just right at the query, it looks kind of like a SPARQL `WHERE` clause. It's a simple query, but one nevertheless.

And this worked great when we had access to the raw data in our own triple store. However, if we need to access a remote SPARQL end-point directly, it's more complicated.

For this recipe, we'll query DBPedia (`http://dbpedia.org`) for information about the United Arab Emirates' currency, the **dirham**. DBPedia extracts structured information from Wikipedia (the summary boxes) and re-publishes it as RDF. Just as Wikipedia is a useful first-stop for humans to get information about something, DBPedia is a good starting point for computer programs gathering data about a domain.

### Getting ready

First, we need to make sure the dependencies are listed in our `project.clj` file:

```
:dependencies [[org.clojure/clojure "1.4.0"]
               [incanter/incanter-core "1.4.1"]
               [edu.ucdenver.ccp/kr-sesame-core "1.4.5"]
               [org.clojure/tools.logging "0.2.4"]
               [org.slf4j/slf4j-simple "1.7.2"]]
```

Then, load the Clojure and Java libraries that we'll use.

```
(require '(clojure.java [io :as io]))
(require '(clojure [xml :as xml]
                   [pprint :as pp]
                   [zip :as zip]))
```

*Importing Data for Analysis*

```
(use 'incanter.core
     '[clojure.set :only (rename-keys)]
     'edu.ucdenver.ccp.kr.kb
     'edu.ucdenver.ccp.kr.rdf
     'edu.ucdenver.ccp.kr.sparql
     'edu.ucdenver.ccp.kr.sesame.kb)
(import [java.io File]
        [java.net URL URLEncoder])
```

## How to do it...

As we work through this, we'll define a series of functions. Finally, we'll create one function, `load-data`, to orchestrate everything, and we'll finish by calling it.

1. We have to create a Sesame triple store and initialize it with the namespaces that we'll use. For both of these we'll use the `kb-memstore` and `init-kb` functions that we discussed in the previous recipe. We define a function that takes a URI for a subject in the triple store and constructs a SPARQL query that returns at most 200 statements about that. It filters out any statements with non-English strings for objects, but it allows everything else through:

   ```
   (defn make-query
     "This creates a query that returns all the
     triples related to a subject URI. It does
     filter out non-English strings."
     ([subject kb]
      (binding [*kb* kb
                *select-limit* 200]
        (sparql-select-query
         (list '(~subject ?/p ?/o)
               '(:or (:not (:isLiteral ?/o))
                     (!= (:datatype ?/o) rdf/langString)
                     (= (:lang ?/o) ["en"])))))))
   ```

2. Now that we have the query, we'll need to encode it into a URL to retrieve the results:

   ```
   (defn make-query-uri
     "This constructs a URI for the query."
     ([base-uri query]
      (URL. (str base-uri
                 "?format="
                 (URLEncoder/encode "text/xml")
                 "&query=" (URLEncoder/encode query)))))
   ```

3. Once we get a result, we'll parse the XML file, wrap it in a zipper, and navigate to the first result. All this will be in a function that we'll write in a minute. Right now, the next function will take that first result node and return a list of all of the results:

   ```
   (defn result-seq
     "This takes the first result and returns a sequence
     of this node, plus all the nodes to the right of it."
     ([first-result]
      (cons (zip/node first-result)
            (zip/rights first-result))))
   ```

4. The following set of functions takes each result node and returns a key-value pair (`result-to-kv`). It uses `binding-str` to pull the results out of the XML file. Then `accum-hash` function pushes those key-value pairs into a map. Keys that occur more than once have their values accumulated in a vector.

   ```
   (defn binding-str
     "This takes a binding, pulls out the first tag's
     content, and concatenates it into a string."
     ([b]
      (apply str (:content (first (:content b))))))

   (defn result-to-kv
     "This takes a result node and creates a key-value
     vector pair from it."
     ([r]
      (let [[p o] (:content r)]
        [(binding-str p) (binding-str o)])))

   (defn accum-hash
     "This takes a map and key-value vector pair and adds
     the pair to the map. If the key is already in the
     map, the current value is converted to a vector and
     the new value is added to it."
     ([m [k v]]
      (if-let [current (m k)]
        (assoc m k (conj current v))
        (assoc m k [v]))))
   ```

5. For the last utility function, we'll define `rekey`. This will convert the keys of a map based on another map:

   ```
   (defn rekey
     "This just flips the arguments for
     clojure.set/rename-keys to make it more
     convenient."
     ([k-map map]
      (rename-keys
        (select-keys map (keys k-map)) k-map)))
   ```

*Importing Data for Analysis*

6. Now, let's add a function that takes a SPARQL endpoint and a subject, and returns a sequence of result nodes. This will use several of the functions we've just defined.

   ```
   (defn query-sparql-results
     "This queries a SPARQL endpoint and returns a
     sequence of result nodes."
     ([sparql-uri subject kb]
      (->>
        kb
        ;; Build the URI query string.
        (make-query subject)
        (make-query-uri sparql-uri)
        ;; Get the results, parse the XML,
        ;; and return the zipper.
        io/input-stream
        xml/parse
        zip/xml-zip
        ;; Find the first child.
        zip/down
        zip/right
        zip/down
        ;; Convert all children into a sequence.
        result-seq)))
   ```

7. Finally, we can pull everything together. Here's `load-data`:

   ```
   (defn load-data
     "This loads the data about a currency for the
     given URI."
     [sparql-uri subject col-map]
     (->>
       ;; Initialize the triple store.
       (kb-memstore)
       init-kb
       ;; Get the results.
       (query-sparql-results sparql-uri subject)
       ;; Generate a mapping.
       (map result-to-kv)
       (reduce accum-hash {})
       ;; Translate the keys in the map.
       (rekey col-map)
       ;; And create a dataset.
       to-dataset))
   ```

8. Now let's use it. We can define a set of variables to make it easier to reference the namespaces that we'll use. We'll use them to create a mapping to column names:

   ```
   (def rdfs "http://www.w3.org/2000/01/rdf-schema#")
   (def dbpedia "http://dbpedia.org/resource/")
   (def dbpedia-ont "http://dbpedia.org/ontology/")
   (def dbpedia-prop "http://dbpedia.org/property/")

   (def col-map {(str rdfs 'label) :name,
                 (str dbpedia-prop 'usingCountries) :country
                 (str dbpedia-prop 'peggedWith) :pegged-with
                 (str dbpedia-prop 'symbol) :symbol
                 (str dbpedia-prop 'usedBanknotes) :used-banknotes
                 (str dbpedia-prop 'usedCoins) :used-coins
                 (str dbpedia-prop 'inflationRate) :inflation})
   ```

9. We call `load-data` with the DBPedia SPARQL endpoint, the resource we want information about (as a symbol), and the column map:

   ```
   user=> (load-data "http://dbpedia.org/sparql"
     #_=>    (symbol (str dbpedia "/United_Arab_Emirates_dirham"))
     #_=>    col-map)
   [:used-coins :symbol :pegged-with :country :inflation :name :used-banknotes]
   ["2550" "!.ב" "U.S. dollar = 3.6725 dirhams" "United Arab Emirates" "14" "United Arab Emirates dirham" "9223372036854775807"]
   ```

## How it works...

The only part of this recipe that has to do with SPARQL, really, is the function `make-query`. It uses the function `sparql-select-query` to generate a SPARQL query string from the query pattern. This pattern has to be interpreted in the context of the triple store that has the namespaces defined. This context is set using the `binding` command. We can see how this function works by calling it from the REPL by itself:

```
user=> (println
  #_=>    (make-query
  #_=>       (symbol (str dbpedia "/United_Arab_Emirates_dirham"))
  #_=>       (init-kb (kb-memstore))))
PREFIX rdf: <http://www.w3.org/1999/02/22-rdf-syntax-ns#>
SELECT ?p ?o
WHERE {   <http://dbpedia.org/resource/United_Arab_Emirates_dirham> ?p ?o .
  FILTER (  ( ! isLiteral(?o)
```

```
      ||  (  datatype(?o)  !=      <http://www.w3.org/1999/02/22-rdf-
syntax-ns#langString> )
      ||  (  lang(?o)   = "en"  )  )
      )
} LIMIT 200
```

The rest of the recipe is concerned with parsing the XML format of the results, and in many ways it's similar to the last recipe.

## See also

- The *Reading RDF data* recipe

# Aggregating data from different formats

Being able to aggregate data from many linked data sources is nice, but most data isn't already formatted for the semantic web. Fortunately, linked data's flexible and dynamic data model facilitates integrating data from multiple sources.

For this recipe, we'll combine several previous ones. We'll load currency data from RDF, as we did in the *Reading RDF data* recipe, and we'll scrape exchange rate data from X-Rates (http://www.x-rates.com) to get information out of a table, just as we did in the *Scraping data from tables in web pages* recipe. Finally, we'll dump everything into a triple store and pull it back out, as we did in the last recipe.

## Getting ready

First, make sure your `project.clj` file has the right dependencies:

```
:dependencies [[org.clojure/clojure "1.4.0"]
               [incanter/incanter-core "1.4.1"]
               [enlive "1.0.1"]
               [edu.ucdenver.ccp/kr-sesame-core "1.4.5"]
               [org.clojure/tools.logging "0.2.4"]
               [org.slf4j/slf4j-simple "1.7.2"]
               [clj-time "0.4.4"]]
```

And we need to declare that we'll use these libraries in our script or REPL:

```
(require '(clojure.java [io :as io]))
(require '(clojure [xml :as xml]
                   [string :as string]
                   [zip :as zip]))
(require '(net.cgrand [enlive-html :as html])
```

```
(use 'incanter.core
     'clj-time.coerce
     '[clj-time.format :only (formatter formatters parse unparse)]
     'edu.ucdenver.ccp.kr.kb
     'edu.ucdenver.ccp.kr.rdf
     'edu.ucdenver.ccp.kr.sparql
     'edu.ucdenver.ccp.kr.sesame.kb)

(import [java.io File]
        [java.net URL URLEncoder])
```

Finally, make sure that you have the file, `data/currencies.ttl`, which we've been using since the *Reading RDF data* recipe.

## How to do it...

Since this is a longer recipe, we'll build it up in segments. At the end, we'll tie everything together.

### Creating the triple store

To begin with, we'll create the triple store. This has become pretty standard. In fact, we'll use the same version of `kb-memstore` and `init-kb` that we've been using from the *Reading RDF data* recipe.

### Scraping exchange rates

1. This is where things get interesting. We'll pull out the timestamp. The first function finds it. The second function normalizes it into a standard format:

```
(defn find-time-stamp
  ([module-content]
   (second
     (map html/text
          (html/select module-content
                       [:span.ratesTimestamp])))))

(def time-stamp-format
     (formatter "MMM dd, yyyy HH:mm 'UTC'"))

(defn normalize-date
  ([date-time]
   (unparse (formatters :date-time)
            (parse time-stamp-format date-time))))
```

2. We'll drill down to get the countries and their exchange rates:

```
(defn find-data
  ([module-content]
    (html/select module-content
                 [:table.tablesorter.ratesTable
                  :tbody :tr])))

(defn td->code
  ([td]
    (let [code (-> td
                   (html/select [:a])
                   first
                   :attrs
                   :href
                   (string/split #"=")
                   last)]
      (symbol "currency" (str code "#" code)))))

(defn get-td-a
  ([td]
    (->> td
      :content
      (mapcat :content)
      string/join
      read-string)))

(defn get-data
  ([row]
    (let [[[td-header td-to td-from]
           (filter map? (:content row))]
      {:currency (td->code td-to)
       :exchange-to (get-td-a td-to)
       :exchange-from (get-td-a td-from)})))
```

3. This function takes the data extracted from the HTML page and generates a list of RDF triples:

```
(defn data->statements
  ([time-stamp data]
    (let [{:keys [currency exchange-to]} data]
      (list [currency 'err/exchangeRate exchange-to]
            [currency 'err/exchangeWith
             'currency/USD#USD]
            [currency 'err/exchangeRateDate
             [time-stamp 'xsd/dateTime]]))))
```

4. And this function ties those two groups of functions together by pulling the data out of the web page, converting it to triples, and adding them to the database:

```
(defn load-exchange-data
  "This downloads the HTML page and pulls the data out
  of it."
  [kb html-url]
  (let [html (html/html-resource html-url)
        div (html/select html [:div.moduleContent])
        time-stamp (normalize-date
                     (find-time-stamp div))]
    (add-statements
      kb
      (mapcat (partial data->statements time-stamp)
              (map get-data (find-data div))))))
```

That's a mouthful, but now that we can get all the data into a triple store, we just need to pull everything back out and into Incanter.

## Loading currency data and tying it all together

Bringing the two data sources together and exporting it to Incanter is fairly easy at this point:

```
(defn aggregate-data
  "This controls the process and returns the aggregated data."
  [kb data-file data-url q col-map]
  (load-rdf-file kb (File. data-file))
  (load-exchange-data kb (URL. data-url))
  (to-dataset (map (partial rekey col-map) (query kb q))))
```

We'll need to do a lot of the setup we've done before. Here we'll bind the triple store, the query, and the column map to names, so that we can refer to them easily:

```
(def t-store (init-kb (kb-memstore)))

(def q
  '((?/c rdf/type money/Currency)
    (?/c money/name ?/name)
    (?/c money/shortName ?/shortName)
    (?/c money/isoAlpha ?/iso)
    (?/c money/minorName ?/minorName)
    (?/c money/minorExponent ?/minorExponent)
    (:optional
      ((?/c err/exchangeRate ?/exchangeRate)
       (?/c err/exchangeWith ?/exchangeWith)
       (?/c err/exchangeRateDate ?/exchangeRateDate)))))
```

*Importing Data for Analysis*

```
(def col-map {'?/name :fullname
              '?/iso :iso
              '?/shortName :name
              '?/minorName :minor-name
              '?/minorExponent :minor-exp
              '?/exchangeRate :exchange-rate
              '?/exchangeWith :exchange-with
              '?/exchangeRateDate :exchange-date})
```

The specific URL that we're going to scrape is `http://www.x-rates.com/table/?from=USD&amount=1.00`. Let's go ahead and put everything together:

```
user=> (aggregate-data t-store "data/currencies.ttl"
  #_ =>          "http://www.x-rates.com/table/?from=USD&amount=1.00"
  #_ =>          q col-map)
[:exchange-date :name :exchange-with :minor-exp :iso :exchange-rate
 :minor-name :fullname]
[#<XMLGregorianCalendarImpl 2012-10-03T10:35:00.000Z> "dirham"
 currency/USD#USD "2" "AED" 3.672981 "fils" "United Arab Emirates
 dirham"]
[nil "afghani" nil "2" "AFN" nil "pul" "Afghan afghani"]
[nil "lek" nil "2" "ALL" nil "qindarkë" "Albanian lek"]
[nil "dram" nil "0" "AMD" nil "luma" "Armenian dram"]
...
```

As you can see, some of the data from `currencies.ttl` doesn't have exchange data (the ones that start with `nil`). We can look in other sources for that, or decide that some of those currencies don't matter for our project.

## How it works...

A lot of this is just a slightly more complicated version of what we've seen before, pulled together into one recipe. The complicated part is scraping the web page, and that's driven by the structure of the page itself.

After looking at the source of the page and playing with it on the REPL the page's structure was clear. First, we needed to pull the timestamp off the top of the table that lists the exchange rates. Then we walked over the table and pulled the data from each row. Both data tables (the short one and the long one) are in a `div` tag with a class `moduleContent`, so everything began there.

Next, we drilled down from the module content into the rows of the `rates` table. Inside each row, we pulled out the currency code and returned it as a symbol in the currency namespace. We also drilled down to the exchange rates and returned them as floats. Then we put everything into a map and converted that to triple vectors, which we added to the triple store.

If you have questions about how we pulled in the main currency data and worked with the triple store, refer to the *Reading RDF data* recipe.

If you have questions about how we scraped the data from the web page, refer to the *Scraping data from tables in web pages* recipe.

If you have questions about the SPARQL query, refer to the *Reading RDF data with SPARQL* recipe.

# 2
# Cleaning and Validating Data

In this chapter, we will cover:

- Cleaning data with regular expressions
- Maintaining consistency with synonym maps
- Identifying and removing duplicate data
- Normalizing numbers
- Rescaling values
- Normalizing dates and times
- Lazily processing very large data sets
- Sampling from very large data sets
- Fixing spelling errors
- Parsing custom data formats
- Validating data with Valip

## Introduction

You probably won't spend as much time getting the data as you will getting it into shape. Raw data is often inconsistent, duplicated, or full of holes. You have to fix it before it's usable.

*Cleaning and Validating Data*

This is often a very iterative, interactive process: If it's a very large dataset, I may create a sample to work with at this stage. Generally, I start by examining the data files. Once I find a problem, I try to code a solution, which I run on the dataset. After each change, I archive the data, either using a ZIP file or—if the data files are small enough—using Git (http://git-scm.com/) or another version control system. Using a version control system is nice, because I can track the code to transform the data along with the data itself, and I can include comments about what I'm doing. Then I look at the data again, and the whole process starts over. Even once I've moved on to analyze the data, I may find more issues or need to change the data somehow to make it easier to analyze, and I'm back in the data cleansing loop once more Clojure is an excellent tool for this kind of work, because the REPL is a great environment for exploring data and fixing it interactively. Also, because many of its sequence functions are lazy by default, Clojure makes it easy to work with a lot of data.

This chapter will highlight a few of the many features Clojure has for cleaning data. Initially, we'll look at regular expressions and some other basic tools. Then, we'll move on to how to normalize specific kinds of values. The next few recipes will turn their attention to process and how to handle very large data sets. Finally, we'll look at some more sophisticated ways of fixing data when we write a simple spell-checker and a custom parser. Finally, the last recipe will introduce a Clojure library that has a nice DSL for writing tests to validate your data.

## Cleaning data with regular expressions

Probably, the most basic and pervasive tool for cleaning data of any kind is regular expressions. Although they're sometimes overused, often regular expressions truly are the best tool for the job. Moreover, Clojure has built-in syntax for compiled regular expressions, so they are convenient too.

In this example, we'll write a function that normalizes US phone numbers.

### Getting ready

For this recipe, we will need to have the `clojure.string` library available for our script or REPL. The expression will be as follows:

```clojure
(require '[clojure.string :as string])
```

### How to do it...

1. For this recipe, let's define the regular expression, using the following:

```clojure
(def phone-regex
  #"(?x)
  (\d{3})      # Area code.
  \D{0,2}      # Separator. Probably one of \(, \), \-,
  \space.
```

```
    (\d{3})       # Prefix.
    \D?           # Separator.
    (\d{4})
    ")
```

2. Now, we'll define a function that uses that regular expression to pull apart a string containing a phone number and put it back together in the form *(999)555-1212*. If the string doesn't appear to be a phone number, it returns nil. This can be done using the following code snippet:

```
(defn clean-us-phone
  [phone]
  (if-let [[_ area-code prefix post]
           (re-find phone-regex phone)]
    (str \( area-code \) prefix \- post)))
```

3. The function works the way we'd expect and we get the following:

```
user=> (clean-us-phone "123-456-7890")"(123)456-7890"
user=> (clean-us-phone "1 2 3 a b c 0 9 8 7")
nil
```

## How it works...

The most complicated part of this is the regular expression. Let's break it down.

- `(?x)`: This is a flag that doesn't match anything itself. Instead, it allows us to spread the regular expression out, and it will ignore whitespace and comments. Writing regular expressions this way makes them considerably easier to read and work with, especially in six months when you try to remember what it does.
- `(\d{3})`: This matches three digits.
- `\D{0,2}`: This matches zero to two non-numeric characters. This is to allow for optional separators between the area code and the prefix.
- `(\d{3})`: This matches another three digits.
- `\D?`: This is an optional non-numeric character. This allows for a dash, for example.
- `(\d{4})`: This is the final four digits of the phone number.

The items in parentheses are captured by the regular expression. If there are no groups in parentheses in the regular expression, `re-find` just returns the matching string. If there are groups, it returns a vector. The entire matching string is the first element, and the groups follow in the order they appear in the regular expression. In this recipe, we use the groups returned to build the output.

*Cleaning and Validating Data*

### There's more...

Regular expressions are complex, and heavy books have been written about them. Here are some more resources:

- The JavaDocs for the Pattern class available at `http://docs.oracle.com/javase/6/docs/api/java/util/regex/Pattern.html`. It summarizes the syntax of Java's style of regular expressions.
- Oracle's Java tutorial on regular expressions available at `http://docs.oracle.com/javase/tutorial/essential/regex/`.
- RegexPlant's online tester available at `http://www.regexplanet.com/advanced/java/index.html`. But the REPL is usually what I use to build and test regular expressions.

### See also...

Jamie Zawinski is credited with saying the following:

> *Some people, when confronted with a problem, think, "I know, I'll use regular expressions." Now they have two problems.*

Regular expressions are a complex, dense, and often fiddly tool. Sometimes they are the right tool, but sometimes not. We'll see a more powerful, and often better, solution in the *Parsing custom data formats* recipe.

## Maintaining consistency with synonym maps

One common problem with data is inconsistency. Sometimes a value is capitalized and sometimes not, sometimes abbreviated and sometimes in full, and sometimes it is misspelled.

When it's an open domain, such as words in a free-text field, the problem can be quite difficult. However, when the data represents a limited vocabulary—like US state names, for our example here—there's a simple trick that can help. A mapping from common forms or mistakes to a normalized form is an easy way to fix variants in a field.

### Getting ready

We just need to make sure that the `clojure.string/upper-case` function is available to us using the following expression:

```
(use '[clojure.string :only (upper-case)])
```

## How to do it...

For this recipe, we'll define the synonym map and a function to use it. Then, we'll see it in action. We'll define the mapping to a normalized form. I don't want to list all states here, but the following code snippet should give you the idea:

```
(def state-synonyms
  {"ALABAMA" "AL",
   "ALASKA" "AK",
   "ARIZONA" "AZ",
   ...
   "WISCONSIN" "WI",
   "WYOMING" "WY"})
```

We'll wrap it in a function that upper-cases the input before querying the mapping.

```
(defn normalize-state
  [state]
  (let [uc-state (upper-case state)]
    (state-synonyms uc-state uc-state)))
```

Then we just call `normalize-state` with the strings we want to fix.

```
user=> (map normalize-state
  #_ =>    ["Alabama" "OR" "Va" "Fla"])
("AL" "OR" "VA" "FL")
```

## How it works...

The only wrinkle here is that we have to normalize the input a little by making sure it's upper case before we can apply the mapping of synonyms to it. Otherwise, we'd also need to have an entry for any possible way that the input could be capitalized.

## See also...

▶ The *Fixing spelling errors* recipe

# Identifying and removing duplicate data

One problem when cleaning up data is what to do with duplicates. How do we find them? What do we do with them once we have them? While some part of this process can be automated, often merging them is a manual task, because a person has to look at potential matches and determine if they are duplicates or not and what to do with the overlapping data. We can code heuristics, of course, but at some point a person may need to make the final call.

*Cleaning and Validating Data*

The first question to answer is what constitutes identity for your data. If you have two items of data, what fields do you have to look at to determine if they are duplicates? And then, how close do they need to be?

For this recipe, we'll examine some data and decide on duplicates by doing a fuzzy comparison of the name fields. We'll simply return all pairs that appear to be duplicates.

## Getting ready

First, we need to add the library to do fuzzy string matching to our Leiningen `project.clj` file using the following instruction:

```
:dependencies [[org.clojure/clojure "1.4.0"]
               [clj-diff "1.0.0-SNAPSHOT"]]
```

And make sure that's available to our script or REPL. This is done using the following instruction:

```
(use 'clj-diff.core)
```

## How to do it...

1. We'll first define a function to test for fuzzy equality. Then, we'll write another function that uses fuzzy equality to test whether two records match. The following are the main parameters for fuzzy string matching. We'll see how we use these later in the recipe.

    ```
    (def fuzzy-max-diff 2)
    (def fuzzy-percent-diff 0.1)
    (def fuzzy-dist edit-distance)
    ```

2. Now, we can define a function that uses those parameters to determine if two strings are equal to each other:

    ```
    (defn fuzzy=
      "This returns a fuzzy match."
      [a b]
      (let [dist (fuzzy-dist a b)]
        (or (<= dist fuzzy-max-diff)
            (<= (/ dist (min (count a) (count b)))
                fuzzy-percent-diff))))
    ```

3. Building on this, we can write a function that determines if two records are the same. It also takes one or more key functions, which return the values that the items should be compared on. This can be done using the following code snippet:

    ```
    (defn records-match
      [key-fn a b]
    ```

```
           (let [kfns (if (sequential? key-fn) key-fn [key-fn])
                 rfn (fn [prev next-fn]
                       (and prev (fuzzy= (next-fn a)
                                         (next-fn b))))]
             (reduce rfn true kfns)))
```

4. These should allow us to test whether two records are approximately equal. Let's create some data to test it out:

   ```
   (def data
     {:mulder  {:given-name "Fox"  :surname "Mulder"}
      :molder  {:given-name "Fox"  :surname "Molder"}
      :mulder2 {:given-name "fox"  :surname "mulder"}
      :scully  {:given-name "Dana" :surname "Scully"}
      :scully2 {:given-name "Dan"  :surname "Scully"}})
   ```

5. Now we can test some of these for "equality" using the following code snippet:

   ```
   user=> (records-match [:given-name :surname]
                         (data :mulder) (data :molder))
   true
   user=> (records-match [:given-name :surname]
                         (data :mulder) (data :mulder2))
   true
   user=> (records-match [:given-name :surname]
                         (data :scully) (data :scully2))
   true
   user=> (records-match [:given-name :surname]
                         (data :mulder) (data :scully))
   false
   ```

## How it works...

The fuzzy string matching function uses several parameters. Let's take a look at each of them individually. The function is as follows:

```
(def fuzzy-dist edit-distance)
```

`fuzzy-dist` is a function that returns a similarity metric for the two strings. Lower numbers indicate that the two strings are more similar. In this case, we're using `clj-diff.core/edit-distance`.

The maximum allowable distance is determined by the following two parameters:

```
(def fuzzy-max-diff 2)
```

*Cleaning and Validating Data*

First, for equality, the distance has to be at most `fuzzy-max-diff`. Setting it to 2 allows for replacements, which are generally two changes (deletion and insertion).

```
(def fuzzy-percent-diff 0.1)
```

Or the maximum distance can be a percentage of the length of the shortest input string. In this case, we're using 10 percent as the maximum difference that the two can be.

If either of these two conditions are met, the strings are determined to be the same. This allows for two cases. No matter what the length of the string is, if only two characters change, it is considered to be the same. This is problematic for very short strings.

On the other hand, a hard maximum distance doesn't work for very long strings, either. If the values are 200 characters or more, say, you'll want to allow more absolute characters of difference than for a string of 20 characters. `fuzzy-percent-diff` provides this flexibility.

### There's more...

As I mentioned, this will not handle short strings very well. For example, it would judge *ace* and *are* to be the same. We could consider making the logic more complicated by adding a clause saying only to use `fuzzy-max-diff` if the length of the string is greater than some value.

In this recipe, we used `clj-diff.core/edit-distance`. This measures the number of changes that need to be made to transform one string into the other with the single-character operations insert and delete. Another option would be to use `clj-diff.core/levenshtein-distance`, which also uses a single-character replace operation.

## Normalizing numbers

If we need to read in numbers as strings, we have to worry about how they're formatted. But we'll probably want the computer to deal with them as *numbers*, not as strings, and that can't happen if the string contains a comma or a period to separate the thousands place.

In this recipe, we'll write a short function that takes a number string and returns the number. The function will strip out all the extra punctuation inside the number, and only leave the last separator: hopefully the one marking the decimal place.

### Getting ready

To write this function, we just need to have access to the `clojure.string` library. We get this access using the following instruction:

```
(require '[clojure.string :as string])
```

## How to do it...

The function itself is pretty short:

```
(defn normalize-number
  [n]
  (let [v (string/split n #"[,.]")
        [pre post] (split-at (dec (count v)) v)]
    (Double/parseDouble (apply str (concat pre [\.] post)))))
```

And using it is also straightforward:

```
user=> (normalize-number "1,000.00")
1000.0
user=> (normalize-number "1.000,00")
1000.0
user=> (normalize-number "3.1415")
3.1415
```

## How it works...

This function is fairly simple, so let's take it apart, step by step:

1. We take the input and use a regular expression to split it on every comma and period. This handles both thousands separators and decimals for most locales, ones that use a comma for thousands and periods for decimals and vice versa.

   ```
   (string/split n #"[,.]")
   ```

2. We take the split input and partition it into the integer part (everything up to the last element) and the fractional part (the last element):

   ```
   (split-at (dec (count v)) v)
   ```

3. We join them back together as a new string, using a period for the decimal and leaving out any thousands separators:

   ```
   (apply str (concat pre [\.] post))
   ```

4. We use the standard Java Double class to parse this into a double:

   ```
   (Double/parseDouble ...)
   ```

This version of the function assumes that the numbers are represented with a decimal component. If that's not the case, there are problems:

```
user=> (normalize-number "1,000")
1.0
```

How would you go about fixing that? It may be easier to have separate versions of this function for integers and floats. In the end, you need to know your data to decide how to handle it best.

*Cleaning and Validating Data*

# Rescaling values

One way to normalize values is to scale frequencies by the size of their groups. For example, say the word *truth* appears three times in a document. That means one thing if the document has 30 words. It means something else if the document has 300 words, or 3,000. And if the dataset has documents of all those lengths, how do we compare the frequencies for words across documents?

The answer is—we rescale the frequency counts. In some cases we could just scale the terms by the length of the documents. Or if we wanted better results, we might use something more complicated like **tf-idf** (**term frequency-inverse document frequency**). Wikipedia has a good overview of this technique at http://en.wikipedia.org/wiki/Tf-idf.

For this recipe, we'll rescale some term frequencies by the total word count for their document.

## Getting ready

We won't need much for this recipe. It will be easier if we have a pretty printer available in the REPL, however. We make use of the following instruction:

```
(require '[clojure.pprint :as pp])
```

## How to do it...

Actually, let's frame this problem more abstractly. If each datum is a map, we can rescale one key (:frequency) by the total of that key's values in the group defined by another key (:document). This is a more general approach, and should be useful in many situations. Refer to the following steps:

1. Let's define a function that rescales by a key's total in a collection. It assigns the scaled value to a new key (dest). This is shown in the following code snippet:

   ```
   (defn rescale-by-total
     [src dest coll]
     (let [total (reduce + (map src coll))
           update (fn [m]
                    (assoc m dest (/ (m src) total)))]
       (map update coll)))
   ```

2. Now let's use that function to define a function to rescale by a group:

   ```
   (defn rescale-by-group
     [src group dest coll]
     (mapcat (partial rescale-by-total src dest)
             (vals (group-by group
                             (sort-by group coll)))))
   ```

3. We can easily make up some data to test this with:

```
(def word-counts
  [{:word 'the, :freq 92, :doc 'a}
   {:word 'a, :freq 76,:doc 'a}
   {:word 'jack, :freq 4,:doc 'a}
   {:word 'the, :freq 3,:doc 'b}
   {:word 'a, :freq 2,:doc 'b}
   {:word 'mary, :freq 1,:doc 'b}])
```

We can finally see how it works:

```
user=> (pprint (rescale-by-group :freq :doc :scaled
word-counts))({:freq 92, :word the, :scaled 23/43, :doc a}
{:freq 76, :word a, :scaled 19/43, :doc a} {:freq 4, :word
jack, :scaled 1/43, :doc a} {:freq 3, :word the, :scaled 1/2,
:doc b} {:freq 2, :word a, :scaled 1/3, :doc b} {:freq 1,
:word mary, :scaled 1/6, :doc b})
 nil
```

We can immediately see that the scaled values are more easily comparable. The scaled frequencies for *the*, for example, are approximately in line with each other in a way the raw frequencies just aren't (0.53 and 0.5 versus 92 and 3). Of course, since this isn't a real dataset, the frequencies are meaningless, but this still does illustrate the method and how it improves the dataset.

## How it works...

For each function, we pass in a couple of keys: a source key and a destination key. The first function, `rescale-by-total`, totals the values for the source key, and then sets the destination key to the ratio of the source key for that item and the total for the source key in all items in the collection.

The second function, `rescale-by-group`, uses another key: the group key. It sorts and groups the items by the group key, and then passes each group to `rescale-by-total`.

# Normalizing dates and times

One difficult issue when normalizing and cleaning up data is dealing with time. People enter dates and times in a bewildering variety of formats, some of them ambiguous. But we have to do our best to interpret them and normalize them into a standard format.

In this recipe, we'll define a function that attempts to parse a date into a standard string format. We'll use the Clojure `clj-time` library, which is a wrapper around the Joda Java library (http://joda-time.sourceforge.net/).

*Cleaning and Validating Data*

## Getting ready

First we need to declare our dependencies in the Leiningen `project.clj` file as shown in the following code snippet:

```
:dependencies [[org.clojure/clojure "1.4.0"]
               [clj-time "0.4.4"]]
```

And, we need to load those into the our script or REPL. This can be done using the following code snippet:

```
(use '[clj-time.core :exclude (extend)]
     '[clj-time.format])
```

## How to do it...

To solve this problem of dealing with time, we'll specify a sequence of date/time formats and walk through them. The first that doesn't throw an exception will be the one we take. Refer to the following steps:

1. Here's a list of formats to try:

    ```
    (def ^:dynamic *default-formats*
      [:date
       :date-hour-minute
       :date-hour-minute-second
       :date-hour-minute-second-ms
       :date-time
       :date-time-no-ms
       :rfc822
       "YYYY-MM-dd HH:mm"
       "YYYY-MM-dd HH:mm:ss"
       "dd/MM/YYYY"
       "YYYY/MM/dd"
       "d MMM YYYY"])
    ```

2. Notice that some of these are keywords and some are strings. Each needs to be handled differently. We'll define a protocol with one method, `->formatter`, that attempts to convert each type to a date formatter, and we'll extend that protocol over both types represented in the format list. This is done using the following code snippet:

    ```
    (defprotocol ToFormatter
      (->formatter [fmt]))

    (extend-protocol ToFormatter
      java.lang.String
      (->formatter [fmt]
    ```

```
      (formatter fmt))

    clojure.lang.Keyword
    (->formatter [fmt] (formatters fmt)))
```

3. Next, `parse-or-nil` will take a format and a date string, attempt to parse the date string, and return `nil` if there are any errors. This is shown in the following code snippet:

```
(defn parse-or-nil
  [fmt date-str]
  (try    (parse (->formatter fmt) date-str)
    (catch Exception ex      nil)))
```

4. With those in place, here is `normalize-datetime`. We just attempt to parse a date string with all of the formats, filter out any `nil` values, and return the first non-nil. Because Clojure is lazy, this will stop processing as soon as one format succeeds. This is shown in the following code snippet:

```
(defn normalize-datetime
  [date-str]
  (first    (remove nil?
             (map #(parse-or-nil % date-str)
                  *default-formats*))))
```

Now, we can try it out using the following:

```
user=> (normalize-datetime "2012-09-12")
#<DateTime 2012-09-12T00:00:00.000Z>
user=> (normalize-datetime "2012/09/12")
#<DateTime 2012-09-12T00:00:00.000Z>
user=> (normalize-datetime "28 Sep 2012")
#<DateTime 2012-09-28T00:00:00.000Z>
user=> (normalize-datetime "2012-09-28 13:45")
#<DateTime 2012-09-28T13:45:00.000Z>
```

## There's more...

This approach to parsing dates has a number of problems. For example, because some date formats are ambiguous, the first match may not be the correct one.

However, trying a list of formats like this is probably about the best we can do. Knowing something about our data allows us to prioritize the list appropriately, and we can augment it with ad-hoc formats as we run across new data. We may also need to normalize data from different sources (for instance, US date formats versus the rest of the world) before we merge the data together.

*Cleaning and Validating Data*

# Lazily processing very large data sets

One of the nice features about Clojure is that most of its sequence processing functions are lazy. This allows us to handle very large datasets with very little effort. However, when combined with reading from files and other IO, there are several things to watch out for.

In this recipe, we'll look at several ways of safely and lazily reading a CSV file. By default, `clojure.data.csv/read-csv` is lazy, so how do we maintain that feature while closing the file at just the right time?

## Getting ready

We need to load the libraries we're going to use into the REPL. This can be done using the following instructions:

```clojure
(require '[clojure.data.csv :as csv]
         '[clojure.java.io :as io])
```

## How to do it...

We'll try several solutions and consider their strengths and weaknesses.

1. We'll try the most straightforward way:

    ```clojure
    (defn lazy-read-bad-1
      [csv-file]
      (with-open [in-file (io/reader csv-file)]
        (csv/read-csv in-file)))
    user=> (lazy-read-bad-1 "data/small-sample.csv")
    IOException Stream closed
      java.io.BufferedReader.
    ensureOpen (BufferedReader.java:97)
    ```

    Oops! At the point the function returns the lazy sequence, it hasn't read any data yet. But when exiting the `with-open` form, the file is closed automatically. What happened?

    First, the file is opened and passed to `read-csv`, which returns a lazy sequence. The lazy sequence is returned from `with-open`, which closes the file. Finally, the REPL tries to print this lazy sequence out. Now, `read-csv` tries to pull data from the file. At this point, however, the file is closed, so the IOException is raised.

    This is a pretty common problem, for the first draft of a function. It especially seems to bite me whenever I'm doing database reads, for some reason.

2. So to fix that, we'll just force all lines to be read:
   ```
   (defn lazy-read-bad-2
     [csv-file]
     (with-open [in-file (io/reader csv-file)]
       (doall     (csv/read-csv in-file))))
   ```
   This one will return data, but everything gets loaded into memory. Now we have safety, but no laziness. Can we get both?

   ```
   (defn lazy-read-ok
     [csv-file]
     (with-open [in-file (io/reader csv-file)]
       (frequencies (map #(nth % 2)
   (csv/read-csv in-file)))))
   ```

   This is one way to do it. Now we've moved what we're going to do to the data into the function that reads it. This works, but has a poor separation of concerns. It is both reading and processing the data, and we really should break those into two functions.

3. Let's try one more time:
   ```
   (defn lazy-read-csv
     [csv-file]
     (let [in-file (io/reader csv-file)
           csv-seq (csv/read-csv in-file)
           lazy (fn lazy [wrapped]
                  (lazy-seq
                    (if-let [s (seq wrapped)]
                      (cons (first s) (lazy (rest s)))
                      (.close in-file))))]
       (lazy csv-seq)))
   ```

This works. Let's see how that happens.

## How it works...

The last version of the function, `lazy-read-csv`, works because it takes the lazy sequence that `csv/read-csv` produces and wraps it in another sequence that closes the input file when there is no more data coming out of the CSV file. This is complicated because we're working with two levels of input: reading from the file and reading CSV. When the higher level (reading CSV) is finished, that triggers an operation on the lower level (reading the file).

However, with this function, we again have a nice, simple interface that we can present to callers, and keep the complexity hidden away.

Unfortunately, this does still have one glaring problem: if we're not going to read the entire file, the file handle won't get closed. For the use case in which only part of the file will be read, `lazy-read-ok` is probably best.

*Cleaning and Validating Data*

# Sampling from very large data sets

One way to deal with very large data sets is to sample them. This can be especially useful when we're first getting started and we want to explore a dataset. A good sample can tell us what's in the full dataset and what we'll need to do to clean and process it.

In this recipe, we'll see a couple of ways of creating samples.

## How to do it...

There are two ways to sample from a stream of values. If we want 10 percent of the larger population, we can just take every tenth item. If we want 1000 out of who-knows-how-many items, the process is a little more complicated.

### Sampling by percentage

Performing a rough sampling by percentage is pretty simple, as shown in the following code snippet:

```
(defn sample-percent
  [k coll]  (filter (fn [_] (<= (rand) k)) coll))
```

Using it is simple also:

```
user=> (sample-percent 0.01 (range 1000))
(141 146 155 292 598 624 629 640 759 815 852 889)
user=> (count *1)
12
```

### Sampling exactly

Sampling for an exact count is a little more complicated. We'll use Donald Knuth's algorithm S from *The Art of Computer Programming, Volume 2*. This takes the sample off the front of the input sequence, and then from that point each new item from the input has a probability of *sample-size / size-of-collection-so-far* to randomly replace one existing item in the sample. To implement this, we'll need one helper function. This takes a map and a new key-value pair. It removes a random key from the map and inserts the new pair, as shown:

```
(defn rand-replace
  [m k v]  (assoc (dissoc m (rand-nth (keys m))) k v))
```

And we'll need another small utility to create an infinite range beginning at a given place:

```
(defn range-from [x] (map (partial + x) (range)))
```

Now we use that to create the function that does the sampling:

```
(defn sample-amount
  [k coll]
```

```
    (->> coll
      (drop k)
      (map vector (range-from (inc k)))
      (filter #(<= (rand) (/ k (first %))))
      (reduce rand-replace
              (into {} (map vector (range k) (take k coll)))))
      (sort-by first)
      (map second)))
```

Using this is as simple as using the first function, though.

```
user=> (sample-amount 10 (range 1000))
(70 246 309 430 460 464 471 547 955 976)
user=> (count *1)
10
```

## How it works...

Sampling by percentage just compares the percentage against a random value for each item in the collection. If the random number is less than the value, it saves the item. Notice, though, that since it's random, the exact number that it pulls out doesn't necessarily exactly match the parameter, 1 percent in this case.

Sampling by a set amount is more complicated. We keep a map of the sample, keyed by each item's position in the original sequence. Originally, we populate this map with the first items off the sequence. Afterwards, we walk through the rest of the collection. At each item, we randomly decide whether to use it or not. If we do use it, we randomly swap it with one item in the sample.

## Fixing spelling errors

One of the issues we'll need to deal with at some point is spelling errors. Especially when you're trying to work with raw text, spelling errors can throw a wrench in the works.

At one time, spell checkers were major pieces of software with lots of optimizations to run in the constrained environments that were once everyday desktops. Now, that's not the case. Peter Norvig has published a piece on the Internet titled, *How to Write a Spelling Corrector* (http://norvig.com/spell-correct.html). It shows how to take some text that is assumed to be spelled correctly and generate a spell checker built on it. He included a 21-line implementation in Python.

For this recipe, we'll convert the Python code to Clojure. Our version will be longer, but less dense. We could certainly implement it shorter than we do, but it will be helpful for our explanation to break it out more.

*Cleaning and Validating Data*

## Getting ready

We need to require `clojure.string` and one function from `clojure.set` shown as follows:

```
(require '[clojure.string :as string])
(use '[clojure.set :only (union)])
```

## How to do it...

1. This algorithm works by comparing a set of permutations of a word against a map of correctly spelled words and their frequencies. The most frequent correct spelling wins. We need a function to tokenize a string into words. We'll use a regular expression for this:

   ```
   (defn words
     [text]
     (re-seq #"[a-z]+" (string/lower-case text)))
   ```

2. The training data structure is just a map of words and their frequencies.

   ```
   (defn train
     [feats] (frequencies feats))
   ```

3. Now we can train our spell checker. We'll use the dataset that Norvig links to in his article (http://norvig.com/big.txt), which I've downloaded locally.

   ```
   (def n-words
       (train (words (slurp "data/big.txt"))))
   (def alphabet
       "abcdefghijklmnopqrstuvwxyz")
   ```

4. We need to define some operations on the words in our training corpus:

   ```
   (defn split-word
     "Split a word into two parts at position i."
     [word I]
     [(.substring word 0 i) (.substring word i)])
   (defn delete-char
     "Delete the first character in the second part."
     [[w1 w2]] (str w1 (.substring w2 1)))
   (defn transpose-split
     "Transpose the first two characters of the second
     part."
     [[w1 w2]]
     (str w1 (second w2) (first w2) (.substring w2 2)))
   (defn replace-split
   ```

```
  "Replace the first character of the second part with
  every letter."
  [[w1 w2]]
  (let [w2-0 (.substring w2 1)]
    (map #(str w1 % w2-0) alphabet)))
(defn insert-split
  "Insert every letter into the word at the split."
  [[w1 w2]] (map #(str w1 % w2) alphabet))
```

5. Now, we're ready to define the two functions that are the heart of the algorithm. The first calculates all the possible edits that can be made to a word, based on the operators we just defined:

```
(defn edits-1
  [word]
  (let [splits (map (partial split-word word)
                    (range (inc (count word))))
        long-splits (filter #(> (count (second %)) 1)
                            splits)
        deletes (map delete-char long-splits)
        transposes (map transpose-split long-splits)
        replaces (mapcat replace-split long-splits)
        inserts (remove nil?
                        (mapcat insert-split
                                splits))]
    (set (concat deletes transposes replaces
                 inserts))))
```

6. And the second primary function gets the edits of a word, but only if they're known in the training set:

```
(defn known-edits-2
  [word]  (set (filter (partial contains? n-words)
               (apply union
                      (map #(edits-1 %)
                           (edits-1 word))))))
```

7. Now we need another utility function that takes a sequence of words and returns the set of those seen in the training corpus:

```
(defn known
  [words]  (set (filter (partial contains? n-words)
                words)))
```

8. Finally, we can put it all together to create the `correct` function:

```
(defn correct
  [word]  (let [candidate-thunks [#(known (list word))
                                  #(known (edits-1 word))
                                  #(known-edits-2 word)
                                  #(list word)]]
    (->>     candidate-thunks
```

*Cleaning and Validating Data*

```
            (map (fn [f] (f)))
            (filter #(> (count %) 0))
            first     (map (fn [w] [(get n-words w 1) w]))
            (reduce (partial max-key first))      second)))
```

Let's see how it works:

```
user=> (correct "deete")
"delete"
user=> (correct "editr")
"editor"
user=> (correct "tranpsose")
"tranpsose"
user=> (correct "eidtor")
"editor"
user=> (correct "eidtr")
"elder"
```

It doesn't recognize transpose, and it mis-corrects `eidtr` as `elder`. Let's look at the training data to see why.

```
user=> (n-words "transpose")
nil
user=> (n-words "elder")
40
user=> (n-words "editor")
17
```

That explains it. `Transpose` doesn't occur in the training set, and `elder` is there more than twice as often as `editor`, so it's the more likely correction.

## How it works...

The heart of this is the `edits-1` and `known-edits-2` functions. They perform a search over the space of strings, looking for all the known words that are one or two edits away from the word to check. Before the operations are applied, the words are split into two by the function `split-word`. The operations that constitute one edit are defined in a series of functions given as follows:

- `delete-char` removes one character from the word (*word* to *wod*)
- `transpose-char` transposes two characters (*word* to *wrod*)
- `replace-split` replaces one letter by another character from the alphabet (*word* to *wobd*)
- `insert-split` inserts a character into the word (*word* to *wobrd*)

The `correct` function looks at all the edits returned that are in the training set and picks the one that was seen most frequently.

## There's more...

If you want more information about the statistics that make this work (and you should—it's quite interesting), see Norvig's explanation in his article (http://norvig.com/spell-correct.html).

# Parsing custom data formats

If you work with data long enough, eventually you'll come across data that you can't find a library for, and you'll need to write your own parser. Some formats may be simple enough for regular expressions, but if you need to balance syntactic structures in the input or do anything too complicated with the output, you're probably better off creating a custom parser. Custom parsers can be slower than regular expressions for very large inputs, but sometimes they're still your best option.

Clojure—and most functional languages—are great for parsing, and many have *parser-combinator* libraries that make writing parsers extremely simple.

For this recipe, as an example of a data format that needs parsing, we'll work with some **FASTA** data (http://en.wikipedia.org/wiki/FASTA_format). FASTA is a file format that's used in bioinformatics to exchange nucleotide and peptide sequences. Of course there are parsers already for this, but it's a simple, yet non-trivial format, which makes a good example case for this recipe.

The first line of FASTA data starts with a > followed by a unique identifier. This line often contains other information about the specimen described, the database it came from, and more. After that line comes one or more lines listing the sequence information. A more detailed explanation of the FASTA format is at http://www.ncbi.nlm.nih.gov/BLAST/blastcgihelp.shtml. An example FASTA record looks like this:

```
>gi|5524211|gb|AAD44166.1| cytochrome b [Elephas maximus maximus]
LCLYTHIGRNIYYGSYLYSETWNTGIMLLLITMATAFMGYVLPWGQMSFWGATVITNLFSAIPY
IGTNLVEWIWGGFSVDKATLNRFFAFHFILPFTMVALAGVHLTFLHETGSNNPLGLTSDSDKIP
FHPYYTIKDFLGLLILILLLLLALLSPDMLGDPDNHMPADPLNTPLHIKPEWYFLFAYAILRS
VPNKLGGVLALFLSIVILGLMPFLHTSKHRSMMLRPLSQALFWTLTMDLLTLTWIGSQPVEYPY
TIIGQMASILYFSIILAFLPIAGXIENY
```

We'll use the parse-ez library (https://github.com/protoflex/parse-ez) to build the parser.

## Cleaning and Validating Data

### Getting ready

We need to make sure that `parse-ez` is listed in our Leiningen `project.clj` file as seen in the following instruction:

```
:dependencies [[org.clojure/clojure "1.4.0"]
               [parse-ez "0.2.0"]]
```

We also need to make it available to our script or REPL using the following instruction:

```
(use 'protoflex.parse)
```

### How to do it...

To define a parser, we just define functions that parse the different parts of the input and then combine them to parse larger structures.

1. We'd like to have a way to parse two things and throw away the results of the second. This function will do that:

   ```
   (defn <|
     [l r]   (let [l-output (l)]    (r)    l-output))
   ```

2. We'll also define a parser for the end of a line. It matches either a carriage return or a newline.

   ```
   (defn nl
     [] (chr-in #{\newline \return}))
   ```

3. Let's start putting the pieces together. The first function parses the sequence definition line by accepting a '>' character followed by anything up to the end of the line:

   ```
   (defn defline
     []   (chr \>)   (<| #(read-to-re #"[\n\r]+") nl))
   ```

4. We parse a sequence of amino- or nucleic acid codes by defining a parser for a single code and then building on that to create a parser for a line of codes:

   ```
   (defn acid-code
     []   (chr-in #{\A \B \C \D \E \F \G \H \I \K \L \M           \N
   \P \Q \R \S \T \U \V \W \X \Y \Z            \- \*}))

   (defn acid-code-line
     [] (<| #(multi+ acid-code) #(attempt nl)))
   ```

5. Next we combine those parsers into one that parses an entire FASTA record and populates a map with our data:

```
(defn fasta
  []
  (ws?)
  (let [dl (defline)
        gls (apply str
                   (flatten (multi+ acid-code-line)))]
    {:defline dl, :gene-seq gls}))
```

6. Finally, we create a wrapper function that passes our parser to parse ez and configures the parsing engine the way we need it to be:

```
(defn parse-fasta
  [input]

  (parse fasta input :eof false :auto-trim false))
```

Now we can use that to parse the example record at the beginning of this recipe:

```
user=> (pprint (parse-fasta test-data))
{:defline
 "gi|5524211|gb|AAD44166.1| cytochrome b
[Elephas maximus maximus]",
 :gene-seq"LCLYTHIGRNIYYGSYLYSETWNTGIMLLL
ITMATAFMGYVLPWGQMSFWGATVITNLFSAIPYIGTNLVEW
IWGGFSVDKATLNRFFAFHFILPFTMVALAGVHLTFLHETGS
NNPLGLTSDSDKIPFHPYYTIKDFLGLLILILLLLLALLSP
DMLGDPDNHMPADPLNTPLHIKPEWYFLFAYAILRSVPNKLG
GVLALFLSIVILGLMPFLHTSKHRSMMLRPLSQALFWTLTMD
LLTLTWIGSQPVEYPYTIIGQMASILYFSIILAFLPIAGXIENY"}
```

## How it works...

At their most abstract level, parsers are functions. They take a string as input and return a data structure. More complex, advanced parsers are built by combining simpler elements.

The <| function is a good example of this. It does not parse anything itself. However, it makes it possible to combine two other parsers in a useful way: it parses both parts, and throws away the result of the second.

The `acid-code` function is an example of creating a parser from a basic component. It matches any of the characters in the set.

`acid-code-line` then combines the `acid-code` parser. It has to match one or more `acid-code` characters, optionally followed by a newline. It uses the `<|` combinator to throw away the newline and return the sequence of `acid-codes`.

This entire parser is built up this way, by composing complex structures from simple parts. While this is a very basic parser, it's possible to create quite complex parsers in this way, leveraging the full power of Clojure while keeping the code readable and maintainable.

## Validating data with Valip

Validating data happens so often, it's good to have a DSL to express the validation rules our data has to pass. This makes the rules easier to create, understand, and maintain.

Valip (`https://github.com/weavejester/valip`) provides this. It's aimed at validating input from web forms, so it expects to validate maps with string values. We'll need to work around that expectation a time or two, but it isn't difficult.

### Getting ready

We need to make sure the Valip library is in our Leiningen `project.clj` file. This can be done using the following code snippet:

```
:dependencies [[org.clojure/clojure "1.4.0"]
               [valip "0.2.0"]]
```

And, we need to load it into our script or REPL. This can be done using the following code snippet:

```
(use 'valip.core
     'valip.predicates)
```

### How to do it...

To validate some data, we have to define predicates to test the data fields against and then define the fields and predicates to validate, plus error messages.

1. First, we need data to validate. This is done using the following code snippet:

   ```
   (def user
     {:given-name "Fox"
      :surname "Mulder"
      :age 51
      :badge "JTT047101111"})
   ```

2. We also need to define a predicate to determine whether a number is present or not. The `present?` predicate defined by Valip fails if its input isn't a string.

   ```
   (defn number-present?
     [x]
     (and (present? (str x))
          (or (instance? Integer x)
              (instance? Long x))))
   ```

3. We'd also like to validate the badge numbers. Taking this one as a template, say they begin with three upper-case letters, followed by one or more digits. We can express that using the following predicate:

   ```
   (defn valid-badge
     [n]
     (not (nil? (re-find #"[A-Z]{3}\d+" n))))
   ```

4. Now we can start to define some validation rules. Rules are vector triples each listing a field, a predicate, and an error message as seen in the following code snippet:

   ```
   (defn validate-user
     [user] (validate    user
       [:given-name present? "Given name required."]
       [:surname present? "Surname required."]
       [:age number-present? "Age required."]
       [:age (over 0) "Age should be positive."]
       [:age (under 150) "Age should be under 150."]
       [:badge present?
        "The badge number is required."]
       [:badge valid-badge
        "The badge number is invalid."]))
   ```

Now we can easily validate data against the following set of rules:

```
user=> (validate-user (assoc user :age -42))
{:age ["Age should be positive."]}
user=> (validate-user (assoc user :age -42 :surname nil))
{:age ["Age should be positive."], :surname ["Surname required."]}
```

## How it works...

Valip provides an easy-to-use DSL for defining validation rules. It then breaks the incoming map structures and validates each field against the rules given. Finally, it returns error messages for any problem data. This system is simple to integrate into a data processing workflow.

# 3
# Managing Complexity with Concurrent Programming

In this chapter, we will cover:

- Managing program complexity with STM
- Managing program complexity with agents
- Getting better performance with commute
- Combining agents and STM
- Maintaining consistency with ensure
- Introducing safe side effects into the STM
- Maintaining data consistency with validators
- Tracking processing with watchers
- Debugging concurrent programs with watchers
- Recovering from errors in agents
- Managing input with sized queues

*Managing Complexity with Concurrent Programming*

# Introduction

Designing and creating a computer system is a balancing act: we constantly try to add features and capabilities while keeping the code simple and the system's performance reasonable. Data analysis systems are no different. In fact, they may be worse. Often, data is only partially consistent, and we need to employ a variety of strategies to extract usable data before we can even begin analysis.

This can get out of hand.

Clojure has a number of tools to help us manage our system's complexity. One of the most powerful of these is **concurrent programming**. This allows us to conceptualize our programs differently. Instead of having monolithic blocks of code that do many things and have direct, tight dependencies, we can structure our program more modularly by composing together many independent modules, each of which do one thing. These communicate by using simple, well-defined protocols. But they all work independently and concurrently—that is, at the same time. Clojure's primary tool for concurrency is one simple thing: a built-in **Software Transactional Memory** (**STM**) system (`http://clojure.org/refs`). This takes the semantics of databases transactions, which most developers are familiar with, and applies it to the computer's memory.

Clojure also has a concurrent message-processing system, its agents, built on top of the STM. Agents contain state information, and we send them function messages to update that state concurrently. Together, the STM and agents provide a way to structure programs to make them maintainable and easy to reason about.

Both of these work very well because all of the native Clojure data structures are **immutable**. They cannot be changed. Because it's working with immutable data, the STM can guarantee the consistency and safety of its transactions even in a highly concurrent environment. These guarantees are good for us because they help us think and reason about our data and our program, and they help us manage the complexity of the systems we're building.

Note that *concurrent* describes how a program is structured to work. Each thread may be doing different things. Hopefully it will result in some speed up, but concurrency is often just a good way to organize your program, to separate out and decouple the different parts of your program that are engaged in different tasks. If you're doing the same thing over and over and want to do it faster, that's **parallelism**. We'll look at recipes related to that in *Chapter 4, Improving Performance with Parallel Programming*.

*Chapter 3*

# Managing program complexity with STM

The basis of Clojure's concurrency is its Software Transactional Memory (STM) system. Basically this extends the semantics of database transactions to the computer's memory.

The way the STM works is that we mark memory locations to be controlled by the STM using the `ref` function. We can then de-reference those anywhere using the `deref` function or the `@` macro. But we can only change the values of a reference inside a `dosync` block. Then, when the point of execution gets to the end of a transaction, the STM performs a check. If any of the references that the transaction altered have been changed by another transaction, the transaction fails, and it's queued to be tried again. However, if none of the references have changed, then the transaction succeeds and is committed.

While we're in the transaction, to code outside it, those values don't appear to have changed. Once the transaction is committed, then any changes we make to those locations with `ref-set` or `alter` will be visible outside that block.

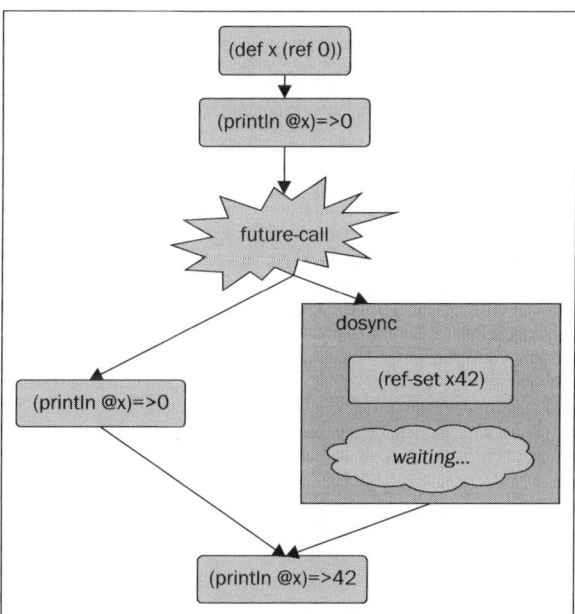

A few warnings: with the STM we should use only Clojure's native, immutable datatypes. This sounds restrictive, but in practice, it isn't a big deal: Clojure has a rich and flexible collection of datatypes. Also, we should limit how much we try to do in each transaction. We only want to bundle together operations that truly must pass or fail as a collection. This keeps transactions from being retried too much, which can hurt performance.

The STM helps us manage complexity by allowing us to divide up our processing in a way that makes the most sense to us, and then to run those processes concurrently. The STM, together with immutable state, keeps this system simple and easy to reason about.

For this recipe, we'll use the STM to calculate the families per housing unit from some US census data. We'll use `future-call` to perform the calculations in the thread pool and spread the execution out over multiple cores.

## Getting ready

To prepare for this recipe, we first need to list our dependencies in the Leiningen `project.clj` file:

```
:dependencies [[org.clojure/clojure "1.5.0-RC2"]
               [org.clojure/data.csv "0.1.2"]]
```

We also need to import these into our script or REPL:

```
(require '[clojure.java.io :as io]
         '[clojure.data.csv :as csv])
```

And finally, we need to have our data file. I downloaded one of the bulk data files from the Investigative Reporters and Editors' US census site: http://census.ire.org/data/bulkdata.html. The data in this recipe will use the family census data for Virginia. I've also uploaded this data to http://www.ericrochester.com/clj-data-analysis/data/all_160_in_51.P35.csv. You can download it easily from there, and save it to a directory named `data/`. Let's bind the file's name to a variable for easy access:

```
(def data-file "data/all_160_in_51.P35.csv")
```

| | A | B | C | D | E | F | G | H | I | J | K | L | M |
|---|---|---|---|---|---|---|---|---|---|---|---|---|---|
| 1 | GEOID | SUMLEV | STATE | COUNTY | CBSA | CSA | NECTA | CNECTA | NAME | POP100 | HU100 | POP100.2 | HU100.20 |
| 2 | 5100148 | 160 | 51 | | | | | | Abingdon town | 8191 | 4271 | 7780 | 3788 |
| 3 | 5100180 | 160 | 51 | | | | | | Accomac town | 519 | 229 | 547 | 235 |
| 4 | 5100724 | 160 | 51 | | | | | | Alberta town | 298 | 163 | 306 | 158 |
| 5 | 5101000 | 160 | 51 | | | | | | Alexandria city | 139966 | 72376 | 128283 | 64251 |
| 6 | 5101256 | 160 | 51 | | | | | | Allisonia CDP | 117 | 107 | | |

## How to do it...

For this recipe, we'll read in the data, break it into chunks, and have separate threads to total the number of housing units and the number of families in each chunk, and each chunk will add its totals to some global references.

1. We need to define two references that the STM will manipulate: one for the total of housing units and one for families.

   ```
   (def total-hu (ref 0))
   (def total-fams (ref 0))
   ```

2. Now we'll need a couple of utility functions to safely read a CSV file into a lazy sequence. The first is `lazy-read-csv` from the *Lazily processing very large datasets* recipe in *Chapter 2, Cleaning and Validating Data*. We'll also define a new `with-header` function that uses the first row to create maps from the rest of the rows in the dataset.

   ```
   (defn with-header [coll]
     (let [headers (map keyword (first coll))]
       (map (partial zipmap headers) (next coll))))
   ```

3. Next, we'll define some utility functions. One (`->int`) will convert a string to an integer. The other (`sum-item`) will take a list of fields, a vector of sums, and a map of data, pull the fields' values from the data map, add those to the running totals in the vector, and return a newly updated vector. Another (`sum-items`) will use `sum-item` to calculate the sums from a collection of data maps.

   ```
   (defn ->int ([i] (Integer. i)))

   (defn sum-item
     ([fields] (partial sum-item fields))
     ([fields accum item]
       (mapv + accum (map ->int (map item fields)))))

   (defn sum-items
     [accum fields coll] (reduce (sum-item fields) accum coll))
   ```

4. Now, we can define the function that will actually interact with the STM. `update-totals` takes a list of fields that contain the housing unit, family data, and a collection of items. It will total those fields from those items and update the STM references with them.

   ```
   (defn update-totals [fields items]
     (let [mzero (mapv (constantly 0) fields)
           [sum-hu sum-fams]
                   (sum-items mzero fields items)]
       (dosync (alter total-hu #(+ sum-hu %))
         (alter total-fams #(+ sum-fams %)))))
   ```

## Managing Complexity with Concurrent Programming

5. In order to call this with `future-call`, we'll write a function to create a **thunk** (a function with no arguments) that just calls `update-totals` with the parameters we give.

   ```
   (defn thunk-update-totals-for
     [fields data-chunk]
       (fn [] (update-totals fields data-chunk)))
   ```

6. With all this in place, we can define a `main` function that controls the whole process and returns the ratio of families to housing units.

   ```
   (defn main
     ([data-file] (main data-file [:HU100 :P035001] 5))
     ([data-file fields chunk-count]
      (doall
        (->>
          (lazy-read-csv data-file)
          with-header
          (partition-all chunk-count)
          (map (partial thunk-update-totals-for fields))
          (map future-call)
          (map deref)))
      (float (/ @total-fams @total-hu))))
   ```

### How it works...

The first reference to the STM in this code is in the definitions of `total-hu` and `total-fams`. Each of these is a reference, initially set to zero.

`update-totals` contains the `dosync` block that updates the references. It uses `alter`, which takes the reference and a function that updates the value. Because of the `dosync` block, if either of these values is changed in another thread summing another chunk of data, the call to `dosync` is repeated. That's why we calculate the items' totals before we enter that block.

Finally, in `main`, we partition the data into chunks and then package calls `update-totals` for each chunk of data into a thunk and run it in Clojure's thread pool using `future-call`. Calling `deref` on future, which is a value returned by `future-call`, blocks until the value is returned from the thread pool.

We wrap this process in a call to `doall` to make sure that all of the processing is completed. Remember that sequences are lazy by default, so without `doall`, the sequence started by `lazy-read-csv` and ending in the series of `map` calls would be garbage collected before any work would be done. `future-call` and `deref` would never actually be called. The `@` macros in the last line would return the values of these references as originally set in the `def` calls (both zero). The `doall` block simply forces all processing to be done before we get to the last line.

As this recipe shows, Clojure provides a lot of easy concurrency without having to worry about synchronizing values, locks, monitors, semaphores, or any of the other things that make threads and concurrency difficult and painful.

## See also

▶ *The Managing program complexity with agents recipe*

## Managing program complexity with agents

Agents build on the STM, and each agent acts a lot like a reference. You use agents by sending the agent messages—functions that manipulate the agent's state—and those are run in the thread pool.

We create agents with the `agent` function, and we send messages to them with `send` and `send-off`. Whatever the function returns is the agent's new state value.

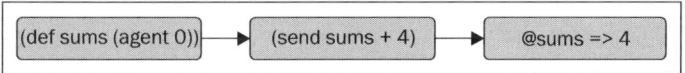

For this recipe, we'll again solve the same problem we did in the last recipe, *Managing program complexity with STM*.

## Getting ready

We will include the same references in the `project.clj` file and the same requirements in the REPL as we did in the *Managing program complexity with STM* recipe. We will also use the same input file, bound to the name `data-file` again.

And we'll also use several utility functions from the last recipe: `lazy-read-csv`, `with-header`, `->int`, `sum-item`, and `sum-items`.

## How to do it...

To use agents, we just need to add a few functions to the ones from the last recipe.

1. The first one is called `accum-sums`. We'll use that to perform pair-wise addition over the agents' outputs.

   ```
   (defn accum-sums [a b] (mapv + a b))
   ```

2. Now, we want a function that takes a pair of numbers and divides them. We'll use this at the very end to generate the ratio of families per housing unit.

   ```
   (defn div-vec [[a b]] (float (/ a b)))
   ```

3. And we'll need a function to make working with agents easier. `force-val` takes an agent and waits for all of the messages currently in its queue to be processed. Then it dereferences the agent. This function will allow us to thread a series of operations on the agents.

   ```
   (defn force-val
     [a]
     (await a)
     @a)
   ```

4. Now that everything's in place, here is the function that controls the process:

   ```
   (defn main
     ([data-file] (main data-file [:P035001 :HU100] 5 5))
     ([data-file fields agent-count chunk-count]
      (let [mzero (mapv (constantly 0) fields)
            agents (map agent
                        (take agent-count
                              (repeat mzero)))]
        (dorun
          (->>
            (lazy-read-csv data-file)
            with-header
            (partition-all chunk-count)
            (map #(send %1 sum-items fields %2)
                 (cycle agents))))
        (->>
          agents
          (map force-val)
          (reduce accum-sums mzero)
          div-vec))))
   ```

5. And we can see this in action:

   ```
   user=> (main data-file)
   0.5888646
   ```

## How it works...

Except for `force-val`, all of the agent-related code is in `main`. Let's walk through the lines that are of interest.

1. We define the number of agents that we want to use. Each agent is initialized to a vector of zeros of the same length as the number of fields.

   ```
   agents (map agent (take agent-count (repeat mzero)))
   ```

2. Next, after reading the input CSV file into a sequence of maps and partitioning them into chunks of equal size, we send each agent the `sum-items` function, including extra parameters. We cycle through the agents until all of the chunks are assigned to an agent.

   ```
   (map #(send %1 sum-items fields %2) (cycle agents))
   ```

3. Now, we block the process until each agent is done by calling `await`, and we dereference each to get its value (both of these take place inside `force-val`).

   ```
   (->>
     agents
     (map force-val)
     …)
   ```

The rest takes place outside the agent system.

## There's more...

See *Agents and Asynchronous Actions* in the Clojure documentation (http://clojure.org/agents) for more on agents.

## See also

Unfortunately, some of the agent tasks are probably being retried because they're all attempting to update the same global values at the same time. We'll see how to prevent this from happening in the next recipe, *Getting better performance with commute*.

# Getting better performance with commute

The STM system we created in the first recipe of this chapter, *Managing program complexity with STM*, has one subtle problem: threads attempting to reference and update `total-hu` and `total-fams` are contending for these two values unnecessarily. Since everything comes down to accessing these two resources, a lot of tasks are probably being retried.

## Managing Complexity with Concurrent Programming

But they don't need to be. Both are simply updating those values with commutative functions (`#(+ sum-? %)`). The order that these updates are applied in doesn't matter. And since we block until all processing is done, we don't have to worry about the two references getting out of sync. They'll get back together eventually, before we access their values, and that's good enough for this situation.

To handle this use case (updating references with a commutative function), instead of `alter`, we should use `commute`. The `alter` function updates the references on the spot; `commute` queues the update to happen later, when the reference isn't otherwise engaged. This prevents contentions on those references and can make the system faster too.

For this recipe, we'll again look at the problem we dealt with in *Managing program complexity with STM*.

### Getting ready

Everything is going to be the same as it was for *Managing program complexity with STM*. We'll use the same dependencies and requirements and even most of the functions as we did for that recipe.

### How to do it...

In fact, the only change will be for the `update-totals` function, and even that change is minor.

```
(defn update-totals [fields items]
  (let [mzero (mapv (constantly 0) fields)
        [sum-hu sum-fams] (sum-itemsmzero fields items)]
    (dosync (commute total-hu #(+ sum-hu %))
            (commute total-fams #(+ sum-fams %)))))
```

Do you see the difference? We just use `commute` instead of `alter`. That's the only change we need to make.

### How it works...

Now the references are updated after the `dosync` block. With `alter`, the changes happen inside the `dosync` block, within the same transaction. However, with `commute`, both changes are run separately. And both are scheduled to run when Clojure knows there will be no conflicts. Depending on the use case, this can dramatically cut down on the number of retries and speed up the overall program.

*Chapter 3*

# Combining agents and STM

Agents by themselves are pretty useful. But if an agent function needs to coordinate the state beyond the agent's own data, we'll need to use both agents and the STM: `send` or `send-off` to coordinate the agent's state, combined with `dosync`, `ref-set`, `alter`, or `commute` inside the agent function to coordinate with the other state.

This combination provides a nice simplicity over complex state- and data-coordination problems. This is a huge help in managing the complexity of a data processing and analysis system.

For this recipe, we'll look at the same problem we have been encountering in the last few recipes: computing the families per housing unit for Virginia from the 2010 US census. This time we'll structure it a little differently. The data sequence will be held in a reference, not in the agent's state. We'll also use a counter to indicate when the agent is finished.

## Getting ready

We'll need to use the same dependencies as we did for the *Managing program complexity with STM* recipe. We'll also need to use the same imports, as well as an import from Java.

```
(import '[java.lang Thread])
```

And we'll use some values and functions from previous recipes. From the *Managing program complexity with STM* recipe, we'll use `data-file`, `lazy-read-csv`, `with-header`, `->int`, `sum-item`, and `sum-items`. From the *Managing program complexity with agents* recipe, we'll use `accum-sums`, `div-vec`, and `force-val`.

## How to do it...

For this recipe, we need to define a few functions to work through a queue of input chunks and then block until all the processing is complete.

1. We'll need a function to pop an item off the input sequence and set the reference to the rest of the sequence.

    ```
    (defn get-chunk
      [data-ref]  (dosync    (when-let [[s & ss] (seq @data-ref)]
      (ref-set data-ref ss)    s)))
    ```

2. Next, we'll need a new function to update the totals. It retrieves new data using `get-chunk`, processes the data, and calls itself recursively. If there's no data, it increments the count of agents that are done and stops processing.

    ```
    (defn update-totals [totals fields coll-ref counter-ref]
      (if-let [items (get-chunk coll-ref)]
        (do
    ```

```
              (send *agent* update-totals fields coll-ref counter-ref)
              (sum-items totals fields items))
          (do
            (dosync (commute counter-ref inc)) totals))))
```

3. We can use the finished agents' counter to block until the report is done.

```
(defn block-to-done
  [counter agent-count]
  (loop []
    (when-not (= agent-count @counter)
      (Thread/sleep 500)
      (recur))))
```

4. The next function takes the agents, which should be finished anyway, and forces their values and accumulates their sums. It then divides the two counts in order to get the final result.

```
(defn get-results [agents fields]
  (->> agents
    (map force-val)
    (reduce accum-sums (mapv (constantly 0) fields))
    (div-vec)))
```

5. Now we're ready for the `main` function, which ties everything together.

```
(defn main
  ([data-file] (main data-file [:P035001 :HU100] 5 5))
  ([data-file fields agent-count chunk-count]
   (let [mzero (mapv (constantly 0) fields)
         agents (map agent
                     (take agent-count (repeat mzero)))
         data (with-header (lazy-read-csv data-file))
         data-ref (ref
                       (doall
                         (partition-all chunk-count
                                        data)))
         finished (ref 0)]
     (dorun
       (map #(send % update-totals
                   fields data-ref finished)
            agents))
     (block-to-done finished (count agents))
     (get-results agents fields))))
```

6. Using this looks exactly like how we'd expect.

```
user=> (main data-file)
0.588864
```

## How it works...

The `get-chunk` function is an example of how the STM can help coordinate the state. Because they're in the same `dosync` block, accessing the data sequence to get its first element and setting it to the rest of the sequence is an atomic operation. We don't have to worry that data is getting processed twice or dropped because of threading issues. And functions that call `get-chunk` don't have to worry about any of this. Hiding this complexity greatly simplifies complicated systems.

## Maintaining consistency with ensure

Sometimes when we use the STM, we'll want to maintain consistency between a set of references, but we won't need to actually change some of them. We can signal that the STM should include these other references in the transaction by using the `ensure` function.

This helps simplify the data-processing system by making sure that the data structures stay synchronized and consistent. The `ensure` function allows us to have more control over what gets managed by the STM.

For this recipe, we'll use a slightly contrived example: we'll process a set of text files, computing the frequency of a term as well as the total number of words. We'll do this concurrently, and we'll be able to watch the results get updated as we progress.

For the set of text files, we'll use the Brown Corpus. Constructed in the 1960s, this was one of the first digital collections of texts (or corpora) assembled for linguists to use to study language. At the time, its size—one million words—seemed huge. Today, similar corpora contain 100 million words or more.

### Getting ready

We'll need to include the `clojure.string` library and have easy access to the `File` class.

```
(require '[clojure.string :as string])
(import '[java.io File])
```

We'll also need to download the Brown Corpus. We can download it at http://nltk.googlecode.com/svn/trunk/nltk_data/index.xml. Really, you can use any large collection of texts, but the Brown Corpus has each word's part of speech listed in the file, so we'll need to parse it specially. If you use a different corpus, you can just change the `tokenize-brown` function to work with your texts.

## How to do it...

For this recipe, we'll walk through pre-processing of the data, to performing the counts in parallel, to looking at the results.

1. Let's get a sequence of the files to process.

   ```
   (def input-files
     (filter #(.isFile %)
             (file-seq (File. "./data/brown"))))
   ```

2. Now, we'll define some references. `finished` will indicate whether processing is done or not; `total-docs` and `total-words` will keep running totals; `freqs` will map the tokens to their frequencies as a whole; and `running-report` is an agent that contains the current state of the report for the term we're interested in.

   ```
   (def finished (ref false))
   (def total-docs (ref 0))
   (def total-words (ref 0))
   (def freqs (ref {}))
   (def running-report
        (agent {:term nil,
     :frequency 0,
     :ratio 0.0}))
   ```

3. Let's create the tokenizer. The text in the Brown Corpus files look like this:

   ```
   The/at Fulton/np-tl County/nn-tl Grand/jj-tl Jury/nn-tl said/vbd
   Friday/nr an/at investigation/nn of/in Atlanta's/np$ recent/jj
   primary/nn election/nn produced/vbd ''/'' no/at evidence/nn ''/''
   that/cs any/dti irregularities/nns took/vbd place/nn ./.
   ```

   We're not interested in the parts of speech, so our tokenizer will remove those and covert each token to a lower-case keyword.

   ```
   (defn tokenize-brown [input-str]
     (->> (string/split input-str #"\s+")
       (map
          #(first (string/split % #"/" 2)))
       (filter #(> (count %) 0))
          (map string/lower-case)
       (map keyword)))
   ```

4. Now, let's write a utility function that increments the frequency map for a token.

   ```
   (defn accum-freq
     [m token]  (assoc m token (inc (m token 0))))
   ```

5. We'll use that function in `compute-file`, which does the primary processing for each file.

   ```
   (defn compute-file
   ```

```
     [fs]
     (dosync
       (if-let [[s & ss] (seq fs)]
         (let [tokens (tokenize-brown (slurp s))
               tc (count tokens)
               fq (reduce accum-freq {} tokens)]
           (commute total-docs inc)
           (commute total-words #(+ tc %))
           (commute freqs #(merge-with + % fq))
           (send-off *agent* compute-file)
           ss)
         (do (alter finished (constantly true)) '()))))
```

6. Another function will update the report in parallel.

   ```
   (defn compute-report
     [{term :term, :as report}] (dosync    (when-not @finished
   (send *agent* compute-report))    (let [term-freq (term (ensure
   freqs) 0)
           tw (ensure total-words)]        (assoc report
               :frequency term-freq
               :ratio (if (zero? tw)
                        nil
                        (float (/ term-freq tw))))))))
   ```

7. Finally, `compute-frequencies` gets the whole thing started.

   ```
   (defn compute-frequencies
     [inputs term]   (let [a (agent inputs)]    (send running-report
   #(assoc % :term term))    (send running-report compute-report)
   (send-off a compute-file)))
   ```

8. To use this, we just call `compute-frequencies` with the inputs and a term, and then we poll `finished` and `running-report` to see how processing is going.

   ```
   user=> (compute-frequencies input-files :committee)
   #<Agent@1830f455: (...)>
   user=> [@finished @running-report]
   [false {:frequency 79, :ratio 6.933839E-4, :term :committee}]
   user=> [@finished @running-report]
   [false {:frequency 105, :ratio 2.5916903E-4, :term :committee}]
   user=> [@finished @running-report]
   [false {:frequency 164, :ratio 1.845714E-4, :term :committee}]
   user=> [@finished @running-report]
   [true {:frequency 168, :ratio 1.4468178E-4, :term :committee}]
   ```

We can see from the ratio of the frequency of `committee` to the total frequency, that initially `committee` occurred relatively frequently (0.07 percent, which is approximately the frequency of it and other common words in the overall corpus), but by the end of processing, it had settled down to about 0.014 percent of the total number of words, which is closer to what we would expect.

## How it works...

In this recipe, `compute-frequencies` kicks everything off. It creates a new agent that processes the input files one by one and updates most of the references in the `compute-file` function.

The `compute-report` function handles updating the running report. It bases that report on the frequency map and the total words. However, it doesn't change either of those. But if we keep everything synchronized, it calls `ensure` on both. Otherwise, there's a chance that the count for total words comes from one set of documents, but the term frequency from another set. This won't happen, since only one agent is updating those values, but if we decide to have more than one agent processing the files, that would be a possibility. To generate a report for a new term without reading all the files again, we can define the following function:

```
(defn get-report [term]
  (send running-report #(assoc % :term term))
  (send running-report compute-report)
  (await running-report)
  @running-report)
```

## Introducing safe side effects into the STM

The STM isn't safe for side effects. Because a `dosync` block may get retried, possibly more than once, any side effects may be executed again and again, whether they should be or not. Values may get written to the screen or logfile multiple times. Worse, values may be written to the database more than once.

However, all programs must produce side effects. The trick is adding them while keeping a handle on complexity. The easiest way to do that is to keep side effects out of transactions.

For this recipe, to illustrate what can happen, we'll simulate **thread starvation**. That sounds serious. It just means that one thread isn't able to access the resources it needs, so it can't do its job. We'll also use an **atom**—a reference that isn't controlled by the STM—to keep track of how many times the STM retries a call to an agent. That way, we can see what creates the problem, and what we need to do to fix it.

### Getting ready

To prepare, we'll need access to `java.lang.Thread` in our REPL.

```
(import [java.lang Thread])
```

## How to do it...

For this recipe, we'll walk through a couple of experiments to simulate thread starvation.

1. For these experiments, we'll use one reference and two agents. The agents will try to read and increment the counter reference simultaneously. But the two will wait for different amounts of time in the transaction, so that one will starve the other out.

    ```
    (def counter (ref 0))
    (def a1 (agent :a1))
    (def a2 (agent :a2))
    ```

2. Now, we'll define a utility to start both the agents on the same message function, with different sleep periods.

    ```
    (defn start-agents [msg a1-sleep a2-sleep]
      (send a1 msg a1-sleep)  (send a2 msg a2-sleep))
    ```

3. For the first experiment, we'll use a `debug` function for the side effect. It just prints out the message and flushes the output stream.

    ```
    (defn debug
      [msg]  (print (str msg \newline))  (.flush *out*))
    ```

4. The first message function will starve out anything.

    ```
    (defn starve-out [tag sleep-for]
      (let [retries (atom 0)]
        (dosync
          (let [c @counter]
            (when-not (zero? @retries)
              (debug (str ":starve-out " tag
                          ", :try " @retries
                          ", :counter " c)))
            (swap! retries inc)
            (Thread/sleep sleep-for)
            (ref-set counter (inc c))
            (send *agent* starve-out sleep-for)
            tag))))
    ```

5. If we send `starve-out` to both agents with very different sleep periods and look through the output, we'll see that :a2 is consistently getting starved out. (You can stop the agents by calling `shutdown-agents`.)

    ```
    user=> (start-agents starve-out 50 1000)
    :starve-out :a2, :try 1, :counter 19
    :starve-out :a2, :try 2, :counter 39
    :starve-out :a2, :try 3, :counter 59
    :starve-out :a2, :try 4, :counter 78
    ```

6. In order to make this safe, we have to move all the side effects out of the `dosync` block. This means that we'll move the `debug` call out of the STM, and while we're at it, we'll move the `send` call, since it's also a side effect. To be extra safe, we'll also use a new output function, one that uses `io!` (highlighted). `io!` blocks will throw an exception if it is executed inside a transaction.

```clojure
(defn debug! [msg]
  (io! (print (str msg \newline)) (.flush *out*)))
(defn starve-safe [tag sleep-for]
    (let [retries (atom 0)]
      (dosync (let [c @counter]
              (swap! retries inc)
              (Thread/sleep sleep-for)
              (ref-set counter (inc c))))
      (when-not (zero? @retries)
        (debug! (str ":safe-starve " tag
                     ", :try " @retries ", " @counter)))
      (send *agent* starve-safe sleep-for)
  tag))
```

This version safely handles I/O in the STM. Moreover, if we forget and refactor the call to `debug!` back inside the transaction, our code will stop working.

## Maintaining data consistency with validators

Clojure has a number of tools for working with agents. One of those is **validators**. When an agent's message function returns a value, any validator functions assigned to that agent receive the agent's data before it does. If the validators return true, all is well: the agent is updated and processing continues. However, if any validator returns false or raises an error, an error is raised on the agent.

This can be a handy tool to make sure that the data assigned to your agent conforms to your expectations, and it can be an important check on the consistency and validity of your data.

For this recipe, we'll read data from a CSV file and convert the values in some of the columns to integers. We'll use a validator to make sure that this actually happens.

### Getting ready

For this recipe, we'll use the dependencies and requirements that we did in the *Managing program complexity with STM* recipe. Also, we'll use the functions `lazy-read-csv` and `with-header` from that recipe and we'll use the data file that we used in that recipe. We'll keep that file name bound to `data-file`.

## How to do it...

This recipe will be built up from a number of shorter functions.

1. Let's define a list of the rows that will need to be converted to integers. Looking at the data file, we can come up with the following:

   ```
   (def int-rows
     [:GEOID :SUMLEV :STATE :POP100 :HU100 :POP100.2000
      :HU100.2000 :P035001 :P035001.2000])
   ```

2. Now, we'll define a predicate function to check whether a value is an integer or not.

   ```
   (defn int?
     [x] (or (instance? Integer x) (instance? Long x)))
   ```

3. And we'll create a function that attempts to read a string to an integer, but if there's an exception, it silently returns the original value.

   ```
   (defn try-read-string
     [x] (try (read-string x) (catch Exception ex x)))
   ```

4. This system will have three agents, each performing a different task. Here is the function for the agent that converts all whole number fields to integer values. It sends the output to another agent and uses the output as its own new value so it can be validated.

   ```
   (defn coerce-row
     [_ row sink]
     (let [cast-row
           (apply assoc row
                  (mapcat
                    (fn [k]
                      [k (try-read-string (k row))])
                    int-rows))]
       (send sink conj cast-row)
       cast-row))
   ```

5. Here is the function for the agent that reads the input. It sends an item of input to the `coerce-row` agent, queues itself to read another item of input, and sets its value to the rest of the input.

   ```
   (defn read-row
     [rows caster sink]
     (when-let [[item & items] (seq rows)]
       (send caster coerce-row item sink)
       (send *agent* read-row caster sink)
       items))
   ```

6. Here is the validator for the `coerce-row` agent. It checks that the integer fields are either integers or empty strings.

   ```
   (defn int-val? [x] (or (int? x) (empty? x)))
   (defn validate
     [row]
     (or (nil? row)
         (reduce #(and %1 (int-val? (%2 row)))
                 true int-rows)))
   ```

7. Finally, we'll define one function that defines the agents, starts their processing, and returns them.

   ```
   (defn agent-ints
     [input-file]
     (let [reader (agent (seque
                           (with-header
                             (lazy-read-csv
                               input-file))))
           caster (agent nil)
           sink (agent [])]
       (set-validator! caster validate)
       (send reader read-row caster sink)
       {:reader reader
        :caster caster
        :sink sink}))
   ```

8. If we run this, we get a map containing the agents. We can get the output data by dereferencing the `:sink` agent.

   ```
   user=> (def ags (agent-ints data-file))
   #'user/ags
   user=> (first @(:sink ags))
   {:SUMLEV 160, :P035001 2056, :HU100.2000 3788, :HU100 4271, :NAME
   "Abingdon town", :GEOID 5100148, :NECTA "", :CBSA "", :CSA "",
   :P035001.2000 2091, :POP100.2000 7780, :CNECTA "", :POP100 8191,
   :COUNTY "", :STATE 51}
   ```

## How it works...

The `agent-ints` function is pretty busy. It defines the agents, sets everything up, and returns the map containing the agents.

Let's break it down.

```
(let [reader (agent (seque
                      (with-header
                        (lazy-read-csv input-file))))
      caster (agent nil)
      sink (agent [])]
```

These lines define the agents. One reads in the data; one converts it to integers; and one accumulates the results.

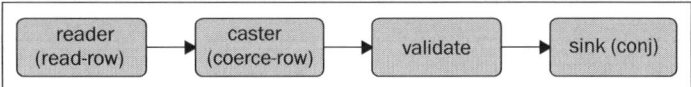

Next, `read-row` simply gets the first item off the input, sends it to the `caster` agent. `coerce-row` tries to coerce the rows listed in `int-rows` to integers. It then passes the results on to the `sink` agent. Before it's completely done, however, its new state is passed to its validator function, `validate`.

The validator allows for nil rows (for the agent's initial state) or integer fields that contain either integers or empty strings. And finally, the `sink` agent is called with `conj`. It accumulates the converted results.

## See also

- To learn how to use a nice DSL for validating data, see the *Validating data with Valip* recipe, in *Chapter 2, Cleaning and Validating Data*.

# Tracking processing with watchers

Another tool that Clojure provides for working with agents is **watchers**. These are just functions that get a chance to peek at the agent's data. This happens after the validators have successfully run and the new data is set as the agent's state. Because of the way it's handled, the state may have changed again since then, but watchers give you the chance to look at and track the data separately.

This can help us keep an eye on the data as it's being processed. We can use it to log progress, sample the data for manual validation, or for a number of other tasks.

*Managing Complexity with Concurrent Programming*

## Getting ready

We'll use the dependencies and requirements that we did in the *Managing program complexity with STM* recipe. We'll also add a new import.

```
(import '[java.lang Thread])
```

And we'll use the data file from the *Managing program complexity with STM* recipe, and the `lazy-read-csv` and `with-header` functions from that recipe.

From the *Maintaining data consistency with validators* recipe, we'll use the `int-rows`, `try-read-string`, and `coerce-row` functions.

## How to do it...

In this recipe, we'll add a watcher to keep track of how many rows are converted, and we'll add a flag that lets us know when processing is finished.

1. The agent that reads the data will use the `read-row` function. This is very similar to the `read-row` function that we saw in the *Maintaining data consistency with validators* recipe. The differences are highlighted in the following code snippet:

   ```
   (defn read-row
     [rows caster sink done]
     (if-let [[item & items] (seq rows)]
       (do
         (send caster coerce-row item sink)
         (send *agent* read-row caster sink done)
         items)
       (do
         (dosync (commute done (constantly true)))
         '())))
   ```

2. The function that watches the agent that coerces the data will just update a counter.

   ```
   (defn watch-caster
     [counter watch-key watch-agent old-state new-state]
     (when-not (nil? new-state)
       (dosync (commute counter inc))))
   ```

3. And we'll define a function that polls until processing is finished.

   ```
   (defn wait-for-it
     [sleep-for ref-var]
     (loop []
       (when-not @ref-var
         (Thread/sleep sleep-for)
         (recur))))
   ```

4.  The last function creates all the agents and references and dispatches their functions. Finally, it blocks until all agents are finished, and at that point, it returns the results. Again, I've highlighted the differences from `agent-ints` in the *Maintaining data consistency with validators* recipe, which is very similar.

    ```
    (defn watch-processing
      [input-file]
      (let [reader (agent (seque
                            (with-header
                              (lazy-read-csv
                                input-file))))
            caster (agent nil)
            sink (agent [])
            counter (ref 0)
            done (ref false)]
        (add-watch caster :counter
                   (partial watch-caster counter))
        (send reader read-row caster sink done)
        (wait-for-it 250 done)
        {:results @sink
         :count-watcher @counter}))
    ```

5.  When we run this, we get the count of data from the watcher.

    ```
    user=> (:count-watcher (watch-processing data-file))
    591
    ```

## How it works...

This time, instead of associating a validator with the agent that coerces the integers, we called `add-watch` on it. Each time the agent is updated, the watch function is called with four parameters: a key, the agent, the old state, and the new state. Our watch function first wants a counter reference, which we supply by partially applying its parameters when we call `add-watch`.

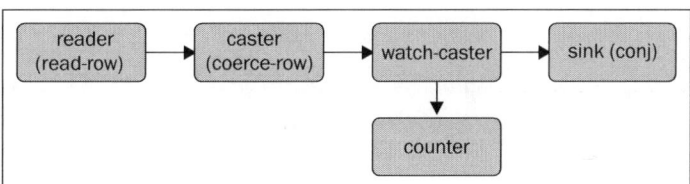

Once everything has been created, `watch-processing` just sends the input agent the first message, and then it waits for the processing to finish.

# Debugging concurrent programs with watchers

Watchers are not only good for logging and counting, but they can also be useful for debugging. If an agent or reference is not getting updated the way we expect, we can temporarily add a watcher to track what's happening, so we can see what's going on.

For this recipe, we'll continue the example we've been working with for the last few recipes. This time, instead of counting the data, the watch function will print the change of state to the console.

## Getting ready

We'll use the dependencies and requirements that we did in the *Managing program complexity with STM* recipe. We'll also add a new import:

```
(import '[java.lang Thread])
```

Also, we'll use the data file from the *Managing program complexity with STM* recipe, and the `lazy-read-csv` and `with-header` functions from that recipe.

From the *Maintaining data consistency with validators* recipe, we'll use the functions `int-rows` and `try-read-string`.

And from the *Tracking processing with watchers* recipe, we'll use the `coerce-row`, `read-row`, `watch-caster`, and `wait-for-it` functions.

## How to do it...

1. The main difference from the last recipe is the watch function. Here's the new one:

   ```
   (defn debug-watch
     [watch-key watch-agent old-state new-state]   (let [output (str
   watch-key                       " : "                     (pr-str old-
   state)                          " => "                    (pr-str new-
   state)                          \newline)]    (print output)))
   ```

2. The main function that creates the system and runs it is also different. I've highlighted the one change in the following code snippet.

   ```
   (defn watch-debugging
     [input-file]
     (let [reader (agent
                    (seque
                      (with-header
                        (lazy-read-csv
   ```

```
                      input-file))))
          caster (agent nil)
          sink (agent [])
          counter (ref 0)
          done (ref false)]
     (add-watch caster :counter
                (partial watch-caster counter))
     (add-watch caster :debug debug-watch)
     (send reader read-row caster sink done)
     (wait-for-it 250 done)
     {:results @sink
      :count-watcher @counter}))
```

3. Now, when we run this processing system, we get a lot of debugging output:

```
user=> (:count-watcher (watch-debugging data-file))
:debug: nil => {:SUMLEV 160, :P035001 2056, :HU100.2000 3788,
:HU100 4271, :NAME "Abingdon town", :GEOID 5100148, :NECTA "",
:CBSA "", :CSA "", :P035001.2000 2091, :POP100.2000 7780, :CNECTA
"", :POP100 8191, :COUNTY "", :STATE 51}
:debug: {:SUMLEV 160, :P035001 2056, :HU100.2000 3788, :HU100
4271, :NAME "Abingdon town", :GEOID 5100148, :NECTA "", :CBSA
"", :CSA "", :P035001.2000 2091, :POP100.2000 7780, :CNECTA "",
:POP100 8191, :COUNTY "", :STATE 51} => {:SUMLEV 160, :P035001
117, :HU100.2000 235, :HU100 229, :NAME "Accomac town", :GEOID
5100180, :NECTA "", :CBSA "", :CSA "", :P035001.2000 126,
:POP100.2000 547, :CNECTA "", :POP100 519, :COUNTY "", :STATE 51}
```

## There's more...

This is a good option for debugging output if you need a lot of flexibility. However, if all you need is to track function calls, arguments, and outputs, `clojure.tools.trace` (https://github.com/clojure/tools.trace) is better. It does this and only this, and it's also less intrusive on your program structure.

## Recovering from errors in agents

Since agents run in a thread pool, the way that exceptions are signaled and handled becomes an issue. Does the offending message function simply stop running? Does the agent stop? What happens to the `Exception` instance?

Clojure has several mechanisms for dealing with errors in agent functions. We'll walk through them in this recipe.

## How to do it...

The agent's **error mode** and its **error handler** determine how the agent handles errors. The error mode can be set when the agent is created or with the function `set-error-mode!`, and the error handler is set with `set-error-handler!`.

### Failing on errors

The default error mode is `:fail`. If we don't specify an error mode when we create an agent, this is what it gets. With this error mode, when one of the agent's message functions throws an exception, the agent stops processing any more messages and stores the exception. We can retrieve the exception with `agent-error`, and we can start processing again with `restart-agent`.

```
user=> (def agent-99 (agent 0))
#'user/agent-99
user=> (send agent-99 #(/ 100 %))
#<Agent@aa711 FAILED: 0>
user=> (agent-error agent-99)
#<ArithmeticExceptionjava.lang.ArithmeticException: Divide by zero>
user=> @agent-99
0
user=> (restart-agent agent-99 0)
0
```

### Continuing on errors

The other option for an error mode is `:continue`. With this error mode, when an agent throws an exception, the exception and the message that caused it are silently swallowed. The agent continues processing as if nothing has happened.

```
user=> (def agent-99 (agent 0 :error-mode :continue))
#'user/agent-99
user=> (send agent-99 #(/ 100 %))
#<Agent@f1b6fa6: 0>
user=> (agent-error agent-99)
nil
user=> @agent-99
0
```

### Using a custom error handler

If the agent's error handler is set, that is used instead of the error mode. The error handler is just a function that is called with the agent and the exception that was thrown. In this example, the new error handler will simply print out the exception.

```
user=> (def agent-99 (agent 0 :error-handler #(prn %2)))
#'user/agent-99
user=> (send agent-99 #(/ 100 %))
#<ArithmeticExceptionjava.lang.ArithmeticException: Divide by zero>
#<Agent@2da13aa9: 0>
user=> (agent-error agent-99)
nil
user=> @agent-99
0
```

Once an error has been caught using a custom error handler, the agent is free to continue processing. If we send `agent-99` a new message, it will process it like nothing has happened.

## There's more...

The canonical source for information about Clojure's agent system and how it handles errors is found in the page **Agents and Asynchronous Actions** in the Clojure documentation (http://clojure.org/agents).

# Managing input with sized queues

When we work with very large datasets, often we talk about structuring our program concurrently. But one big problem when dealing with very large datasets concurrently is coordinating and managing the flow of data between different parts of our program. If one part produces data too quickly, or another part processes it too slowly, depending on how you look at it, the message queue between the two can get backed up. If that happens, memory will get filled up with the messages and data waiting to be processed.

## How to do it...

The solution for this in Clojure is quite simple: use `seque`. This uses an instance of `java.util.concurrent.LinkedBlockingQueue` to pull values from a lazy sequence. It works ahead of where we're pulling values out of the queue, but not too far ahead. And once we've wrapped a sequence with `seque`, we can treat it just like any other sequence.

```
user=> (take 20 (seque 5 (range Integer/MAX_VALUE)))
(0 1 2 3 4 5 6 7 8 9 10 11 12 13 14 15 16 17 18 19)
```

*Managing Complexity with Concurrent Programming*

### How it works...

The `seque` function reads ahead a bit (usually a little more than what we specify). It then waits until some of the items it's read have been consumed, and then it reads ahead a little more. This makes sure that the rest of our system always has input to process, but its memory won't get filled by the input waiting to be processed. This is an easy solution to balancing input and processing, and this function's simplicity helps keep an often complex problem from introducing incidental complexity into our processing system.

# 4
# Improving Performance with Parallel Programming

In this chapter, we will cover:

- Parallelizing processing with pmap
- Parallelizing processing with Incanter
- Partitioning Monte Carlo simulations for better pmap performance
- Finding the optimal partition size with simulated annealing
- Parallelizing with reducers
- Generating online summary statistics with reducers
- Harnessing your GPU with OpenCL and Calx
- Using type hints
- Benchmarking with Criterium

## Introduction

If concurrent processing is a way of structuring our programs that has performance implications, parallel processing is a way of getting better performance that has implications in how we structure our programs. Although often conflated, concurrent processing and parallel processing are really different solutions to different problems. Concurrency is good for expressing programs that involve different tasks that can be, or must be, carried on at the same time. Parallelization is good for doing the same task many, many times, all at once.

## Improving Performance with Parallel Programming

It used to be that the easiest, and often best, strategy for improving performance was to go on vacation. Moore's law implies that processor speed would double approximately every 18 months, so in the 1990s, we could go on vacation, return, buy a new computer, and our programs were faster. It was magic.

Today, we're no longer under Moore's law, however. Instead, as the saying goes, "the free lunch is over." Now, processor speeds have plateaued, or even declined. Instead, computers are made faster by packing more processors into them. To make use of those, we have to employ **parallel programming**.

Of course, the processor isn't always the slowest part of the program (that is, our programs aren't always CPU bound). Sometimes it's the disk or network. If that's the case, we have to read from multiple disks or network connections simultaneously in order to see any improvement in speed.

The recipes in this chapter focus on leveraging multiple cores by showing different ways to parallelize Clojure programs. It also includes a few recipes on related topics. For instance, consider the last two recipes: *Using type hints* talks about how to optimize our code, and *Benchmarking with Criterium* discusses how to get good data for optimizing our code.

## Parallelizing processing with pmap

The easiest way to parallelize data is to take a loop we already have and handle each item in it in a thread.

That is essentially what `pmap` does. If we replace a call to `map` with `pmap`, it takes each call to the function argument and executes it in a thread pool. `pmap` is not completely lazy, but it's not completely strict, either: it stays just ahead of the output consumed. So if the output is never used, it won't be fully realized.

For this recipe, we'll calculate the Mandelbrot set. Each point in the output takes enough time that this is a good candidate to parallelize. We can just swap `map` for `pmap` and immediately see a speed-up.

### How to do it...

The Mandelbrot set can be found by looking for points that don't settle on a value after passing through the formula that defines the set quickly.

1. We need a function that takes a point and the maximum number of iterations to try and return the iteration that it escapes on. That just means that the value gets above 4.

    ```
    (defn get-escape-point
      [scaled-x scaled-y max-iterations]
      (loop [x 0, y 0, iteration 0]
    ```

```
         (let [x2 (* x x),
      y2 (* y y)]
        (if (and (< (+ x2 y2) 4)
                 (< iteration max-iterations))
          (recur (+ (- x2 y2) scaled-x)
                 (+ (* 2 x y) scaled-y)
                 (inc iteration))
          iteration))))
```

2. The scaled points are the pixel points in the output, scaled to relative positions in the Mandelbrot set. Here are the functions that handle the scaling. Along with a particular x-y coordinate in the output, they're given the range of the set and the number of pixels each direction.

```
(defn scale-to
  ([pixel maximum [lower upper]]
   (+ (* (/ pixel maximum)
         (Math/abs (- upper lower))) lower)))

(defn scale-point
  ([pixel-x pixel-y max-x max-y set-range]
   [(scale-to pixel-x max-x (:x set-range))
    (scale-to pixel-y max-y (:y set-range))]))
```

3. The function `output-points` returns a sequence of x, y values for each of the pixels in the final output.

```
(defn output-points
  ([max-x max-y]
   (let [range-y (range max-y)]
     (mapcat (fn [x] (map #(vector x %) range-y))
             (range max-x)))))
```

4. For each output pixel, we need to scale it to a location in the range of the Mandelbrot set and then get the escape point for that location.

```
(defn mandelbrot-pixel
  ([max-x max-y max-iterations set-range]
   (partial mandelbrot-pixel
            max-x max-y max-iterations set-range))
  ([max-x max-y max-iterations set-range
    [pixel-x pixel-y]]
   (let [[x y] (scale-point pixel-x pixel-y
                            max-x max-y
                            set-range)]
     (get-escape-point x y max-iterations))))
```

## Improving Performance with Parallel Programming

5. At this point, we can simply map `mandelbrot-pixel` over the results of `output-points`. We'll also pass in the function to use (`map` or `pmap`).

   ```
   (defn mandelbrot
     ([mapper max-iterations max-x max-y set-range]
      (doall
        (mapper (mandelbrot-pixel
                  max-x max-y max-iterations set-range)
                (output-points max-x max-y)))))
   ```

6. Finally, we have to define the range that the Mandelbrot set covers.

   ```
   (def mandelbrot-range
        {:x [-2.5, 1.0], :y [-1.0, 1.0]})
   ```

How do these two compare? A lot depends on the parameters we pass them. (For more precise and robust times, we could use Criterium—see the *Benchmarking with Criterium* recipe—but to get a rough idea of how the parameter affect the running times, `time` should be sufficient.)

```
user=> (def m (time (mandelbrot map 500 1000 1000
                       mandelbrot-range)))
"Elapsed time: 28981.112 msecs"
#'user/m
user=> (def m (time (mandelbrot pmap 500 1000 1000
                       mandelbrot-range)))
"Elapsed time: 34205.122 msecs"
#'user/m
user=> (def m (time (mandelbrot map 1000 10001000
                       mandelbrot-range)))
"Elapsed time: 85308.706 msecs"
#'user/m
user=> (def m (time (mandelbrot pmap 1000 10001000
                       mandelbrot-range)))
"Elapsed time: 49067.584 msecs"
#'user/m
```

Refer to the following chart:

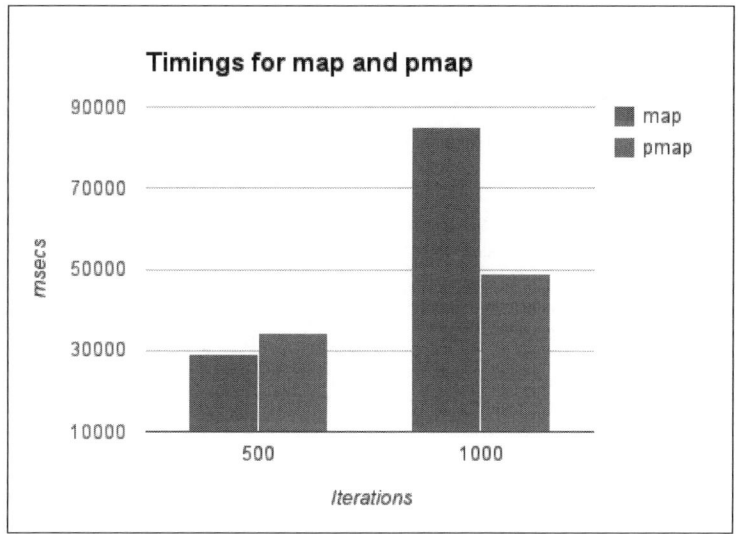

If we only iterate at most 500 times for each point, it's slightly faster to use map and work sequentially. However, if we iterate 1,000 times each, pmap is faster.

## How it works...

This shows that parallelization is a balancing act. If each separate work item is small, the overhead of creating the threads, coordinating them, and passing data back and forth takes more time than doing the work itself. However, when each thread has enough to do to make it worth it, we can get nice speed-ups just by using pmap.

Behind the scenes, pmap takes each item and uses future to run it in a thread pool. It forces only a couple more items than you have processors, so it keeps your machine busy, without generating more work or data than you need.

## There's more...

For an in-depth, excellent discussion of the nuts and bolts of pmap, along with pointers about things to watch out for, see David Liebke's talk, *From Concurrency to Parallelism* (http://blip.tv/clojure/david-liebke-from-concurrency-to-parallelism-4663526).

*Improving Performance with Parallel Programming*

### See also

▶ The *Partitioning Monte Carlo Simulations for better pmap performance* recipe

# Parallelizing processing with Incanter

In the coming chapters, many recipes will feature Incanter. One of its nice features is that it uses the Parallel Colt Java library (http://sourceforge.net/projects/parallelcolt/) to actually handle its processing, so when you use a lot of the matrix, statistical, or other functions, they're automatically executed on multiple threads.

For this, we'll revisit the Virginia housing-unit census data from the *Managing program complexity with STM* recipe. This time, we'll fit it to a linear regression.

### Getting ready

We'll need to add Incanter to our list of dependencies in our Leiningen `project.clj` file:

```
:dependencies [[org.clojure/clojure "1.5.0"]
               [incanter "1.3.0"]]
```

We'll also need to pull those libraries into our REPL or script:

```
(use '(incanter core datasets io optimize charts stats))
```

And we'll use the data file from the *Managing program complexity with STM* recipe in *Chapter 3, Managing Complexity with Concurrent Programming*. We can bind that file name to the name `data-file`, just as we did in that recipe:

```
(def data-file "data/all_160_in_51.P35.csv")
```

### How to do it...

For this recipe, we'll extract the data to analyze and perform the linear regression. We'll then graph the data afterwards.

1. First, we'll read in the data and pull the population and housing unit columns into their own matrix.

    ```
    (def data (to-matrix
                (sel (read-dataset data-file :header true)
                     :cols [:POP100 :HU100]))))
    ```

2. From this matrix, we can bind the population and the housing unit data to their own names.

   ```
   (def population (sel data :cols 0))
   (def housing-units (sel data :cols 1))
   ```

3. Now that we have those, we can use Incanter to fit the data.

   ```
   (def lm (linear-model housing-units population))
   ```

4. We'll talk more about graphing and plotting in a later chapter, but Incanter makes it so easy, it's hard *not* to look at it.

   ```
   (def plot (scatter-plot population housing-units
               :legend true))
   (add-lines plot population (:fitted lm))
   (view plot)
   ```

Here we can see that the graph of housing units to families makes a very straight line:

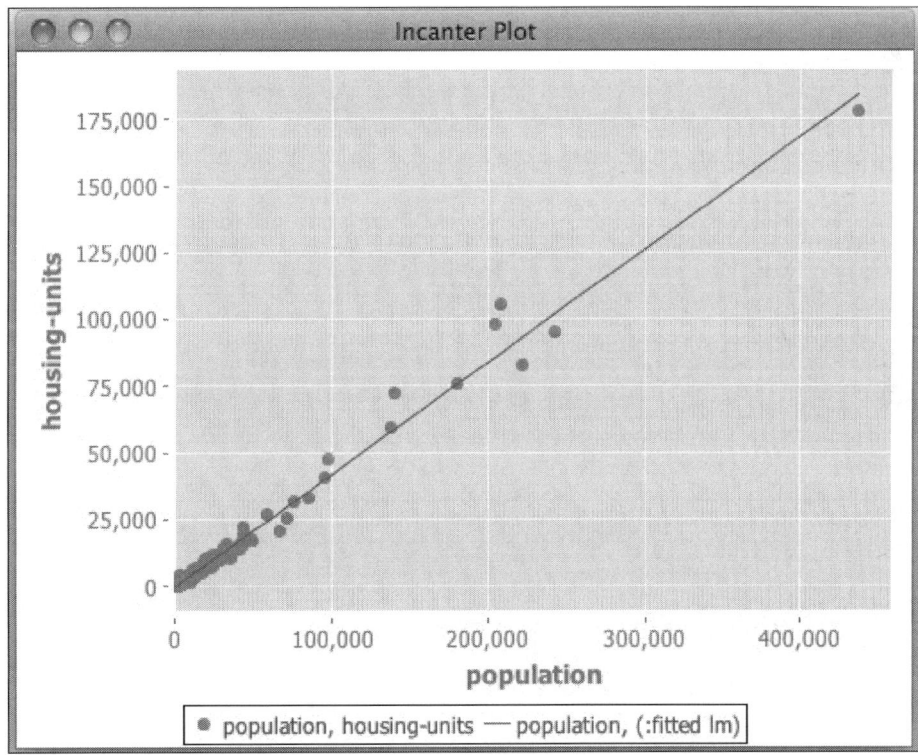

*Improving Performance with Parallel Programming*

## How it works...

Under the covers, Incanter takes the data matrix and partitions it into chunks. It then spreads those over the available CPUs to speed up processing. Of course, we don't have to worry about this. That's part of what makes Incanter so powerful.

# Partitioning Monte Carlo simulations for better pmap performance

In the *Parallelizing processing with pmap* recipe, we found that while using `pmap` is easy enough, knowing when to use it is more complicated. Processing each task in the collection has to take enough time to make the costs of threading, coordinating processing, and communicating the data worth it. Otherwise, the program will spend more time concerned with *how* (parallelization) and not enough time with *what* (the task).

The way to get around this is to make sure that `pmap` has enough to do at each step that it parallelizes. The easiest way to do that is to partition the input collection into chunks and run `pmap` on groups of the input.

For this recipe, we'll use Monte Carlo methods to approximate *pi*. We'll compare a serial version against a naïve parallel version against a version that uses parallelization and partitions.

## Getting ready

We'll use Criterium to handle benchmarking, so we'll need to include it as a dependency in our Leiningen `project.clj` file, shown as follows:

```
:dependencies [[org.clojure/clojure "1.5.0"]
               [criterium "0.3.0"]]
```

We'll use these dependencies and the java.lang.Math class in our script or REPL.

```
(use 'criterium.core)
(import [java.lang Math])
```

## How to do it...

To implement this, we'll define some core functions and then implement a Monte Carlo method for estimating pi that uses `pmap`.

1. We need to define the functions necessary for the simulation. We'll have one that generates a random two-dimensional point that will fall somewhere in the unit square.

   ```
   (defn rand-point [] [(rand) (rand)])
   ```

2. Now, we need a function to return a point's distance from the origin.

   ```
   (defn center-dist
     [[x y]] (Math/sqrt (+ (* x x) (* y y))))
   ```

3. Next we'll define a function that takes a number of points to process, and creates that many random points. It will return the number of points that fall inside a circle.

   ```
   (defn count-in-circle
     [n]
     (->>
       (repeatedly n rand-point)
       (map center-dist)
       (filter #(<= % 1.0))
       count))
   ```

4. That simplifies our definition of the base (serial) version. This calls `count-in-circle` to get the proportion of random points in a unit square that fall inside a circle. It multiplies this by 4, which should approximate pi.

   ```
   (defn mc-pi
     [n]
     (* 4.0 (/ (count-in-circle n) n)))
   ```

5. We'll use a different approach for the simple `pmap` version. The function that we'll parallelize will take a point and return 1 if it's in the circle, or 0 if not. Then we can add those up to find the number in the circle.

   ```
   (defn in-circle-flag
     [p]
     (if (<= (center-dist p) 1.0)
       1
       0))

   (defn mc-pi-pmap
     [n]
     (let [in-circle (->>
                       (repeatedly n rand-point)
                       (pmap in-circle-flag)
                       (reduce + 0))]
       (* 4.0 (/ in-circle n))))
   ```

6. For the version that chunks the input, we'll do something different again. Instead of creating the sequence of random points and partitioning that, we'll have a sequence that tells how large each partition should be and have `pmap` walk across that, calling `count-in-circle`. This means that creating the larger sequences are also parallelized.

   ```
   (defn mc-pi-part
     ([n] (mc-pi-part 512 n))
   ```

## Improving Performance with Parallel Programming

```
  ([chunk-size n]
   (let [step (int
                 (Math/floor (float (/ n chunk-size))))
         remainder (mod n chunk-size)
         parts (lazy-seq
                 (cons remainder
                       (repeat step chunk-size)))
         in-circle (reduce + 0
                           (pmap count-in-circle
                                 parts))]
     (* 4.0 (/ in-circle n)))))
```

Now, how do these work? We'll bind our parameters to names, and then we'll run one set of benchmarks before we look at a table of all of them. We'll discuss the results in the next section.

```
user=> (def chunk-size 4096)
#'user/chunk-size
user=> (def input-size 1000000)
#'user/input-size
user=> (quick-bench (mc-pi input-size))
WARNING: Final GC required 4.001679309213317 % of runtime
Evaluation count : 6 in 6 samples of 1 calls.
             Execution time mean :634.387833 ms
    Execution time std-deviation : 33.222001 ms
   Execution time lower quantile : 606.122000 ms ( 2.5%)
   Execution time upper quantile : 677.273125 ms (97.5%)
nil
```

Here's all the information in the form of a table:

| Function | Input Size | Chunk Size | Mean | Std Dev. | GC Time |
|---|---|---|---|---|---|
| mc-pi | 1,000,000 | NA | 634.39ms | 33.22 ms | 4.0% |
| mc-pi-pmap | 1,000,000 | NA | 1.92 sec | 888.52 ms | 2.60% |
| mc-pi-part | 1,000,000 | 4,096 | 455.94 ms | 4.19 ms | 8.75% |

Here's a chart with the same information:

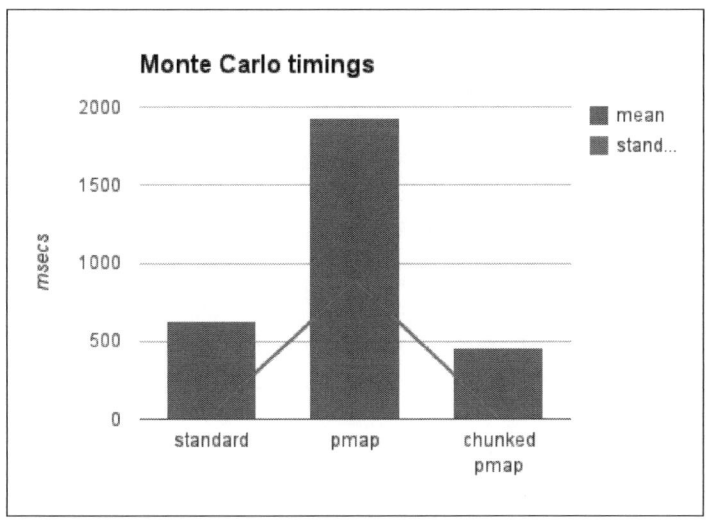

## How it works...

There are a couple of things we should talk about here. Primarily, we'll need to look at chunking the inputs for pmap, but we should also discuss Monte Carlo methods.

### Estimating with Monte Carlo simulations

Monte Carlo simulations work by throwing random data at a problem that is fundamentally deterministic, but when it's practically infeasible to attempt a more straightforward solution. Calculating pi is one example of this. By randomly filling in points in a unit square, π/4 will be approximately the ratio of points that will fall within a circle centered on 0, 0. The more random points that we use, the better the approximation.

I should note that this makes a good demonstration of Monte Carlo methods, but it's a terrible way to calculate pi. It tends to be both slower and less accurate than the other methods.

Although not good for this task, Monte Carlo methods have been used for designing heat shields, simulating pollution, ray tracing, financial option pricing, evaluating business or financial products, and many, many more things.

For a more in-depth discussion, Wikipedia has a good introduction to Monte Carlo methods at http://en.wikipedia.org/wiki/Monte_Carlo_method.

### Chunking data for pmap

The table we saw earlier makes it clear that partitioning helped: the partitioned version took just 72 percent of the time that the serial version did, while the naïve parallel version took more than three times longer. Based on the standard deviations, the results were also more consistent.

The speed up is because each thread is able to spend longer on each task. There is a performance penalty to spreading the work over multiple threads. Context switching (that is, switching between threads) costs time, and coordinating between threads does as well. But we expect to be able to make that time and more up by doing more things at once. However, if each task itself doesn't take long enough, then the benefit won't out-weigh the costs. Chunking the input—and effectively creating larger individual tasks for each thread—gets around this by giving each thread more to do, and thereby spending less time context switching and coordinating, relative to the overall time spent running.

## Finding the optimal partition size with simulated annealing

In the last recipe, *Partitioning Monte Carlo simulations for better pmap performance*, we more or less guessed what would make a good partition size. We tried a few different values and saw what gives us the best result. However, it's still largely guesswork, since just making the partitions larger or smaller doesn't give consistently better or worse results.

This is the type of task that computers are good at: searching a complex space to find the function parameters that results in an optimal output value. For this recipe, we'll use a fairly simple optimization algorithm called **simulated annealing**. Like many optimization algorithms, this one is based on a natural process: the way that molecules settle into low-energy configurations as the temperature drops to freezing. This is what allows water to form efficient crystal lattices as it freezes.

In simulated annealing, we feed a state to a cost function. At each point, we evaluate a random neighboring state, and possibly move to it. As the energy in the system (the temperature) goes down, we are less likely to jump to a new state, especially if that state is worse than the current one, according to the cost function. Finally, after either reaching a target output or iterating through a set number of steps, we take the best match found. Like many optimization algorithms, this doesn't guarantee that the result will be the absolute best match, but it should be a good one.

For this recipe, we'll use the Monte Carlo pi approximation function that we did in the *Partitioning Monte Carlo simulations for better pmap performance* recipe, and we'll use simulated annealing to find a better partition size.

## Getting ready

We'll need to use the same dependencies, uses, imports, and functions as we did in the *Partitioning Monte Carlo simulations for better pmap performance* recipe. In addition, we'll also need the `mc-pi-part` function from that recipe.

## How to do it...

For this recipe, we'll first define a generic simulated annealing system, and then we'll define some functions to pass it as parameters.

1. Everything will be driven by the simulated annealing function that takes all the function parameters for the process as arguments. We'll discuss them in more detail in a minute.

    ```
    (defn annealing
      [initial max-iter max-cost
        neighbor-fn cost-fn p-fn temp-fn]
      (let [get-cost (memoize cost-fn)
            cost (get-cost initial)]
        (loop [state initial
               cost cost
               k 1
               best-seq [{:state state, :cost cost}]]
          (println '>>> 'sa k \. state \$ cost)
          (if (and (< k max-iter)
                   (or (nil? max-cost)
                       (> cost max-cost)))
            (let [t (temp-fn (/ k max-iter))
                  next-state (neighbor-fn state)
                  next-cost (get-cost next-state)
                  next-place {:state next-state,
                              :cost next-cost}]
              (if (> (p-fn cost next-cost t) (rand))
                (recur next-state next-cost (inc k)
                       (conj best-seq next-place))
                (recur state cost (inc k) best-seq)))
            best-seq))))
    ```

2. For parameters, `annealing` takes an initial state, a limit to the number of iterations, a target output value, and a series of functions. The first function takes the current state and returns a new neighboring state.

*Improving Performance with Parallel Programming*

To write this function, we have to decide how best to handle the state for this problem. Often, if the function to evaluate has multiple parameters we'd use a vector and randomly slide one value in that around. However, for this problem, we only have one input value, the partition size.

So for this problem, we'll instead use an integer between 0 and 20. The actual partition size will be 2 raised to that power. To find a neighbor, we just randomly slide the `state` value up or down at most five, within the range of 0 to 20.

```
(defn get-neighbor
  [state]
  (max 0 (min 20 (+ state (- (rand-int 11) 5)))))
```

3. The next function parameter for `annealing` is the `cost` function. This will take the state and return the value that we're trying to minimize. In this case, we benchmark `mc-pi-part` with the given partition size (2 raised to the power) and return the average time.

```
(defn get-pi-cost
  [n state]
  (let [chunk-size (long (Math/pow 2 state))]
    (first (:mean (quick-benchmark
                    (mc-pi-part chunk-size n))))))
```

4. The next function takes the current state's cost, a potential new state's cost, and the current energy in the system (from 0 to 1). It returns the odds that the new state should be used. Currently, this will skip to an improved state always, or to a worse state 25 percent of the time (both of these are pro-rated by the temperature).

```
(defn should-move
  [c0 c1 t] (* t (if (< c0 c1) 0.25 1.0)))
```

5. The final function parameter takes the current percent through the iteration count and returns the energy or temperature as a number from 0 to 1. This can use a number of easing functions, but for this we'll just use a simple linear one.

```
(defn get-temp [r] (- 1.0 (float r)))
```

That's it. We can let this find a good partition size. We'll start with the value that we used in the *Partitioning Monte Carlo simulations for better pmap performance* recipe. We'll only allow ten iterations, since the search space is relatively small.

```
user=> (annealing 12 10 nil get-neighbor
  #_ =>               (partial get-pi-cost 1000000)
  #_ =>               should-move get-temp)
>>> sa 1 . 12 $ 0.5805938333333334
>>> sa 2 . 8 $ 0.38975950000000004
>>> sa 3 . 8 $ 0.38975950000000004
>>> sa 4 . 8 $ 0.38975950000000004
```

```
>>> sa 5 . 8 $ 0.38975950000000004
>>> sa 6 . 8 $ 0.38975950000000004
>>> sa 7 . 6 $ 0.357514
>>> sa 8 . 6 $ 0.357514
>>> sa 9 . 6 $ 0.357514
>>> sa 10 . 6 $ 0.357514
[{:state 12, :cost 0.5805938333333334}
 {:state 8,  :cost 0.38975950000000004}
 {:state 6,  :cost 0.357514}]
```

We can see that a partition size of 64 (26) is the best time, and re-running the benchmarks verifies this.

## How it works...

In practice, this algorithm won't help if we run it over the full input data. But if we can get a large enough sample, this can help us process the full dataset more efficiently by taking a lot of the guesswork out of picking the right partition size for the full evaluation.

What we did was kind of interesting. Let's take the annealing function apart to see how it works.

1. The process is handled by a `loop` inside the `annealing` function. Its parameters are a snapshot of the state of the annealing process.

   ```
   (loop [state initial
          cost cost
          k 1
          best-seq [{:state state, :cost cost}]]
   ```

2. We only continue if we need more iterations or if we haven't bested the maximum cost.

   ```
   (if (and (< k max-iter)
            (or (nil? max-cost)
                (> cost max-cost)))
   ```

3. If we continue, we calculate the next energy and get a potential state and cost to evaluate.

   ```
   (let [t (temp-fn (/ k max-iter))
         next-state (neighbor-fn state)
         next-cost (get-cost-cache next-state)
         next-place {:state next-state, :cost next-cost}]
   ```

4. If the probability function (`should-move`, in this case) indicates so, we move to the next `state` and `loop`. Otherwise, we stay at the current `state` and `loop`.

   ```
   (if (> (p-fn cost next-cost t) (rand))
     (recur next-state next-cost (inc k)
   ```

```
            (conj best-seq next-place))
   (recur state cost (inc k) best-seq)))
```

5. If we're done, we return the sequence of best states and costs seen.

   ```
   best-seq)))))
   ```

This provides a systematic way to explore the problem space: in this case to find a better partition size for this problem.

### There's more...

Simulated annealing is one of a class of algorithms known as **optimization algorithms**. All of these take a function (the `cost-fn` function that we saw) and try to find the largest or smallest value for it. Other optimization algorithms include genetic algorithms, ant colony optimization, particle swarm optimization, and many others. This is a broad and interesting field, and being familiar with these algorithms can be helpful for anyone doing data analysis.

## Parallelizing with reducers

Clojure 1.5 introduced the `clojure.core.reducers` library. This library provides a lot of interesting and exciting features, including composing multiple calls to `map` and other sequence-processing high-order functions and abstracting `map` and other functions for different types of collections while maintaining the collection type.

Looking at the following chart, initial operations on individual data items such as `map` and `filter` operate on items of the original dataset. Then the output of the operations on the items are combined using a reduce function. Finally, the outputs of the reduction step are progressively combined until the final result is produced. This could involve a reduce-type operation such as addition, or an accumulation, such as the `into` function.

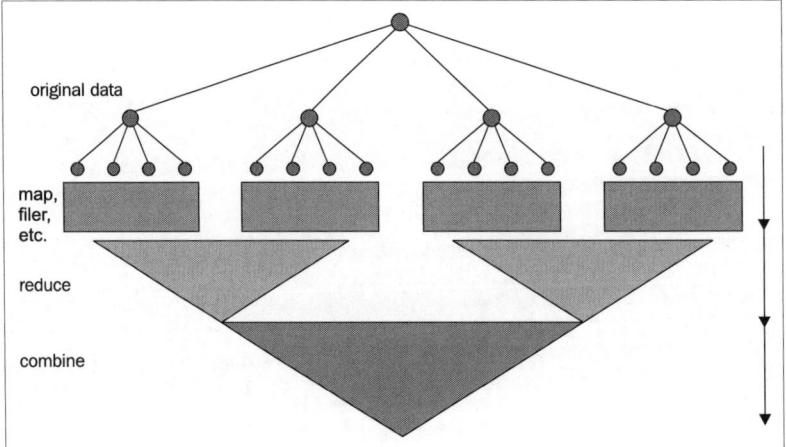

Another feature of reducers is that they can automatically partition and parallelize the processing of tree-based data structures. This includes Clojure's native vectors and hash maps.

For this recipe, we'll continue the Monte Carlo simulation example that we started in the *Partitioning Monte Carlo simulations for better pmap performance* recipe. In this case, we'll write a version that uses reducers and see how it performs.

## Getting ready

From the *Partitioning Monte Carlo simulations for better pmap performance* recipe, we'll use the same imports, as well as the `rand-point` function, the `center-dist` function, and the `mc-pi` function.

Along with these, we'll also need to require the reducers and Criterium libraries:

```
(require '[clojure.core.reducers :as r])
(use 'criterium.core)
```

Also, if you're using Java 1.6, you'll need the ForkJoin library, which you can get by adding this to your `project.clj` dependencies:

```
[org.codehaus.jsr166-mirror/jsr166y "1.7.0"]
```

## How to do it...

This version of the Monte Carlo pi approximation algorithm will be structured similarly to how `mc-pi` was in the *Partitioning Monte Carlo simulations for better pmap performance* recipe. First, we'll define a `count-in-circle-r` function that uses the reducers library to compose the processing and spread it over the available cores.

```
(defn count-items [c _] (inc c))
(defn count-in-circle-r
  [n]
  (->>
    (repeatedly n rand-point)
    vec
    (r/map center-dist)
    (r/filter #(<= % 1.0))
    (r/fold + count-items)))

(defn mc-pi-r
  [n]
  (* 4.0 (/ (count-in-circle-r n) n)))
```

## Improving Performance with Parallel Programming

Now, we can use Criterium to compare the two functions.

```
user=> (quick-bench (mc-pi 1000000))
WARNING: Final GC required 3.023487696312759 % of runtime
Evaluation count : 6 in 6 samples of 1 calls.
             Execution time mean :1.999605 sec
    Execution time std-deviation : 217.056295 ms
   Execution time lower quantile : 1.761563 sec ( 2.5%)
   Execution time upper quantile : 2.235991 sec (97.5%)
nil
user=> (quick-bench (mc-pi-r 1000000))
WARNING: Final GC required 6.398394257011045 % of runtime
Evaluation count : 6 in 6 samples of 1 calls.
             Execution time mean :947.908000 ms
    Execution time std-deviation : 306.273266 ms
   Execution time lower quantile : 776.947000 ms ( 2.5%)
   Execution time upper quantile : 1.477590 sec (97.5%)

Found 1 outliers in 6 samples (16.6667 %)
low-severe       1 (16.6667 %)
 Variance from outliers : 81.6010 % Variance is severely inflated by outliers
nil
```

Not bad. The version with reducers is over 50 percent faster than the serial one. This is more impressive because we've made relatively minor changes to the original code, especially compared to the version of this algorithm that partitioned the input before passing it to `pmap`, which we also saw in the *Partitioning Monte Carlo simulations for better pmap performance* recipe.

### How it works...

The reducers library does a couple of things in this recipe. Let's look at some lines from `count-in-circle-r`. Converting the input to a vector was important, because vectors can be parallelized, but generic sequences cannot be.

Next, these two lines are composed into one reducer function that doesn't create an extra sequence between the call to `r/map` and `r/filter`. This is a small, but important, optimization, especially if we'd stacked more functions into this stage of the process.

```
(r/map center-dist)
(r/filter #(<= % 1.0))
```

The bigger optimization is in the line for `r/fold`. `r/reduce` processes serially always, but if the input is a tree-based data structure, `r/fold` will employ a fork-join pattern to parallelize it. This line takes the place of a call to count by incrementing a counter function for every item in the sequence so far.

```
(r/fold + count-items))))
```

Graphically this process looks something like the following chart:

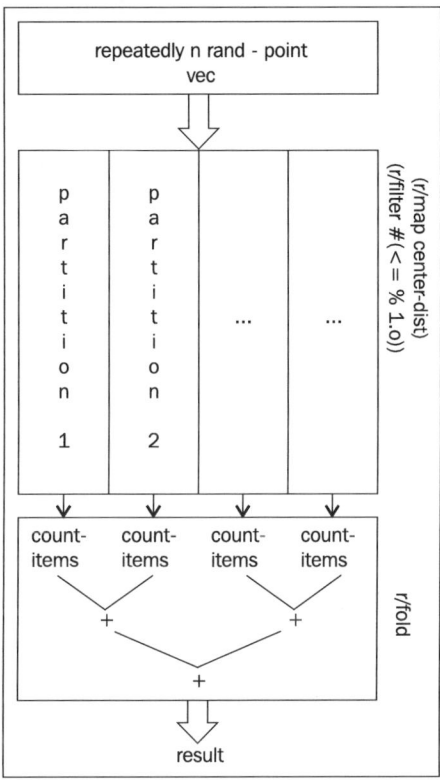

The reducers library is still fairly new to Clojure, but it has a lot of promise to automatically parallelize structured operations with a control and simplicity that we haven't seen elsewhere.

## There's more...

For more about reducers, see Rich Hickey's blog posts at http://clojure.com/blog/2012/05/08/reducers-a-library-and-model-for-collection-processing.html and http://clojure.com/blog/2012/05/15/anatomy-of-reducer.html. Also, his presentation on reducers for EuroClojure 2012 (http://vimeo.com/45561411) has a lot of good information.

### See also

- The *Generating online summary statistics with reducers* recipe

# Generating online summary statistics with reducers

We can use reducers in a lot of different situations, but sometimes we'll need to change how we process data to do so.

For this example, we'll show how to compute summary statistics with reducers. We'll use some algorithms and formulas first proposed by Tony F. Chan, Gene H. Golub, and Randall J. LeVeque in 1979 and later extended by Timothy B. Terriberry in 2007. These allow us to approximate mean, standard deviation, and skew for online data—that is, for streaming data that we may only see once—so we'll need to compute all the statistics on one pass without holding the full collection in memory.

The following formulae are a little complicated and difficult to read in lisp-notation. But there's a good overview of this process, with formulae, on the Wikipedia page for *Algorithms for calculating variance* (http://en.wikipedia.org/wiki/Algorithms_for_calculating_variance). And to simplify this example somewhat, we'll only calculate the mean and variance.

### Getting ready

For this, we'll need to have easy access to the reducers library and the Java `Math` class.

```
(require '[clojure.core.reducers :as r])
(import '[java.lang Math])
```

### How to do it...

For this recipe, first we'll define the accumulator data structures and then the accumulator functions. Finally, we'll put it all together.

1. We need to define a data structure to store all the data that we want to accumulate and keep track of.

   ```
   (def zero-counts
     {:n (long 0), :s 0.0,
    :mean 0.0,
    :m2 0.0})
   ```

2. Now, we'll need some way to add a datum to the counts and accumulation. The function `accum-counts` will take care of this.

   ```
   (defn accum-counts
     ([] zero-counts)
     ([{:keys [n mean m2 s] :as accum} x]
      (let [new-n (long (inc n))
            delta (- x mean)
            delta-n (/ delta new-n)
            term-1 (* delta delta-n n)
            new-mean (+ mean delta-n)]
        {:n new-n
         :mean new-mean
         :s (+ s x)
         :m2 (+ m2 term-1)})))
   ```

3. Next, we'll need a way to combine two accumulators. This has the complete, unsimplified versions of the formulae from `accum-counts`. Because some of the numbers can get very large and overflow the range of the primitive Java types, we'll use `*'`. This is a variant of the multiplication operator that automatically promotes values into Java's BigInteger types instead of overflowing.

   ```
   (defn op-fields
     "A utility function that calls a function on
     the values of a field from two maps."
     [op field item1 item2]
     (op (field item1) (field item2)))

   (defn combine-counts
     ([] zero-counts)
     ([xa xb]
      (let [n (long (op-fields + :n xa xb))
            delta (op-fields - :mean xb xa)
            nxa*xb (*' (:n xa) (:n xb))]
        {:n n
         :mean (+ (:mean xa) (* delta (/ (:n xb) n)))
         :s (op-fields + :s xa xb)
         :m2 (+ (:m2 xa) (:m2 xb)
                (* delta delta (/ nxa*xb n)))})))
   ```

4. Now we need a way to take the accumulated counts and values and turn them into the final statistics.

   ```
   (defn stats-from-sums
     [{:keys [n mean m2 s] :as sums}]
     {:mean (double (/ s n))
      :variance (/ m2 (dec n))})
   ```

5. Finally, we combine all these functions to produce results.

```
(defn summary-statistics
  [coll]
  (stats-from-sums
    (r/fold combine-counts accum-counts coll)))
```

For a pointless example, we can use this to find summary statistics on 1,000,000 random numbers:

```
user=> (summary-statistics (repeatedly 1000000 rand))
{:mean 0.5004908831693459, :variance 0.08346136740444697}
```

## Harnessing your GPU with OpenCL and Calx

For calculations involving matrixes and floating point math, in today's computers our best option is executing them on the **graphical processing unit**, or **GPU**. Because these have been so highly tuned for 3D shading and rendering, they can handle these operations very quickly, sometimes an order of magnitude more quickly than general CPUs can.

But programming GPUs is a little different than general programming. For the most part, we're stuck coding in a subset of C with very specific parameters for the parts of the process that are handled by the GPU. There are some projects that convert Java byte-code to GPU code (https://github.com/pcpratts/rootbeer1, http://www.jocl.org/, or http://code.google.com/p/aparapi/). Unfortunately, at this time, none of them support using a dynamic JVM language, such as Clojure.

For this recipe, we'll use the Calx library (https://github.com/ztellman/calx/). This project has a warning about not being under active development, but it's already usable. This is a wrapper around an OpenCL (http://www.khronos.org/opencl/) library, which supports a wide range of video card vendors.

In general, you'll receive the most payoff from the GPU when doing floating point math, especially vector and matrix operations. Because of this, we'll once again calculate the Mandelbrot set. This will be an example that would see improvement from running on the GPU and having an existing implementation to compare to. This will also allow us to see just how much of a speed increase we're getting.

### Getting ready

We need to include a dependency on Calx in our `project.clj` file.

```
:dependencies [[org.clojure/clojure "1.5.0"]
               [calx "0.2.1"]]
```

And we'll need to import `Calx` and `java.lang.Math` into our REPL or script.

```
(use 'calx)
(import [java.lang Math])
```

We'll also use the `output-points` function from the *Parallelizing processing with pmap* recipe.

## How to do it...

Even using Calx, most of this has to be in C. This is encoded as a string that is processed and compiled by Calx.

```
(def src
  "// scale from -2.5 to 1.
float scale_x(float x) {
    return (x / 1000.0) * 3.5 - 2.5;
  }

  // scale from -1 to 1.
float scale_y(float y) {
    return (y / 1000.0) * 2.0 - 1.0;
  }

    __kernel void escape(
        __global float *out) {
    int i = get_global_id(0);
    int j = get_global_id(1);
    int index = j * get_global_size(0) + i;
    float point_x = scale_x(i);
    float point_y = scale_y(j);
    int max_iterations = 1000;
    int iteration     = 0;
    float x = 0.0;
    float y = 0.0;

    while (x*x + y*y <= 4 && iteration <max_iterations) {
      float tmp_x = (x*x - y*y) + point_x;
      y = (2 * x * y) + point_y;
      x = tmp_x;
      iteration++;
    }

    out[index] = iteration;
  }")
```

## Improving Performance with Parallel Programming

We'll also need a function to handle compiling the source code and passing data around.

```
(defn -main
  []
  (let [max-x 1000, max-y 1000]
    (with-cl
      (with-program
        (compile-program src)
        (time
          (let [out (wrap (flatten
                            (output-points max-x max-y))
                          :float32-le)]
            (enqueue-kernel :escape (* max-x max-y) out)
            (let [out-seq (vec @(enqueue-read out))]
              (spit "mandelbrot-out.txt" (prn-str out-seq))
              (println
                "Calculated on " (platform) "/" (best-device))
              (println
                "Output written to mandelbrot-out.txt")))))))))
```

If we run this, we'll see how fast it is.

```
user=> (-main)
Calculated on  #<CLPlatform Apple {vendor: Apple, version: OpenCL 1.0
(Dec 26 2010 12:52:21), profile: FULL_PROFILE, extensions: []}> /
#<CLDevice ATI Radeon HD 6750M>
Output written to mandelbrot-out.txt
"Elapsed time: 9659.691 msecs"
nil
```

We can compare that 9.7 seconds to the parallel version of the Mandelbrot set program that we wrote in the *Parallelizing processing with pmap* recipe.

```
user=> (def mset (time (mandelbrot pmap
max-iterations max-x max-y
  #_=>                                    mandelbrot-range)))
"Elapsed time: 19126.335 msecs"
#'user/mset
```

That's about twice as fast. This was a very invasive change, but the results are quite good.

### How it works...

There are two parts to this. First, the C code and GPU processing in general, and then the Calx interface to the GPU.

## Writing the GPU code in C

A full explanation—or for that matter, even just an introduction—of GPU programming is beyond the scope of this recipe, so we'll just try to understand what's going on in this specific example. See the *There's more...* section of this recipe for where to go to learn more.

First, the code to run on the GPU needs to be marked `__kernel`. Notice that we're just passing one parameter into this function, the output array. The GPU function, `escape`, will be called many times, based upon the shape of the data.

Each time the GPU calls `escape`, we have to figure out which index into the data it's executing on. We do that by calling `get_global_id` (dimension). Instead of scaling the pixel point to the Mandelbrot range in Clojure, I've moved those functions into C (`scale_x` and `scale_y`). Otherwise, the code is more or less the same as we were doing before to calculate the Mandelbrot set, just in C.

This pattern—let the GPU handle the looping and only code the inner part of the loop—is generally how we'll structure everything that runs on the GPU.

## Wrapping it in Calx

While this all may seem very low-level, Calx is still taking a lot of the pain out of GPU processing. Let's look at what else we have to do. After compiling everything in the call to `compile-program`, the `-main` function breaks the process down into three steps. First, we need to move the data over to the GPU. This is done by converting the list of pixel coordinates to a float array on the GPU.

```
(let [out (wrap (flatten
                  (output-points max-x max-y))
                :float32-le)]
```

Next, we queue the `escape` function written in C for processing on the GPU. We tell it how many data items we'll need and the parameters to pass to it (in this case, only the float array we just allocated).

```
(enqueue-kernel :escape (* max-x max-y) out)
```

Finally, we queue a `read` operation on the `out` array, so that we can access its data. This returns a reference, which will block when we dereference it until the data is available.

```
(let [out-seq (vec @(enqueue-read out))]
```

GPU processing can be a bit different than the general-purpose programming we're probably used to, but as we saw, it also allows us to get some spectacular performance improvements.

## There's more...

To go further with the GPU, you'll want to find some more material. Personally, I found AMD's tutorial to be helpful (`http://developer.amd.com/tools/heterogeneous-computing/amd-accelerated-parallel-processing-app-sdk/introductory-tutorial-to-opencl/`). There are a number of other tutorials out on the Internet, and there seemed to be a lot of variance in them. Google can help you there.

And as usual, your mileage may vary, so start on a few tutorials until you find one that makes sense to you.

## Using type hints

Most problems that are good targets for parallelization involve doing calculations in tight loops. These places are good for all kinds of performance optimizations, from hoisting conditionals out of them to fine-tuning compiler hints, which we will do here.

Being a dynamic language, Clojure doesn't require type declarations. However, if we know what types we are using, we can get better performance by including type hints in our code. This is helpful for object types, where Clojure can then resolve method calls at compile time, and also for primitive types, where Clojure can generate well-tuned code that doesn't include boxing, or wrapping the primitive type in a heavier Java object. For more information about this, see the documentation about interacting with Java from Clojure for information about type hints and working with Java primitives (`http://clojure.org/java_interop`). Type hints are expressed as metadata tags for return types and object types. We'll see examples of both in the following section.

For this recipe, we'll revisit the Monte Carlo simulation to estimate the value of pi. We first saw this in the *Partitioning Monte Carlo simulations for better pmap performance* recipe. This example has enough low-level math to make it a good candidate for this kind of optimization.

### Getting ready

We'll use the Criterium library for benchmarking, so include these in our Leiningen `project.clj` file:

```
:dependencies [[org.clojure/clojure "1.5.0"]
               [criterium "0.3.0"]]
```

We use it and the `java.lang.Math` class in our script or REPL.

```
(use 'criterium.core)
(import [java.lang Math])
```

From the *Partitioning Monte Carlo simulations for better pmap performance* recipe, we'll use the functions `rand-point` and `center-dist`.

## How to do it...

We'll implement the Monte Carlo simulation without type hints, benchmark it, and then re-implement with type hints to see if we can get better performance.

1. The simulation itself places n random points in the unit square and tests to see how many of them fall within the upper-right quadrant of a circle centered on 0, 0. The ratio of them that falls within the circle, multiplied by 4, should approximate pi.

   ```
   (defn mc-pi
     [n]
     (let [in-circle (->>
                       (repeatedly n rand-point)
                       (map center-dist)
                       (filter #(<= % 1.0))
                       count)]
       (* 4.0 (/ in-circle n))))
   ```

2. If we benchmark the existing implementation with Criterium, it will give us something to shoot for. It shows that the average run time was 47.6 milliseconds.

   ```
   user=> (bench (mc-pi 100000))
   Evaluation count : 1320 in 60 samples of 22 calls.
                Execution time mean : 47.615120 ms
       Execution time std-deviation : 610.350153 us
      Execution time lower quantile : 46.690273 ms ( 2.5%)
      Execution time upper quantile : 48.966694 ms (97.5%)
   nil
   ```

3. Now, we'll add casts for the primitive doubles in `center-dist`, and we'll add type hint metadata for the return type also.

   ```
   (defn center-dist-hint
     (^double [[x y]]
        (Math/sqrt (+ (Math/pow (double x) (double 2.0))
                      (Math/pow (double y)
                                (double 2.0))))))
   ```

4. Next, we change `mc-pi` to call `center-dist-hint` and add a type hint to it.

   ```
   (defn mc-pi-hint
     (^double [n]
        (let [in-circle (double
                          (->>
                            (repeatedly n rand-point)
                            (map center-dist-hint)
                            (filter #(<= % (double 1.0)))
   ```

```
                              count))]
              (double
                (* (double 4.0) (/ in-circle (double n)))))))
```

Finally, let's see if this helps.

```
user=> (report-result (benchmark (mc-pi-hint 100000)))
Evaluation count : 1740 in 60 samples of 29 calls.
            Execution time mean :35.626201 ms
    Execution time std-deviation : 608.936601 us
    Execution time lower quantile : 34.653523 ms ( 2.5%)
    Execution time upper quantile : 36.880537 ms (97.5%)
nil
```

This is a 25 percent improvement in average run times. Not too bad for adding a little metadata to help the Clojure compiler out a little.

## How it works...

The first type hint we used is the ^double, which indicates the functions' return types and parameters. These allow the Clojure compiler to generate byte-code that's well optimized for those types and for working with the Java primitives.

The other use of type hints allows the Clojure compiler to resolve methods at compile time. The clojure.string namespace has a nice example of that:

```
user=> (require '[clojure.string :as string])
nil
user=> (source string/trim)
(defn ^String trim
  "Removes whitespace from both ends of string."
  {:added "1.2"}
  [^CharSequence s]
  (.. s toString trim))
nil
```

We can see that the parameter to the string/trim function is a CharSequence, and the compiler can use that information to know which toString to dispatch to.

## See also

- The *Benchmarking with Criterium* recipe
- The *Partitioning Monte Carlo simulations for better pmap performance* recipe

# Benchmarking with Criterium

Benchmarking can be an important part of the data analysis process. Especially when faced with very large datasets that need to be processed in multiple ways, choosing algorithms that will finish in a reasonable amount of time is important. Benchmarking gives us an empirical basis on which to make these decisions.

For some of the recipes in this chapter, we've used the `time` macro. For others we've used the Criterium library (https://github.com/hugoduncan/criterium). Why would we want to go to the trouble of using a whole library, just to see how fast our code is?

Generally, when we want to benchmark our code, we'll often start by using something like the `time` macro. This means:

1. Get the start time.
2. Execute the code.
3. Get the end time.

If you've done this often, you will realize that this has a number of problems, especially for benchmarking small functions that execute quickly. The times are often inconsistent, and they can be dependant on a number of factors external to our program, such as the memory or disk cache. Using this benchmarking method often ends up as an exercise in frustration.

Fortunately, Criterium takes care of all of this. It makes sure that the caches are warmed up, it runs our code multiple times, and it presents a statistical look at the execution times.

This presents more information than just a single raw time. It also presents a lot of other useful information, like how much time is spent in garbage collection.

For this recipe, we'll take the functions that we created for doing Monte Carlo pi estimates in the *Using type hints* recipe and compare the timings we get with the `time` macro against those we get from Criterium.

## Getting ready

To use Criterium, we just need to add it to the list of dependencies in our `project.clj` file:

```
:dependencies [[org.clojure/clojure "1.5.0"]
               [criterium "0.3.0"]]
```

We need to use it in our script or REPL.

```
(use 'criterium.core)
```

We'll also need to benchmark the code. This means the `mc-pi` and `mc-pi-hint` functions from the *Using type hints* recipe, along with their dependencies.

*Improving Performance with Parallel Programming*

## How to do it...

First, let's look at the results running the `time` macro several times on each function. Here's how we do it once:

```
user=> (time (mc-pi 1000000))
"Elapsed time: 590.074msecs"
```

The following chart shows the results of all five calls on each:

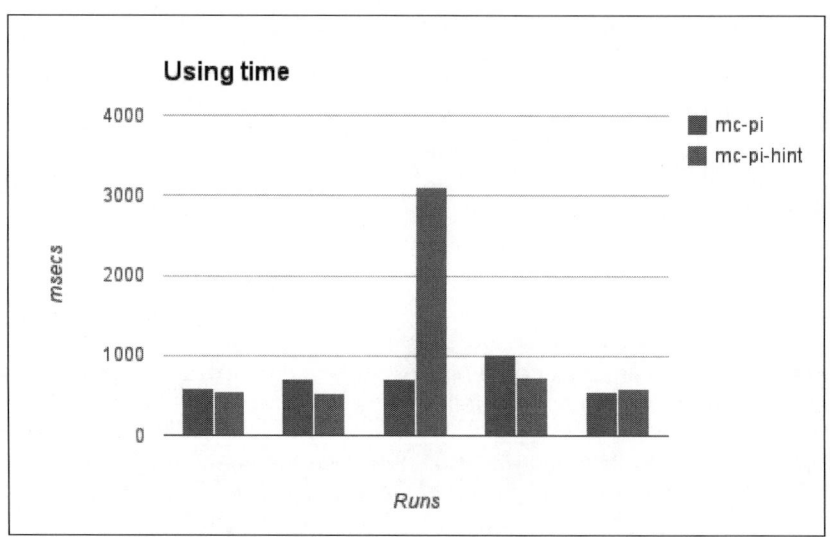

We can see that the results are all over the map on this. Some of the middle runs are suspiciously high, possibly from garbage collection, and the rest of them seem to wander around over the span of a couple of hundred milliseconds.

For comparison, here are the results with Criterium:

```
user=> (bench (mc-pi 1000000))
Evaluation count : 60 in 60 samples of 1 calls.
          Execution time mean :1.347967 sec
 Execution time std-deviation : 2.231000 sec
Execution time lower quantile : 459.251000 ms ( 2.5%)
Execution time upper quantile : 4.772331 sec (97.5%)

Found 6 outliers in 60 samples (10.0000 %)
low-severe       1 (1.6667 %)
low-mild         5 (8.3333 %)
 Variance from outliers : 98.3241 % Variance is severely inflated by outliers
```

```
nil
user=> (bench (mc-pi-hint 1000000))
Evaluation count : 120 in 60 samples of 2 calls.
             Execution time mean :878.054242 ms
    Execution time std-deviation : 1.047811 sec
   Execution time lower quantile : 439.007000 ms ( 2.5%)
   Execution time upper quantile : 2.454926 sec (97.5%)

Found 6 outliers in 60 samples (10.0000 %)
low-severe       1 (1.6667 %)
low-mild         5 (8.3333 %)
 Variance from outliers : 98.3157 % Variance is severely inflated by
outliers
nil
```

The version with type hints isn't quite twice as fast. The results are immediately clear (without having to type them into a spreadsheet, which I did to create the chart). And there's a lot more information given.

## How it works...

So how does Criterium help us? First, it runs the code several times, and just throws away the results. This means we don't have to worry about initial inconsistencies while the JVM, memory cache, and disk cache get settled.

Second, it runs the code a lot more than five times. Quick benchmarking runs it six times. Standard benchmarking runs it sixty times. This gives us a lot more data and a lot more confidence in our interpretation.

Third, it provides us with a lot more information about the runs. With `time`, we have to eyeball the results and go with our gut for what all those numbers mean. If we want to be more precise, we can re-type all the numbers into a spreadsheet and generate some statistics. Criterium does that for us. It also analyzes the results, to tell us if some outliers are throwing off the statistics.

Criterium gives us a much better basis on which to make decisions about how best to optimize our code and improve its performance.

## There's more...

We've really just touched the surface on the functionality that Criterium provides and the functions it exports. For more information about this fantastic library, see the documentation at `https://github.com/hugoduncan/criterium`.

# 5
# Distributed Data Processing with Cascalog

In this chapter, we will cover:

- Distributed processing with Cascalog and Hadoop
- Querying data with Cascalog
- Distributing data with Apache HDFS
- Parsing CSV files with Cascalog
- Executing complex queries with Cascalog
- Aggregating data with Cascalog
- Defining new Cascalog operators
- Composing Cascalog queries
- Handling errors in Cascalog workflows
- Transforming data with Cascalog
- Executing Cascalog queries in the Cloud with Pallet

# Introduction

Over the course of the last few chapters, we've been progressively moving outward. We started assuming that everything would run on one processor, probably in a single thread. Then we looked at how to structure our program without that assumption, performing different tasks on many threads. Next we tried to speed up processing by getting multiple threads and cores working on the same task. Now we've pulled back about as far as we can, and we're going to look at how to break the work to execute on multiple computers. For large amounts of data, this can be especially useful.

In fact, big data has become more and more common. The definition of big data is a moving target as disk sizes grow, but you work with big data if you have trouble processing it in memory, or even storing it on disk. There's a lot of information locked in, but getting it out can be a real problem. The recipes in this chapter will help address those issues.

The most common way of distributing computations currently is to use an algorithm described by Google called **MapReduce** (http://research.google.com/archive/mapreduce.html). The MapReduce process should be familiar to anyone who uses Clojure, as MapReduce is directly inspired by functional programming. The data is partitioned over all of the computers in the cluster. An operation is mapped across the input data, with each computer in the cluster performing part of the processing. The outputs of the map function are then accumulated using a Reduce operation. Conceptually, this is very similar to the reducers library that we discussed in some of the recipes in *Chapter 4, Improving Performance with Parallel Programming*. The following diagram illustrates the three stages of processing:

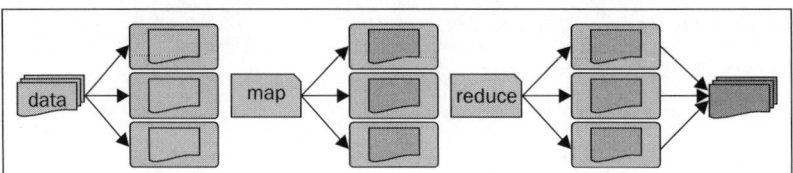

Clojure itself doesn't have any features for distributed processing. However, it does have excellent interoperability with the Java Virtual Machine, and Java has a number of libraries and systems for creating and using distributed systems. In the recipes of this chapter, we'll primarily use **Hadoop** (http://hadoop.apache.org/), and we'll especially focus on **Cascading** (http://www.cascading.org/) and the Clojure wrapper for that library, **Cascalog** (https://github.com/nathanmarz/cascalog). This tool chain makes distributed processing simple.

All of these systems also work in a single-server/development mode. That's what we'll use in most of the recipes in this chapter. The code should work in a multi-server, clustered environment also, and for the last recipe, we'll show how to set up such a system on EC2 using **Pallet** (http://palletops.com/).

# Distributed processing with Cascalog and Hadoop

Hadoop was developed by Yahoo to implement Google's MapReduce algorithm and then open-sourced. Since then, it's become one of the most widely-tested and used systems for creating distributed processing.

The central part of this ecosystem is Hadoop, but it's also complemented by a range of other tools, including the **Hadoop Distributed File System** (**HDFS**) and **Pig**, a language for writing jobs to run on Hadoop.

One tool to make the working with Hadoop easier is Cascading. This provides a workflow-like layer on top of Hadoop that can make expressing some tasks much easier. Cascalog is a Clojure-idiomatic interface for Cascading and, ultimately, for Hadoop.

This recipe will show us how to access and query data in Clojure sequences using Cascalog.

## Getting ready

First, we have to add a new repository to the Leiningen `project.clj` file. This will allow it to find the Cascading Java library, which Cascalog depends on.

```
:repositories [["conjars.org" "http://conjars.org/repo"]]
```

Next, we have to add Cascalog to the dependencies in our `project.clj` file.

```
:dependencies [[org.clojure/clojure "1.4.0"]
               [cascalog "1.10.0"]
               [org.slf4j/slf4j-api "1.7.2"]]
```

And we'll also want to include the Hadoop libraries in our development environment. We can do that by adding the following to the `project.clj` file:

```
:profiles
  {:dev
    {:dependencies
 [[org.apache.hadoop/hadoop-core "1.1.1"]]}}
```

Finally, we'll require the packages that we'll use, including the `clojure.string` library.

```
(require '[clojure.string :as string])
(require '(cascalog [workflow :as w] [ops :as c] [vars :as v]))
(use 'cascalog.api)
```

## How to do it...

Most of this recipe will define the data we'll query. For this, we will use the sequences of information about the companions and actors from the British television program, *Doctor Who*. This is in a sequence of maps, so we'll need to transform it into several sequences of vectors, which is what Cascalog can access. One will be a list of companion "keys": lowercased given names. One will be the name key and the full name. And the final one will be a table of the companions' keys to a doctor they're tagged along with. We'll also define a list of the actors who played the doctors and the number of years they played them.

At the time of writing this book, there were about 50 companions. I've only listed 10 here, but the examples may show others. The full data is available in the source code. You can also download the code to create this dataset from `http://www.ericrochester.com/clj-data-analysis/data/companions.clj`.

```clojure
(def input-data
  [{:given-name "Susan", :surname "Forman", :doctors [1]}
   {:given-name "Katarina", :surname nil, :doctors [1]}
   {:given-name "Victoria", :surname "Waterfield", :doctors [2]}
   {:given-name "Sarah Jane", :surname "Smith", :doctors [3 4 10]}
   {:given-name "Romana", :surname nil, :doctors [4]}
   {:given-name "Kamelion", :surname nil, :doctors [5]}
   {:given-name "Rose", :surname "Tyler", :doctors [9 10]}
   {:given-name "Martha", :surname "Jones", :doctors [10]}
   {:given-name "Adelaide", :surname "Brooke", :doctors [10]}
   {:given-name "Craig", :surname "Owens", :doctors [11]}])

(def companion (map string/lower-case
                    (map :given-name input-data)))
(def full-name
  (map (fn [{:keys [given-name surname]}]
         [(string/lower-case given-name)
          (string/trim
            (string/join \space [given-name surname]))])
       input-data))
(def doctor
  (mapcat #(map (fn [d] [(string/lower-case (:given-name %)) d])
                (:doctors %))
          input-data))

(def actor
  [[1 "William Hartnell" "1963-66"]
   [2 "Patrick Troughton" "1966-69"]
```

```
            [3 "Jon Pertwee" "1970-74"]
            [4 "Tom Baker" "1974-81"]
            [5 "Peter Davison" "1981-84"]
            [6 "Colin Baker" "1984-86"]
            [7 "Sylvester McCoy" "1987-89, 1996"]
            [8 "Paul McGann" "1996"]
            [9 "Christopher Eccleston" "2005"]
            [10 "David Tennant" "2005-10"]
            [11 "Matt Smith" "2010-present"]])
```

We'll explain the syntax for the query in more detail in the following *How it works...* section. In the meantime, let's just dive in.

```
(?<- (stdout) [?companion] (companion ?companion))
```

When you execute the preceding statement, you may see a lot of logging messages from Hadoop. Towards the end, you should see the following:

```
RESULTS
----------------------
susan
barbara
ian
vicki
steven
...
```

We can also query the other tables.

```
(?<- (stdout) [?name] (full-name _ ?name))
...
RESULTS
----------------------
Susan Forman
Barbara Wright
Ian Chesterton
Vicki
Steven Taylor
...
```

## How it works...

The structure for query statements is not hard to understand. Let's break one apart.

```
(?<- (stdout) [?name] (full-name _ ?name))
```

The ?<- operator creates a query and executes it. It's really a combination of the <- macro, which creates a query from output variables and predicates, and the ?- function that executes a query to a sink.

```
(?<- (stdout) [?name] (full-name _ ?name))
```

The first parameter is a Cascading **tap** sink. This is a destination for the data. Obviously, if there's a lot of data being output, just dumping it to the console won't be a good idea. In such cases, you could send it to a file. Since there's not much data, we'll just write it to the screen.

```
(?<- (stdout) [?name] (full-name _ ?name))
```

The preceding is a vector of output variables. The names here must occur in the predicates that follow.

```
(?<- (stdout) [?name] (full-name _ ?name))
```

This is the list of predicates. In this example, there's only one. It queries the `full-name` table. It doesn't care about the values in the first column, so it just uses an underscore as a placeholder (_).

> Using the underscore as a variable name in this way is a convention in Clojure and similar languages for values that we want to ignore.

The values in the second column are bound to the name ?name, which is also found in the vector of output columns.

Of course working with in-memory data isn't that useful. It's good for development and debugging, though. And later we'll see how to connect to a data file, and the query syntax is exactly the same.

## See also

We'll see how to access data that's not held in memory in the following recipes:

- The *Distributing data with Apache HDFS* recipe
- The *Parsing CSV files with Cascalog* recipe

# Querying data with Cascalog

In the *Distributed processing with Cascalog and Hadoop* recipe, we started looking at how to query data in Cascalog with a couple of small examples. However, Cascalog's query language is much more powerful than we saw there. We'll dive in further in this recipe and start looking at some of the logical predicates available. Recipes later in this chapter will have still more examples of querying with Cascalog.

## Getting ready

For this recipe, we'll need the `project.clj` file dependencies and imports from the *Distributed processing with Cascalog and Hadoop* recipe. We'll also use the data from that recipe: the sequences of information about the companions and actors from the British television program, *Doctor Who*.

## How to do it...

1. For the first example, we'll get the first five actors who played the doctor.

   ```
   (?<- (stdout) [?n ?actor ?period]
        (actor ?n ?actor ?period) (<= ?n 5))
   ```
   …
   ```
   RESULTS
   ----------------------
   1       William Hartnell        1963-66
   2       Patrick Troughton       1966-69
   3       Jon Pertwee     1970-74
   4       Tom Baker       1974-81
   5       Peter Davison   1981-84
   ```

2. For the next, we'll get all the companions of the tenth doctor (David Tennant).

   ```
   (?<- (stdout) [?companion] (doctor ?companion ?n) (= ?n 10))
   ```
   …
   ```
   RESULTS
   ----------------------
   sarahjane
   rose
   jack
   mickey
   donna
   martha
   astrid
   jackson
   rosita
   christina
   adelaide
   wilfred
   ```

   Well, he's a popular guy.

## How it works...

Let's look at the second example in a little more detail.

```
(?<- (stdout) [?companion] (doctor ?companion ?n) (= ?n 10))
```

The predicates are evaluated once for each row in the input data. Once a name has been bound in one predicate, it will keep that value throughout all predicates. And a row is the only output when *all* predicates pass.

```
(?<- (stdout) [?companion] (doctor ?companion ?n) (= ?n 10))
```

This predicate only passes where ?n is bound to 10. Since all predicates have to pass successfully, this only returns the companions for doctor number 10.

## There's more...

**Variable binding**, which we saw in this recipe, is a well-known feature of data-oriented systems. **Prolog** (http://en.wikipedia.org/wiki/Prolog), for example, uses it extensively.

# Distributing data with Apache HDFS

One of the nicest features of Hadoop is the Hadoop Distributed File System. This creates a network of computers that automatically synchronizes their data, making our input data available to all computers. Not having to worry about how our data gets distributed makes our lives much, much easier.

For this recipe, we'll put a file into the HDFS and read it back out using Cascalog, line by line.

## Getting ready

The previous recipes in this chapter all used the version of Hadoop that Leiningen downloaded as one of Cascalog's dependencies. For this recipe, however, we'll need to have Hadoop installed and running separately. Go to http://hadoop.apache.org/ and download and install Hadoop. You may also be able to use your operating system's package manager. Alternatively, Cloudera has a VM with a 1-node Hadoop cluster that we can download and use (https://ccp.cloudera.com/display/SUPPORT/CDH+Downloads#CDHDownloads-CDH4PackagesandDownloads).

You'll still need to configure everything. Look on the Hadoop website for the **Getting Started** documentation for your version. Get a **Single Node Setup** working.

Once it's installed and configured, go ahead and start the servers. There's a script in the `bin` directory for doing this:

```
$ ./bin/start-all.sh
startingnamenode, logging to /usr/local/Cellar/hadoop/1.0.4/libexec/
bin/../logs/hadoop-err8n-namenode-eris.out
localhost: starting datanode, logging to /usr/local/Cellar/
hadoop/1.0.4/libexec/bin/../logs/hadoop-err8n-datanode-eris.out
localhost: starting secondarynamenode, logging to /usr/local/Cellar/
hadoop/1.0.4/libexec/bin/../logs/hadoop-err8n-secondarynamenode-eris.
out
startingjobtracker, logging to /usr/local/Cellar/hadoop/1.0.4/libexec/
bin/../logs/hadoop-err8n-jobtracker-eris.out
localhost: starting tasktracker, logging to /usr/local/Cellar/
hadoop/1.0.4/libexec/bin/../logs/hadoop-err8n-tasktracker-eris.out
```

We still need to have everything working with Clojure, however. For that, we just use the same dependencies and references that we did in the *Distributed processing with Cascalog and Hadoop* recipe. However, this time don't worry about the REPL. We'll take care of that separately.

## How to do it...

For this recipe, we'll insert a file into the distributed filesystem, run the Clojure REPL inside Hadoop, and read the data back out.

1. First, the data file must be in the HDFS. For this example, we'll use a CSV version of the *Doctor Who* companion data from the *Distributed processing with Cascalog and Hadoop* recipe. You can download this file from http://www.ericrochester. com/clj-data-analysis/data/companions.txt. Once it's on our local filesystem, we can insert it into HDFS with the following command:

   ```
   $ hadoop fs -put companions.txt /tmp/companions.txt
   ```

2. Now, in order to run our code in the Hadoop environment, we have to use the `hadoop` command on a JAR file created from our project. Create an empty namespace to give the JAR file a little content. For example, I created a file named `src/distrib_data/cascalog_setup.clj` with the following content:

```clojure
(ns distrib-data.cascalog-setup
  (:require (cascalog
              [workflow :as w]
              [ops :as c]
              [vars :as v])
            [clojure.string :as string])
  (:use cascalog.api))
```

3. Once that's in place, we create a JAR file containing this file and all of its dependencies.

   ```
   $ lein uberjar
   Created /Users/err8n/p/cljbook/distrib-data/target/distrib-data-
   0.1.0.jar
   Including distrib-data-0.1.0.jar
   Including janino-2.5.16.jar
   Including commons-httpclient-3.1.jar
   Including jsr305-1.3.9.jar
   ...
   ```

    If you're using Windows, Mac, or another OS with a case-insensitive filesystem, you'll need to remove the LICENSE file, because it will clash with a license directory. To do that, you can use the following command:
   ```
   $ zip -d target/distrib-data-0.1.0-standalone.jar \
   META-INF/LICENSE
   deleting: META-INF/LICENSE
   ```

4. Now, we can start the Clojure REPL from within Hadoop by using the hadoop command on the JAR file we just created.

   ```
   $ hadoop jar target/distrib-data-0.1.0-standalone.jar \
           clojure.main
   Clojure 1.4.0
   user=>
   ```

5. Inside the REPL that just started, we need to import the libraries that we're going to use.

   ```
   user=> (require '(cascalog [workflow :as w] [ops :as c]
                              [vars :as v]))
   nil
   user=> (use 'cascalog.api)
   nil
   ```

6. And finally, once that's in place, we can execute the Cascalog query to read the companions.txt file.

   ```
   user=> (?<- (stdout) [?line]
           ((hfs-textline "hdfs:///tmp/companions.txt")
               :> ?line))
   ...
   ```

```
RESULTS
----------------------
susan,Susan Forman
barbara,Barbara Wright
ian,Ian Chesterton
vicki,Vicki
steven,Steven Taylor
katarina,Katarina
...
```

## How it works...

There are several moving parts to this recipe. The primary one is Hadoop. It has its own configuration, environment variables, and libraries that the process executing the Cascalog queries must access. The easiest way to manage that is to run everything through the `hadoop` command, so that's what we did.

The `hadoop` command has an `fs` task, which provides access to a whole range of operations for working with the HDFS. In this case, we used its `-put` option to move a data file into the HDFS.

Once there, we can refer to that file using the `hdfs:` URI scheme. Hadoop knows how to find these URIs.

In the Cascalog query, `hfs-textline` reads the file line by line. We use the `:>` operator to bind each line to the `?line` name, which gets returned as the output of the query.

## Parsing CSV files with Cascalog

In the last recipe, the file we read was a CSV file, but we read it line-by-line. That's not optimal. Cascading provides a number of taps—sources of data or sinks to send data to—including one for CSV and other delimited data formats. Cascalog also has some very nice wrappers for several of these taps, but not for the CSV one.

And in truth, creating a wrapper that exposed all the functionality of the delimited text format tap would be complex. There are options for delimiter characters, for quote characters, for including a header row, for the types of the columns, and other things. That's a lot of options, and dispatching to the right method can be tricky.

We won't worry about handling all of the options right here. For this recipe, we will create a simple wrapper around the delimited text file tap that includes some of the more common options for reading CSV files.

*Distributed Data Processing with Cascalog*

## Getting ready

First, we'll need to use some of the same dependencies we've been using, as well as some new ones. Here are the full dependencies that we'll need in our `project.clj` file.

```clojure
:dependencies [[org.clojure/clojure "1.4.0"]
               [cascalog "1.10.0"]
               [cascading/cascading-core "2.1.3"]
               [cascading/cascading-hadoop "2.1.3"]]
:repositories [["conjars.org" "http://conjars.org/repo"]]
```

And we'll need to import a number of namespaces from these libraries into our script or REPL.

```clojure
(require '(cascalog [workflow :as w]
                    [ops :as c]
                    [vars :as v]
                    [tap :as tap]))
(use 'cascalog.api)
(import [cascading.tuple Fields]
        [cascading.scheme.hadoop.TextDelimited])
```

We'll also use the data file that we did in the *Distributing data with Apache HDFS* recipe. You can access it either locally or through HDFS, as we did before. I'll access it locally in the rest of this recipe.

## How to do it...

1. We just need to write a function that creates a `cascading.scheme.hadoop.TextDelimited` tap scheme with the correct options and then calls the Cascalog function `cascalog.tap/hfs-tap` with it. That will handle the rest.

```clojure
(defn hfs-text-delim
  ([path & {:keys [fields has-header delim quote-str]
            :as opts
            :or {fields Fields/ALL, has-header false, delim ",",
                 quote-str "\""}}]
   (let [scheme (TextDelimited. (w/fields fields) has-header delim
                                quote-str)
         tap-opts (select-keys opts [:sinkmode
                                     :sinkparts
                                     :source-pattern
                                     :sink-template
                                     :templatefields])]
     (apply tap/hfs-tap scheme path tap-opts))))
```

2. Now let's try it out.

   ```
   user=> (?<- (stdout)
               [?companion-id ?name]
               ((hfs-text-delim "data/companions.txt")
                ?companion-id ?name))
   ...
   RESULTS
   --------------------
   susanSusan Forman
   barbaraBarbara Wright
   ianIan Chesterton
   vickiVicki
   ...
   ```

## How it works...

This function takes the a number of options: `fields`, `has-header`, `delim`, and `quote-str`. The defaults are for CSV files, but it could be easily overridden for a variety of other formats.

With the options in hand, it creates a `TextDelimited` scheme object.

Finally, it passes it to the `hfs-tap` function, which wraps the scheme object in a tap. The tap serves as a data generator, and we bind the values from it to the names in our query.

## There's more...

Hadoop can consume a number of different file formats. Avro (http://avro.apache.org/) uses JSON schemas to store data in a fast, compact, binary data format. Sequence files (http://wiki.apache.org/hadoop/SequenceFile) contain a binary key-value store. XML and JSON are also common data formats.

If we want to parse our own data formats in Cascading or Cascalog, we'll need to write our own source tap (http://docs.cascading.org/cascading/1.2/userguide/html/ch03s03.html). If it's a delimited text format like CSV or TSV, we can base the new tap on `cascading.scheme.hadoop.TextDelimited`, just as we did in this recipe. See the JavaDocs for this class at http://docs.cascading.org/cascading/2.0/javadoc/cascading/scheme/hadoop/TextDelimited.html for more information on this.

# Complex queries with Cascalog

So far we've seen very basic Cascalog predicates and queries. We've seen queries that pull data from one source generator and maybe include one predicate test. In this recipe, we'll see several more complex queries.

*Distributed Data Processing with Cascalog*

## Getting ready

For this recipe, we'll need the dependencies from the *Distributed processing with Cascalog and Hadoop* recipe. We'll also use the *Doctor Who* companion data that we defined in that recipe. The source code for this data is available in the code for the book, and you can also download just the code to create this dataset from `http://www.ericrochester.com/clj-data-analysis/data/companions.clj`.

## How to do it...

We'll start with simple queries and build up from there.

1. First, let's look at a simple join:

   ```
   user=> (?<- (stdout) [?name ?dr]
            (full-name ?c ?name) (doctor ?c ?dr))
   …
   RESULTS
   ----------------------
   Ace              7
   Adam Mitchell    9
   Adelaide Brooke  10
   Adric            4
   Adric            5
   Amy Pond         11
   Astrid Peth      10
   …
   ```

   This pulls each companion's full name from one table and the numbers of the doctors they accompanied from another table. The binding for the companion's key, `?c`, stays the same across all generators and predicates for each row of the output. Notice too that the second predicate, `(doctor ?c ?dr)`, can generate more than one row of output for each value of `?c`, like it did for Adric.

2. Let's look at one that's slightly more complex.

   ```
   user=> (?<- (stdout)
            [?name ?dr ?actor ?tenure]
            (full-name ?c ?name) (doctor ?c ?dr)
            (actor ?dr ?actor ?tenure))
   …
   RESULTS
   ----------------------
   Ace              7     Sylvester McCoy       1987-89, 1996
   Adam Mitchell    9     Christopher Eccleston 2005
   Adelaide Brooke  10    David Tennant         2005-10
   Adric            4     Tom Baker             1974-81
   Adric            5     Peter Davison         1981-84
   ```

```
Amy Pond          11     Matt Smith      2010-present
Astrid Peth       10     David Tennant   2005-10
...
```

This time we've re-used the same query as the previous one, but we've also joined on the table of actors who've played *Doctor Who*.

3. Even with more than one generator, we can still include one or more test predicates. The following is a query that only returns the companions for the modern-era doctors.

```
user=> (?<- (stdout) [?name]
            (full-name ?c ?name) (doctor ?c ?dr)
       (>= ?dr 9))
...
RESULTS
----------------------
Adelaide Brooke
Amy Pond
Astrid Peth
Christina de Souza
Craig Owens
Donna Noble
...
```

4. Test predicates are useful for more than just filtering data. We can also use them to generate data. For example, in the next query, we add a *modern* flag to each row to indicate whether they are from the modern era or not. We do that by assigning the test predicate's output to a variable binding using the :> operator.

```
user=> (?<- (stdout)
            [?name ?modern]
            (full-name ?c ?name) (doctor ?c ?dr)
            (>= ?dr 9 :> ?modern))
...
RESULTS
----------------------
Ace             false
Adam Mitchell   true
Adelaide Brooke true
Adric           false
Adric           false
Amy Pond        true
Astrid Peth     true
...
```

Out of the simple building blocks of generator and predicates, Cascalog makes it easy to build complex queries in an intuitive way. We'll see even more complex queries in coming recipes, but composing generators and predicates and sharing bindings are the basis of all of them.

*Distributed Data Processing with Cascalog*

# Aggregating data with Cascalog

So far, the Cascalog queries we've seen have all returned tables of results. However, sometimes we'll want to aggregate the tables, to boil them down to a single value, or into a table where groups from the original data are aggregated.

Cascalog makes this easy to do also, and it includes a number of aggregate functions. For this recipe, we'll only use one—cascalog.ops/count—but you can find more easily in the API documentation on the Cascalog website (http://nathanmarz.github.com/cascalog/cascalog.ops.html).

## Getting ready

We'll use the same dependencies and imports as we did in the *Distributed processing with Cascalog and Hadoop* recipe. We'll also use the same data that we defined in that recipe.

## How to do it...

We'll look at a couple of examples of aggregating with the count function.

1. First, we'll query how many companions the doctor has had (If you're using just the data listed earlier in this chapter, you'll only have 10 companions).

    ```
    user=> (?<- (stdout) [?count] (companion _) (c/count ?count))
    …
    RESULTS
    ----------------------
    47
    ----------------------
    ```

    For this, we just include the aggregate operator as a predicate and give it a new name binding. We use that binding—and only that binding—in the results. The other predicates in the query are used to select the data that we want aggregated.

2. Now let's try something more complicated. We'll find out how many doctors each companion has accompanied.

    ```
    user=> (?<- (stdout)
      #_ =>       [?name ?count]
      #_ =>       (full-name ?c ?name) (doctor ?c _)
      #_ =>       (c/count ?count))
    …
    RESULTS
    ----------------------
    ```

```
Adam Mitchell        1
Adelaide Brooke      1
Adric        2
Amy Pond             1
Astrid Peth          1
Barbara Wright       1
Ben Jackson          2
Brigadier Lethbridge-Stewart     1
...
```

This query is very similar. We use predicates to return the results that we want aggregated. We also include an aggregator predicate. Next, in the output bindings, we include both the value that we want the data grouped on (?name) and the aggregated binding (?count).

It's that simple. Cascalog takes care of the rest.

### There's more...

Cascalog provides a number of other aggregator functions. Some that you'll want to use regularly include count, max, min, sum, and avg. See the documentation for the built-in operations (https://github.com/nathanmarz/cascalog/wiki/Built-in-operations) for a more complete list.

## Defining new Cascalog operators

Cascalog comes with a number of operators; however, for most analyses, we'll need to define our own.

For different uses, Cascalog defines a number of different categories of operators, each with different properties. Some are run in the Map phase of processing, and some are run in the Reduce phase. The ones in the Map phase can use a number of extra optimizations, so if we can push some of our processing into that stage, we'll get better performance. In this recipe, we'll see which categories of operators are Map-side and which are Reduce-side. We'll also provide an example of each, and see how they fit into the larger processing model.

### Getting ready

For this recipe, we'll use the same dependencies and includes that we did in the *Distributed processing with Cascalog and Hadoop* recipe. We'll also use the *Doctor Who* companion data from that recipe.

## How to do it...

As I mentioned, Cascalog allows us to specify a number of different operator types. Each type is used in a different situation and with different classes of problems and operations. Let's take a look at each type of operator.

### Creating Map operators

Map operators transform data in the Map phase, with one input row being mapped to one output row. A simple example of a custom Map operator is an operator that triples all numbers that pass through it.

```
(defmapop triple-value [x] (* 3 x))
```

Something similar to this could be used to rescale all the values in a field.

### Creating Map concatenation operations

Map concatenation operators transform data in the Map phase, but each input row can map to one output row, many output rows, or none. They return a sequence, and each item in the sequence is a new output row. For example, this operator splits a string on whitespace, and each token is a new output row. We'll use that in the following predicate to count the number of names that each companion had.

```
(defmapcatop split [string] (string/split string #"\s+"))
(?<- (stdout)
[?name ?count]
     (full-name _ ?name) (split ?name :> ?token) (c/count ?count))
```

### Creating filter operators

Filter operators remove rows from the output in the Map phase. They take one item, and return a Boolean value. If true, the item should be included in the results; if false, then the item should be held back. For example, this filter returns true if the input is an even number, and we use it in a query to return only the companions who accompanied an even number of doctors.

```
(deffilterop is-even? [x] (even? x))
(?<- (stdout)
[?companion ?dr-count]
     (doctor ?companion _)
     (c/count ?dr-count)
     (is-even? ?dr-count))
```

## Creating buffer operators

Buffer operators work in the Reduce phase. They process a group of rows as a single input. They take an entire list of input rows to process and return one or more items for output. For example, the following buffer operator takes rows of strings and returns the total number of characters in all the strings. We use it in the query to count the characters in the full names of the companions for each doctor.

```
(defbufferop count-chars [strings]
  [(reduce + 0 (mapcat #(map count %) strings))])
(?<- (stdout)
[?dr ?companion-chars]
     (doctor ?c ?dr)
     (full-name ?c ?name)
     (count-chars ?name :> ?companion-chars))
```

## Creating aggregate operators

Aggregate functions work in the Reduce phase to combine input rows into one value. Compared to buffer operators, aggregate operators are in some ways more flexible—they can be used with other aggregators—but are more restricted in other ways. Each aggregator function has to be callable with no parameters, one parameter, or two parameters. The call with no parameters returns the initial value; the call with one parameter takes the aggregator's state and returns the final value; and the call with two parameters takes the state and a new value and folds the two together into a new state.

For example, this returns the average length of their companions' names for each doctor.

```
(defaggregateop mean-count
  ([] [0 0])
  ([[n total] string]
   [(inc n) (+ total (count string))])
  ([[n total]] [(float (/ total n))]))
(?<- (stdout)
[?dr ?companion-chars]
     (doctor ?c ?dr)
     (full-name ?c ?name)
     (mean-count ?name :> ?companion-chars))
```

## Creating parallel aggregate operators

Parallel aggregate operators are the most restricted, but they also give the best performance. Unlike the rest, they can be run in the Map phase of the computation. These aggregators are defined by two functions. One is called on each row, and one is called to combine the results of calling the first function on two rows.

This example returns the average length of the name of each doctor's companions.

1. First, we have to define the aggregator functions as named functions. Cascalog serializes them as names, so we can't use anonymous functions.

   ```
   (defn mean-init [x] [1 (count x)])
   (defn mean-step [n1 t1 n2 t2] [(+ n1 n2) (+ t1 t2)])
   ```

2. Then we use these to define the parallel aggregator.

   ```
   (defparallelagg
     mean-count-p
     :init-var #'mean-init
     :combine-var #'mean-step)
   ```

3. The aggregator returns both the item count and the total number of characters, so we have to divide the two in the query that calls the aggregator.

   ```
   (?<- (stdout)
        [?dr ?companion-chars]
        (doctor ?c ?dr)
        (full-name ?c ?name)
        (mean-count-p ?name :> ?n ?total)
        (div ?total ?n :> ?companion-chars))
   ```

Having so many options to build operators provides us with a lot of flexibility and power in how we define and create queries and transformations in Cascalog. And this allows us to create powerful, custom workflows.

# Composing Cascalog queries

One of the nicest things about Cascalog queries is that they can be composed together. Like composing functions, this can be a nice way to build a complex process from smaller, easy-to-understand parts.

In this recipe, we'll parse the Virginia census data we first used in the *Managing program complexity with STM* recipe in *Chapter 3, Managing Complexity with Concurrent Programming*. You can download this data from `http://www.ericrochester.com/clj-data-analysis/data/all_160_in_51.P35.csv`. We'll also use a new census data file containing the race data. You can download it from `http://www.ericrochester.com/clj-data-analysis/data/all_160_in_51.P3.csv`.

## Getting ready

Since we're reading a CSV file, we'll need to use the dependencies and imports from the *Parsing CSV files with Cascalog* recipe. We'll also use the `hfs-text-delim` function from that recipe. And we'll also need the data files from http://www.ericrochester.com/clj-data-analysis/data/all_160_in_51.P35.csv and http://www.ericrochester.com/clj-data-analysis/data/all_160_in_51.P3.csv. We'll put them into the `data/` directory.

```
(def families-file "data/all_160_in_51.P35.csv")
(def race-file "data/all_160_in_51.P3.csv")
```

## How to do it...

We'll read these datasets and convert some of the fields in each of them to integers. Then we'll join the two together and select only a few of the fields.

1. We'll define a custom operation that converts a string to a number. We'll call it `->long`.

   ```
   (defmapop ->long [value] (Long/parseLong value))
   ```

2. Now we'll define a query that reads the families data file and converts the integer fields to numbers.

   ```
   (def family-data
     (<- [?GEOID ?SUMLEV ?STATE
          ?NAME ?POP100 ?HU100 ?P035001]
         ((hfs-text-delim families-file
                          :has-header true)
              ?GEOID ?SUMLEV ?STATE _ _ _ _
              ?NAME ?spop100 ?shu100 _ _ ?sp035001 _)
         (->long ?spop100      :> ?POP100)
         (->long ?shu100       :> ?HU100)
         (->long ?sp035001     :> ?P035001)))
   ```

3. We also need to read in the race data file.

   ```
   (def race-data
     (<- [?GEOID ?SUMLEV ?STATE
          ?NAME ?POP100 ?HU100 ?P003001 ?P003002
          ?P003003 ?P003004 ?P003005 ?P003006 ?P003007
          ?P003008]
         ((hfs-text-delim race-file :has-header true)
   ```

## Distributed Data Processing with Cascalog

```
              ?GEOID ?SUMLEV ?STATE _ _ _ _ _
              ?NAME ?spop100 ?shu100 _ _
              ?sp003001 _ ?sp003002 _ ?sp003003 _
              ?sp003004 _ ?sp003005 _ ?sp003006 _
              ?sp003007 _ ?sp003008 _)
         (->long ?spop100   :> ?POP100)
         (->long ?shu100    :> ?HU100)
         (->long ?sp003001 :> ?P003001)
         (->long ?sp003002 :> ?P003002)
         (->long ?sp003003 :> ?P003003)
         (->long ?sp003004 :> ?P003004)
         (->long ?sp003005 :> ?P003005)
         (->long ?sp003006 :> ?P003006)
         (->long ?sp003007 :> ?P003007)
         (->long ?sp003008 :> ?P003008)))
```

4. We'll use those queries to build a query that joins those two queries on the `?GEOID` field. It will also rename some of the fields.

```
(def census-joined
  (<- [?name ?pop100 ?hu100 ?families
       ?white ?black ?indian ?asian ?hawaiian ?other
       ?multiple]
      (family-data ?geoid _ _
                   ?name ?pop100 ?hu100 ?families)
      (race-data ?geoid _ _ _ _ _
                 ?white ?black ?indian ?asian
                 ?hawaiian ?other ?multiple)))
```

5. Now we can run this and send the results to standard output.

```
user=> (?- (stdout) census-joined)
...
RESULTS
-----------------------
```

| | | | | | | | |
|---|---|---|---|---|---|---|---|
| Abingdon town | 8191 | 4271 | 2056 | 7681 | 257 | 15 | 86 |
| 6 | | | | | | | |
| Accomac town | 519 | 229 | 117 | 389 | 106 | 0 | 3 |
| 1 | | | | | | | |
| Adwolf CDP | 1530 | 677 | 467 | 1481 | 17 | 1 | 4 |
| 0 | | | | | | | |
| Alberta town | 298 | 163 | 77 | 177 | 112 | 4 | 0 |
| 0 | | | | | | | |
| Alexandria city | 139966 | 72376 | 30978 | 85186 | 30491 | 589 | |
| 8432 | 141 | | | | | | |

```
Altavista town    3450    1669    928     2415    891     5       20
0
Amherst town      2231    1032    550     1571    550     17      14
0
Annandale CDP     41008   14715   9790    20670   3533    212
10103   53
Appalachia town   1754    879     482     1675    52      4       2
0
Appomattox town   1733    849     441     1141    540     8       3
0
Aquia Harbour CDP         6727    2300    1914    5704    521     38
150
...
```

## How it works...

In every recipe so far, we've used the ?<- macro, which is a combination of <- and ?-. The arrow, <-, allows us to create and compose queries. The ?- macro executes the query and sends the results to a sink. Using the combined ?<- macro is convenient, but using the separate ones can be much more powerful.

# Handling errors in Cascalog workflows

No one's perfect, and there will certainly be errors in our Cascalog workflows. By default, Cascalog handles errors by stopping the processing. However, we may want to save the errors for later to allow the processing to continue. Cascalog (and Cascading) allows us to do that by defining a **trap**. This sends errors to a special sink tap and continues working.

## Getting ready

Since we're extending the previous recipe, we'll use all the dependencies, imports, functions, and variables from there.

## How to do it...

For this recipe, we'll extend the previous *Composing Cascalog queries* recipe. We'll define a custom operator that throws an error occasionally, and we'll call that operator in a query.

1. First, here's the new custom operator. If the value passed in is too low (less than 125), it causes an exception by dividing by zero.

   ```
   (defmapop throw-error [value]
     (if (< value 125) (div value 0) 0))
   ```

2. Now we can define a query that calls the queries from the last recipe, calls `throw-error`, and traps any exceptions raised.

   ```
   (def families-per-hu  (<- [?name ?pop100 ?hu100
         ?p035001 ?fam-hu]
       (census-joined ?name ?pop100 ?hu100
                      ?families ?white ?black ?indian
                      ?asian ?hawaiian ?other ?multiple)
       (throw-error ?families :> ?err)
       (div ?families ?hu100 :> ?fam-hu)
     (:trap (hfs-textline "data/trap"))))
   ```

3. Now, when we run this, we'll get the following results:

   ```
   user=>(?- (stdout) families-per-hu)
   ...
   RESULTS
   -----------------------
   Fort Chiswell CDP      939     417    911    380    271
   264      0.6498800959232613
   Fries town        484    340    614    337    144    177
   0.4235294117647059
   Greenville CDP   832    259    886    251    178    194
   0.6872586872586872
   Irvington town   432    374    673    325    142    175
   0.37967914438502676
   Jarratt town     638    304    589    293    176    176
   0.5789473684210527
   Keysville town   832    401    817    398    192    195
   0.47880299251870323
   ...
   ```

4. And if we look in the `data/trap` directory, there's a file named `part-m-00001-00000`. It contains the numbers that raised an exception:

   ```
   117
   77
   99
   34
   88
   ...
   ```

*Chapter 5*

# Transforming data with Cascalog

Often, simply querying data won't do everything we need. For instance, the data may not be in a form we can use. In that case, we'll need to transform the data. We can do that easily in Cascalog too.

For this recipe, we'll define a custom operation and use it to split year ranges in the form 2000-2010 into two fields.

## Getting ready

We'll use the same dependencies and includes that we did in the *Distributed processing with Cascalog and Hadoop* recipe. We'll also use the *Doctor Who* companion data from that recipe.

## How to do it...

1. We'll define a new, custom operation to take a date range string and split it into two values. In this dataset, we're splitting them on an N-dash (#"\u2013"). If the input isn't a range (that is, it's just a year), then the year is returned for both the start and end of the range.

   ```
   (defmapop split-range [date-range]
     (let [[from to] (string/split (str date-range) #"\u2013" 2)]
       [from (if (nil? to) from (str (.substring from 0 2) to))]))
   ```

2. Then we can use this to transform the tenure dates in the actor data.

   ```
   user=> (?<- (stdout)
               [?n ?name ?from ?to]
               (actor ?n ?name ?range)
               (split-range ?range :> ?from ?to))
   ...
   RESULTS
   -----------------------
   1      William Hartnell        1963    1966
   2      Patrick Troughton       1966    1969
   3      Jon Pertwee      1970   1974
   ...
   ```

## How it works...

In the `split-range` operator, we return a vector containing two years for the output. Then, in the query, we use the `:>` operator to bind the output values from `split-range` to the names `?from` and `?to`. Destructuring makes this especially easy.

# Executing Cascalog queries in the Cloud with Pallet

So far we've run everything in the single-server mode. This is good for experimenting and for working out the bugs in our process, but it's not very good for actually analyzing data. So for this recipe, we'll use Pallet (http://palletops.com/) to provision a cluster of EC2 instances to run one of the previous recipes.

Pallet is a platform for provisioning cloud systems. We define the hardware, OS, and software for nodes and groups of nodes. We connect those to a service provider, such as EC2, and use the Clojure REPL to spin up those nodes and bring them back down. One of the nice things about Pallet is that, unlike many other provisioning systems, nothing has to be installed on the systems being created. Everything is done via SSH.

Sam Ritchie (https://github.com/sritchie) and the Pallet team have put together a library and a sample project that shows how to use Pallet to provision a Hadoop cluster on EC2. For this recipe, we'll follow these instructions, but apply them to running the queries from the *Composing Cascalog queries* recipe.

## Getting ready

For this, we'll need to have the Pallet Hadoop project on our machine (https://github.com/pallet/pallet-hadoop-example). You can clone it from Github with this command.

```
$ git clone git://github.com/pallet/pallet-hadoop-example.git
```

You can also download it from https://github.com/pallet/pallet-hadoop-example/archive/master.zip.

And you'll need to have SSH keys set up. If you're not familiar with SSH, there are a number of good tutorials. The one by Glenn Murray at http://inside.mines.edu/~gmurray/HowTo/sshNotes.html appears complete. There are a number of other SSH tutorials around, too. Typically, setting up SSH is very operating-system specific. Look for a tutorial that directly addresses your OS.

## How to do it...

In this recipe, we'll get set up with **Amazon Web Services** (**AWS**) and EC2, and then we'll use Pallet to set up a cluster. Finally, we'll log in to our cluster and run some queries before we shut everything down.

1. If you don't already have an account on AWS, visit `https://aws-portal.amazon.com/gp/aws/developer/registration/index.html` and sign up.

2. Visit your account page at `http://aws.amazon.com/account/`. Click on **Security Credentials**. Under **Access Credentials** and the **Access Keys** tab, note your **Access Key ID** and **Secret Access Key**. If you don't have one, create one and write it down.

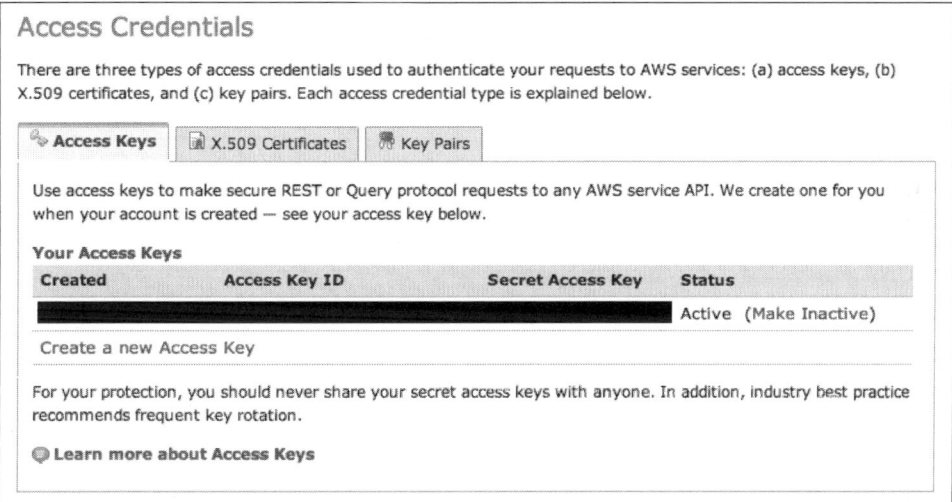

3. In the directory for the `pallet-hadoop-example` project, open `project.clj` and add the following lines:

   ```
   :profiles
   {:dev
     {:dependencies
       [[org.cloudhoist/pallet "0.7.2"
         :classifier "tests"]]
      :plugins
        [[org.cloudhoist/pallet-lein "0.5.2"]]}}
   ```

4. Now, from the command line in that project's directory, we can add our AWS credentials, so that Pallet knows what they are. This command places them in a configuration directory so they're accessible to all Pallet projects.

   ```
   $ lein pallet add-service aws aws-ec2 "AWS_KEY" \
        "AWS_SECRET_KEY"
   ```

5. Start the Clojure REPL on your local machine:

   ```
   $ lein repl
   ```

6. Now, the next set of commands will be executed in the REPL. We'll need to import the `pallet-hadoop-example` namespace and call its `bootstrap` function.

   ```
   (use 'pallet-hadoop-example.core)
   ```

   ```
   (bootstrap)
   ```

7. We define the EC2 service from the configuration we created earlier.

   ```
   (def ec2-service (service :aws))
   ```

8. We create an example cluster.

   ```
   (def eg (make-example-cluster 2 512))
   ```

9. And then we start it.

   ```
   (create-cluster eg ec2-service)
   ```

10. Now we'll wait. In the background, Pallet creates the clusters and provisions them with the software and users that we'll need. When it's ready, the REPL prompt will come back. Our cluster now has two slaves and one master.

11. Once we have a prompt again, we can get the IP address of the `jobtracker` node.

    ```
    user=> (jobtracker-ip :public ec2-service)
    "50.16.175.26"
    ```

12. We'll use this address to access the jobtracker web interface. In this case, it will be at `http://50.16.175.26:50030/`.

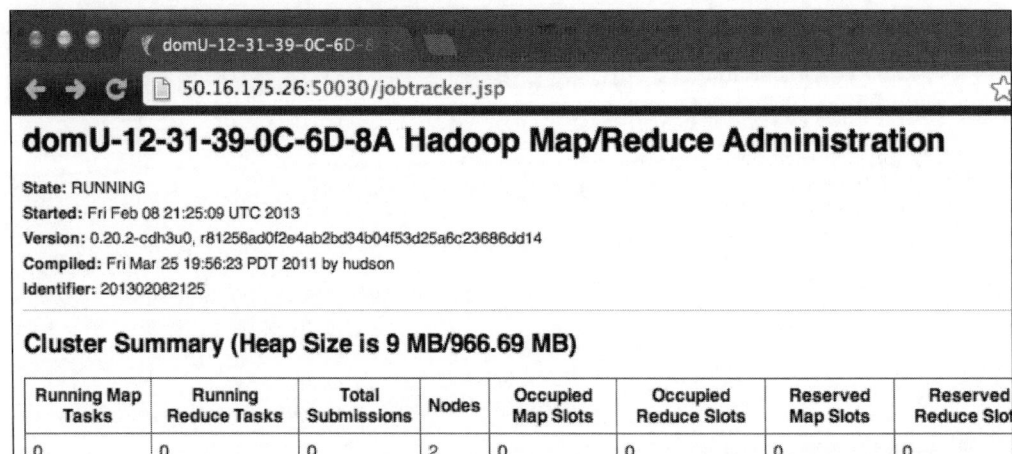

13. From the command line again, let's create a JAR file containing all of the code for this recipe, just as we did in the *Distributing data with Apache HDFS* recipe. I've been using a project named `distrib-data`. It contains the dependencies and code for the queries of the recipe we'll be executing, that is, the *Composing Cascalog queries* recipe. The following command will create the JAR file for us:

    ```
    $ lein uberjar
    ```

14. We want to transfer this to the `jobtracker` node. We have to use secure copy (`scp`).

    ```
    $ scp \
        distrib-data/target/distrib-data-0.1.0-standalone.jar \
        50.16.175.26:/tmp/
    ```

15. And we transfer the two data files that we'll use from the `data/` directory.

    ```
    $ scp data/all_160*.csv 50.16.175.26:/tmp/
    ```

16. Finally, we log in to the node. Pallet has created a user with the same username as we have on our local machine. And it's transferred our SSH keys, so we don't have to input a password.

    ```
    $ ssh 50.16.175.26
    ```

17. On this node, we first need to add the data files into the `/user/hadoop/census/` directory of Hadoop's distributed filesystem. To do this, we first change users to the `hadoop` user and then change directories to the Hadoop distribution.

    ```
    $ sudo su - hadoop
    $ cd /usr/local/hadoop-0.20.2/
    ```

18. Now we'll create the `census` directory in the distributed filesystem and copy the data files there.

    ```
    $ hadoop dfs -mkdir census
    $ hadoop dfs -copyFromLocal /tmp/all_160_in_51*.csv census
    ```

19. Now we'll run the Clojure REPL from the JAR file we created earlier.

    ```
    $ hadoop jar /tmp/distrib-data-0.1.0-standalone.jar \
        clojure.main
    ```

20. In the REPL on the `jobtracker` node, we should be able to access the namespaces that we'll use.

    ```
    (require '(cascalog [workflow :as w]
                       [ops :as c]
                       [vars :as v]
                       [tap :as tap]))
    (use 'cascalog.api
         'distrib-data.parse-csv)
    ```

21. And we create references to the locations of the data files.

    ```
    (def families-file
      "hdfs:///user/hadoop/census/all_160_in_51.P35.csv")
    (def race-file
      "hdfs:///user/hadoop/census/all_160_in_51.P3.csv")
    ```

22. We define the queries for the two datasets.

    ```
    (def family-data
      (<- [?GEOID ?SUMLEV ?STATE
           ?NAME ?POP100 ?HU100 ?P035001]
          ((hfs-text-delim families-file
                           :has-header true)
             ?GEOID ?SUMLEV ?STATE _ _ _ _
             ?NAME ?spop100 ?shu100 _ _ ?sp035001 _)
          (->long ?spop100   :> ?POP100)
          (->long ?shu100    :> ?HU100)
          (->long ?sp035001 :> ?P035001)))
    (def race-data
      (<- [?GEOID ?SUMLEV ?STATE ?NAME ?POP100 ?HU100
           ?P003001 ?P003002 ?P003003 ?P003004 ?P003005
           ?P003006 ?P003007 ?P003008]
          ((hfs-text-delim race-file :has-header true)
             ?GEOID ?SUMLEV ?STATE _ _ _ _
             ?NAME ?spop100 ?shu100 _ _
             ?sp003001 _ ?sp003002 _ ?sp003003 _
             ?sp003004 _ ?sp003005 _ ?sp003006 _
             ?sp003007 _ ?sp003008 _)
          (->long ?spop100   :> ?POP100)
          (->long ?shu100    :> ?HU100)
          (->long ?sp003001 :> ?P003001)
          (->long ?sp003002 :> ?P003002)
          (->long ?sp003003 :> ?P003003)
          (->long ?sp003004 :> ?P003004)
          (->long ?sp003005 :> ?P003005)
          (->long ?sp003006 :> ?P003006)
          (->long ?sp003007 :> ?P003007)
          (->long ?sp003008 :> ?P003008)))
    ```

23. And we define the query that joins these two queries.

    ```
    (def census-joined
      (<- [?name ?pop100 ?hu100 ?families
           ?white ?black ?indian ?asian ?hawaiian
           ?other ?multiple]
    ```

```
            (family-data ?geoid _ _
                         ?name ?pop100 ?hu100 ?families)
            (race-data ?geoid _ _ _ _ _
                       ?white ?black ?indian ?asian
                       ?hawaiian ?other ?multiple)))
```

24. When we run this, we can see the same output that was created before, but now in the cloud.

    **(?- (stdout) census-joined)**

    **RESULTS**

    ----------------------

    | Abingdon town | 8191 | 4271 | 2056 | 7681 | 257 | 15 | 86 |
    | 6    64 | 82 | | | | | | |
    | Accomac town | 519 | 229 | 117 | 389 | 106 | 0 | 3 |
    | 1    17 | 3 | | | | | | |
    | Adwolf CDP | 1530 | 677 | 467 | 1481 | 17 | 1 | 4 |
    | 0    21 | 6 | | | | | | |

    ...

25. To clean up, we log out of Clojure, the `hadoop` user session, and our original login on the cluster.

26. Finally, we switch back to the REPL that we created the cluster from, and run the following command to terminate and remove the instances. They will still show up for a while after they're terminated, but they'll disappear eventually:

    (destroy-cluster eg ec2-service)

## How it works...

The `pallet-hadoop-example` is based on the Pallet-Hadoop library (https://github.com/pallet/pallet-hadoop). This has a lot of functionality for using Pallet to deploy Hadoop in the cloud, and it makes setting up the distributed cluster on EC2 much easier. This library also makes a good starting point for other analyses that we want to distribute to the cloud.

# 6
# Working with Incanter Datasets

In this chapter, we will cover:

- Loading Incanter's sample datasets
- Loading Clojure data structures into datasets
- Viewing datasets interactively with view
- Converting datasets to matrices
- Using infix formulas in Incanter
- Selecting columns with $
- Selecting rows with $
- Filtering datasets with $where
- Grouping data with $group-by
- Saving datasets to CSV and JSON
- Projecting from multiple datasets with $join

## Introduction

We've seen Incanter (http://incanter.org/) earlier in this book, but we'll spend a lot more time with that library over the next few chapters. Incanter combines the power of doing statistics using a fully-featured statistical language such as R with the ease and joy of Clojure.

*Working with Incanter Datasets*

Incanter's core data structure is the dataset, so we'll be spending some time in this chapter looking at how to use them effectively. Learning basic tools like this is often not the most exciting way to spend our time, but it can still be incredibly useful. At its most fundamental level, an Incanter dataset is a table of rows. Each row has the same set of columns, much like a spreadsheet. The data in each cell of an Incanter dataset can be a string or numeric.

First, we'll learn how to populate and view datasets, and then we'll learn different ways to query and project the parts of the dataset that we're interested in onto a new dataset. Finally, we'll look at saving datasets and merging multiple datasets together.

## Loading Incanter's sample datasets

Incanter comes with a set of default datasets that are useful for exploring Incanter's functions. I haven't made use of them in this book, since there is so much data available at other places, but they're a great way to get a feel for what we can do with Incanter. Some of these datasets, for instance, the Iris dataset, are widely used for teaching. That's the dataset we'll access today.

In this recipe, we'll load a dataset and see what it contains.

### Getting ready

We'll need to include Incanter in our Leiningen `project.clj` file.

```
:dependencies [[org.clojure/clojure "1.4.0"]
               [incanter "1.4.1"]]
```

We'll also need to include the right Incanter namespaces into our script or REPL.

```
(use '(incanter core datasets))
```

### How to do it...

Once the namespaces are available, we can access the datasets easily.

```
user=> (def iris (get-dataset :iris))
#'user/iris
user=> (col-names iris)
[:Sepal.Length :Sepal.Width :Petal.Length :Petal.Width :Species]
user=> (nrow iris)
150
user=> (set ($ :Species iris))
#{"versicolor" "virginica" "setosa"}
```

## How it works...

We use the `get-dataset` function to access the built-in datasets. In this case, we're loading the Fisher's or Anderson's Iris data. This is a multivariate dataset for discriminant analysis. It gives petal and sepal measurements for fifty each of three different species of Iris.

Incanter's sample datasets cover a wide variety of topics—from US arrests, to plant growth, to ultrasonic calibration. They can be used for testing different algorithms and analyses and for working with different types of data.

## There's more...

Incanter's API documentation for `get-dataset` (http://liebke.github.com/incanter/datasets-api.html#incanter.datasets/get-dataset) lists more sample datasets, and you should refer to that for the latest information about the data that Incanter bundles.

# Loading Clojure data structures into datasets

While good for learning, Incanter's built-in datasets probably won't be that useful for your work (unless you work with Irises). Other recipes cover ways to get data from CSV files and other sources into Incanter (refer to *Chapter 1, Importing Data for Analysis*). Incanter also accepts native Clojure data structures in a number of formats. We'll look at a couple of those in this recipe.

## Getting ready

We'll just need Incanter listed in our `project.clj` file.

```
:dependencies [[org.clojure/clojure "1.4.0"]
               [incanter "1.4.1"]]
```

We'll need to include it in our script or REPL.

```
(use 'incanter.core)
```

*Working with Incanter Datasets*

## How to do it...

The primary function for converting data into a dataset is `to-dataset`. While it can convert single, scalar values into a dataset, we'll start with slightly more complicated inputs:

1. Generally, we'll be working with at least one matrix. If we pass that to `to-dataset`, what do we get?

   ```
   user=> (def matrix-set (to-dataset [[1 2 3] [4 5 6]]))
   #'user/matrix-set
   user=> (nrow matrix-set)
   2
   user=> (col-names matrix-set)
   [:col-0 :col-1 :col-2]
   ```

2. All the data is there, but it could be labeled better. Does `to-dataset` handle maps?

   ```
   user=> (def map-set (to-dataset {:a 1, :b 2, :c 3}))
   #'user/map-set
   user=> (nrow map-set)
   1
   user=> (col-names map-set)
   [:a :c :b]
   ```

3. So map keys become the column labels. That's much more intuitive. Let's throw a sequence of maps at it.

   ```
   user=> (def maps-set (to-dataset [{:a 1, :b 2, :c 3},
                                     {:a 4, :b 5, :c 6}]))
   #'user/maps-set
   user=> (nrow maps-set)
   2
   user=> (col-names maps-set)
   [:a :c :b]
   ```

4. That's much more useful. We can also create a dataset by passing the column vector and the row matrix separately to `dataset`.

   ```
   user=> (def matrix-set-2
            (dataset [:a :b :c]
                     [[1 2 3] [4 5 6]]))
   #'user/matrix-set-2
   user=> (nrow matrix-set-2)
   2
   user=> (col-names matrix-set-2)
   [:c :b :a]
   ```

## How it works...

The function `to-dataset` looks at the input and tries to process it intelligently. If given a sequence of maps, the column names are taken from the keys of the first map in the sequence.

Ultimately, it uses the `dataset` constructor to create the dataset. It requires the dataset to be passed in as a column vector and a row matrix. When the data is in this format, or when we need to most control—to rename the columns, for instance—we can use `dataset`.

## See also

Several recipes in *Chapter 1, Importing Data for Analysis*, look at how to load data from different external sources into Incanter datasets.

# Viewing datasets interactively with view

Being able to interact with our data programmatically is important, but sometimes it's also helpful to be able to look at it. This can be especially useful while doing data exploration.

## Getting ready

We'll need to have Incanter in our `project.clj` file and script or REPL, so we'll use the same set up as we did for the *Loading Incanter's sample datasets* recipe. We'll also use the Iris dataset from that recipe.

## How to do it...

Incanter makes this very easy. Let's look at just how simple it is:

1. First, we need to load the dataset.

   ```
   user=> (def iris (get-dataset :iris))
   #'user/iris
   ```

2. Then we just call `view` on the dataset:

   ```
   user=> (view iris)
   #<JFrame javax.swing.JFrame[frame0,0,22,400x600,invalid,layout
   =java.awt.BorderLayout,title=Incanter
   Dataset,resizable,normal,defaultCloseOperation=
   HIDE_ON_CLOSE,rootPane=javax.swing.JRootPane
   [,0,22,400x578,invalid,layout=javax.swing.
   JRootPane$RootLayout,alignmentX=0.0,alignmentY=
   0.0,border=,flags=16777673,maximumSize=,minimumSize=
   ,preferredSize=],rootPaneCheckingEnabled=true]>
   ```

*Working with Incanter Datasets*

This function returns the Swing window frame, which contains our data. That window should also be open on your desktop, although for me it's usually hiding behind another window. It is shown in the following screenshot:

| :Sepal.Leng... | :Sepal.Width | :Petal.Length | :Petal.Width | :Species |
|---|---|---|---|---|
| 5.1 | 3.5 | 1.4 | 0.2 | setosa |
| 4.9 | 3.0 | 1.4 | 0.2 | setosa |
| 4.7 | 3.2 | 1.3 | 0.2 | setosa |
| 4.6 | 3.1 | 1.5 | 0.2 | setosa |
| 5.0 | 3.6 | 1.4 | 0.2 | setosa |
| 5.4 | 3.9 | 1.7 | 0.4 | setosa |
| 4.6 | 3.4 | 1.4 | 0.3 | setosa |
| 5.0 | 3.4 | 1.5 | 0.2 | setosa |
| 4.4 | 2.9 | 1.4 | 0.2 | setosa |

## How it works...

Incanter's `view` function takes any object and tries to display it graphically. In this case, it simply displays the raw data as a table. We'll use this function a lot in *Chapter 10, Graphing in Incanter* when we talk about Incanter's graphing functionality.

## See also

In *Chapter 10, Graphing in Incanter*, we'll see more sophisticated, exciting ways to visualize Incanter datasets.

# Converting datasets to matrices

Although datasets are often convenient, many times we'll want something a bit faster. Incanter matrices store a table of doubles. This provides good performance in a compact data structure. We'll also need matrices many times because some of Incanter's functions, `trans`, for example, only operate on a single matrix.

Also, it implements Clojure's ISeq interface, so interacting with matrices is also convenient.

## Getting ready

For this recipe, we'll need the Incanter libraries, so we'll use this `project.clj` file:

```
:dependencies [[org.clojure/clojure "1.4.0"]
               [incanter "1.4.1"]]
```

We'll use the `core` and `io` namespaces, so we'll load those into our script or REPL:

```
(use '(incanter core io))
```

We'll use the Virginia census data that we've used periodically throughout the book. Refer to the *Managing program complexity with STM* recipe from *Chapter 3, Managing Complexity with Concurrent Programming,* for information on how to get this dataset. You can also download it from http://www.ericrochester.com/clj-data-analysis/data/all_160_in_51.P35.csv.

```
(def data-file "data/all_160_in_51.P35.csv")
```

## How to do it...

For this recipe, we'll create a dataset, convert it to a matrix, and then perform some operations on it using the following steps:

1. First, we need to read the data into a dataset.

    ```
    (def va-data (read-dataset data-file :header true))
    ```

2. Then, to convert it to a matrix, we just pass it to the `to-matrix` function. Before we do that, we'll pull out a few of the columns, since matrices can only contain floating point numbers.

    ```
    (def va-matrix
        (to-matrix ($ [:POP100 :HU100 :P035001] va-data)))
    ```

3. Now that it's a matrix, we can treat it like a sequence. Here we pass it to `first` to get the first row, to `take` to get a subset of the matrix, and to `count` to get the number of rows in the matrix:

    ```
    user=> (first va-matrix)
    [8191.0000 4271.0000 2056.0000]

    user=> (take 5 va-matrix)
    ([8191.0000 4271.0000 2056.0000]
     [519.0000 229.0000 117.0000]
     [298.0000 163.0000 77.0000]
     [139966.0000 72376.0000 30978.0000]
     [117.0000 107.0000 32.0000]
    )
    user=> (count va-matrix)
    591
    ```

4. We can also use Incanter's matrix operators to get the sum of each column, for instance:

    ```
    user=> (reduce plus va-matrix)
    [5433225.0000 2262695.0000 1332421.0000]
    ```

*Working with Incanter Datasets*

## How it works...

The `to-matrix` function takes a dataset of floating-point values and returns a compact matrix. Matrices are used by many of Incanter's more sophisticated analysis functions, as they're easy to work with.

## There's more...

In this recipe, we saw the `plus` matrix operator. Incanter defines a full suite of these. You can learn more about matrices and see what operators are available at https://github.com/liebke/incanter/wiki/matrices.

## See also

- The *Selecting columns with $* recipe

# Using infix formulas in Incanter

There's a lot to like about lisp: macros, the simple syntax, and the rapid development cycle. Most of the time, it is fine that we treat math operators like functions and use prefix notation, which is a consistent, function-first syntax. This allows us to treat math operators the same as everything else so that we can pass them to `reduce`, or anything else we want to do.

But we're not taught to read math expressions using prefix notation (with the operator first). Especially when formulas get even a little complicated, tracing out exactly what's happening can get hairy.

## Getting ready

For this, we'll just need Incanter in our `project.clj` file, so we'll use the dependencies statement—as well as the `use` statement—from the *Loading Clojure data structures into datasets* recipe.

For data, we'll use the matrix that we created in the *Converting datasets to matrices* recipe.

## How to do it...

Incanter has a macro that converts standard math notation to lisp notation. We'll explore that in this recipe:

1. The `$=` macro changes its contents to use infix notation, which is what we're used to from math class.

   ```
   user=> ($= 7 * 4)
   ```

```
28
user=> ($= 7 * 4 + 3)
31
```

2. We can also work on whole matrices or just parts of matrices. In this example, we perform scalar multiplication of the matrix.

   ```
   user=> ($= va-matrix * 4)
   [  32764.0000   17084.0000    8224.0000
       2076.0000     916.0000     468.0000
       1192.0000     652.0000     308.0000
   ...
   user=> ($= (first va-matrix) * 4)
   [32764.0000 17084.0000 8224.0000]
   ```

3. Using this we can build complex expressions, such as the following one that takes the mean of the values in the first row of the matrix:

   ```
   user=> ($= (sum (first va-matrix)) /
   (count (first va-matrix)))
   4839.333333333333
   ```

4. Or the following expression, which takes the mean of each column:

   ```
   user=> ($= (reduce plus va-matrix) / (count va-matrix))
   [9193.2741 3828.5871 2254.5195]
   ```

## How it works...

Whenever we're working with macros and we wonder how they work, we can always get at their output expressions easily, so that we can see what the computer is actually executing. The tool to do this is macroexpand-1. This expands the macro one step and returns the result. Its sibling function, macroexpand, expands the expression until there is no longer a macro expression. Usually, this is more than we want, so we just use macroexpand-1.

Let's see what the following macros expand into:

```
user=> (macroexpand-1 '($= 7 * 4))
(incanter.core/mult 7 4)
user=> (macroexpand-1 '($= 7 * 4 + 3))
(incanter.core/plus (incanter.core/mult 7 4) 3)
user=> (macroexpand-1 '($= 3 + 7 * 4))
(incanter.core/plus 3 (incanter.core/mult 7 4))
```

Here we can see that it doesn't expand into Clojure's * or + functions, but instead it uses Incanter's matrix functions, mult and plus. This allows it to handle a variety of input types, including matrices, intelligently.

*Working with Incanter Datasets*

Otherwise, it switches the expressions around the way we'd expect. We can also see by comparing the last two that it even handles operator precedence correctly.

## Selecting columns with $

Often we need to cut down the data to make it more useful. One common transformation is to pull out all the values from one or more columns into a new dataset. This can be useful for generating summary statistics or aggregating the values of some columns.

The Incanter macro $ slices out parts of a dataset. In this recipe, we'll see this in action.

### Getting ready

For this recipe, we'll need to have Incanter listed in our `project.clj` file:

```
:dependencies [[org.clojure/clojure "1.4.0"]
               [incanter "1.4.1"]]
```

We'll also need to include `incanter.core` and `incanter.io` in our script or REPL.

```
(use '(incanter core io))
```

We'll also need some data. This time we'll use the race data from the US census data available at `http://censusdata.ire.org/`. However, instead of using the data for one state we'll use all states' data. These have to be downloaded separately and joined together. I've already done this, and the file is available for download at `http://www.ericrochester.com/clj-data-analysis/data/all_160.P3.csv`.

To make this data easy to access, we can bind the file name for that data to `data-file`. We'll then load the dataset and bind it to the name `race-data`.

```
(def data-file "data/all_160.P3.csv")
(def race-data (read-dataset data-file :header true))
```

### How to do it...

We'll use the $ macro several different ways to get different results as seen in the following steps:

1. We can select columns to pull out from the dataset by passing the column names or numbers to the $ macro. It returns a sequence of the values in the column.

   ```
   user=> ($ :POP100 race-data)
   (192 2688 4522 758 356 30352 21160 14875 3917 2486 …)
   ```

2. We can select more than one column by listing all of them in a vector. This time, the results are in a dataset.

```
user=> ($ [:STATE :POP100 :POP100.2000] race-data)
[:STATE :POP100 :POP100.2000]
[1 192 ""]
[1 2688 2987]
[1 4522 4965]
[1 758 723]
[1 356 521]
…
```

3. We can list as many columns as we want.

```
user=> ($ [:STATE :POP100 :P003002 :P003003
          :P003004 :P003005 :P003006 :P003007
          :P003008]
         race-data)
[:STATE :POP100 :P003002 :P003003 :P003004 :P003005 :P003006
:P003007 :P003008]
[1 192 129 58 0 0 0 2 3]
[1 2688 1463 1113 2 26 0 53 31]
[1 4522 2366 2030 23 14 1 50 38]
[1 758 751 1 0 1 0 0 5]
[1 356 47 308 0 0 0 0 1]
…
```

## How it works...

The $ function is just a wrapper over the Incanter's `sel` function. It provides a nice way of slicing columns out of the dataset so we can focus only on the data that actually pertain to our analysis.

## There's more...

The column headers for this dataset are a little cryptic. The IRE download page for the census data (http://census.ire.org/data/bulkdata.html) has a link for the column header information, or you can access that data in CSV format directly at https://raw.github.com/ireapps/census/master/tools/metadata/sf1_labels.csv.

In this recipe, I pulled out a number of columns:

- The total population (:POP100)
- The population for whites (:P003002)

*Working with Incanter Datasets*

- African-Americans (`:P003003`)
- American Indians or Alaska natives (`:P003004`)
- Asians (`:P003005`)
- Native Hawaiians or Pacific islanders (`:P003006`)
- Some other race (`:P003007`)
- Two or more races (`:P003008`)

## See also

- The *Selecting rows with $* recipe

# Selecting rows with $

The Incanter macro $ also pulls rows out of a dataset. In this recipe, we'll see this in action.

## Getting ready

For this recipe, we'll use the same dependencies, imports, and data that we did in the *Selecting columns with $* recipe.

## How to do it...

Like using $ to select columns, there are several ways we can use it to select rows. Refer to the following steps:

1. We can create a sequence of the values of one row by using $ and passing it the index of the row we want and `:all` for the columns.

   ```
   user=> ($ 0 :all race-data)
   (100100 160 1 "" "" "" "" "" "Abanda CDP" 192 79 "" "
   " 192 "" 129 "" 58 "" 0 "" 0 "" 0 "" 2 "" 3 "")
   ```

2. We can also pull out a dataset containing multiple rows by passing more than one index into $ with a vector.

   ```
   user=> ($ [0 1 2 3 4] :all race-data)
   [:GEOID :SUMLEV :STATE :COUNTY :CBSA :CSA :NECTA :CNECTA :NAME
   :POP100 :HU100 :POP100.2000 :HU100.2000 :P003001 :P003001.2000
   :P003002 :P003002.2000 :P003003 :P003003.2000 :P003004
   :P003004.2000 :P003005 :P003005.2000 :P003006 :P003006.2000
   :P003007 :P003007.2000 :P003008 :P003008.2000]
   ```

*Chapter 6*

```
[100100 160 1 "" "" "" "" "" "Abanda CDP" 192 79 "" "
" 192 "" 129 "" 58 "" 0 "" 0 "" 0 "" 2 "" 3 ""]
[100124 160 1 "" "" "" "" "" "Abbeville city" 2688 1255 2987 1353
2688 2987 1463 1692 1113 1193 2 0 26 2 0 0 53 85 31 15]
[100460 160 1 "" "" "" "" "" "Adamsville city" 4522 1990 4965 2042
4522 4965 2366 3763 2030 1133 23 20 14 7 1 1 50 8 38 33]
[100484 160 1 "" "" "" "" "" "Addison town" 758 351 723 339 758
723 751 719 1 1 0 1 1 1 0 0 0 0 5 1]
[100676 160 1 "" "" "" "" "" "Akron town" 356 205 521 239 356 521
47 93 308 422 0 0 0 0 0 0 0 1 6]
```

3. We can also combine the two ways to slice data to pull specific columns and rows. We can either pull out a single row or multiple rows.

```
user=> ($ 0 [:STATE :POP100 :P003002 :P003003 :P003004 :P003005
             :P003006 :P003007 :P003008]
          race-data)
(1 192 129 58 0 0 0 2 3)
user=> ($ [0 1 2 3 4]
          [:STATE :POP100 :P003002 :P003003 :P003004 :P003005
           :P003006 :P003007 :P003008]
          race-data)
[:STATE :POP100 :P003002 :P003003 :P003004 :P003005 :P003006
:P003007 :P003008]
[1 192 129 58 0 0 0 2 3]
       1463 1113 2 26 0 53 31]
              14 1 50 38]
```

g rows and projecting (or selecting) columns from exing parameters, the first is the row or rows, and

## s with $where

we import them into Incanter, Incanter makes it easy to existing ones. We'll take a look at its query language in

*Working with Incanter Datasets*

## Getting ready

We'll use the same dependencies, imports, and data that we did in the *Using infix formulas in Incanter* recipe.

## How to do it...

Once we have the data, we query it using the `$where` function.

1. For example, the following creates a dataset with the row for Richmond:

   ```
   user=> (def richmond ($where {:NAME "Richmond city"}
   va-data))
   #'user/richmond
   user=> richmond
   [:GEOID :SUMLEV :STATE :COUNTY :CBSA :CSA :NECTA :CNECTA :NAME
   :POP100 :HU100 :POP100.2000 :HU100.2000 :P035001 :P035001.2000]
   [5167000 160 51 "" "" "" "" "" "Richmond city"
   204214 98349 197790 92282 41304 43649]
   ```

2. The queries can be more complicated, too. The following one picks out the small towns, ones with population less than 1,000:

   ```
   user=> (def small ($where {:POP100 {:lte 1000}} va-data))
   #'user/small
   user=> (nrow small)
   232
   user=> ($ [0 1 2 3] :all small)
   [:GEOID :SUMLEV :STATE :COUNTY :CBSA :CSA :NECTA :CNECTA :NAME
   :POP100 :HU100 :POP100.2000 :HU100.2000 :P035001 :P035001.2000]
   [5100180 160 51 "" "" "" "" "" "Accomac town" 519 229 547 235 117
   126]
   [5100724 160 51 "" "" "" "" "" "Alberta town" 298 163 306 158 77
   86]
   [5101256 160 51 "" "" "" "" "" "Allisonia CDP" 117 107 "" "" 32
   ""]
   [5102248 160 51 "" "" "" "" "" "Arcola CDP" 233 96 "" ""
   59 ""]
   ```

3. This one picks out the medium-sized towns, ones with populations between 1,000 and 40,000:

   ```
   user=> (def medium ($where {:POP100 {:gt 1000 :lt 40000}}
   va-data))
   #'user/medium
   user=> (nrow medium)
   ```

```
                            333
user=> ($ [0 1 2 3] :all medium)
[:GEOID :SUMLEV :STATE :COUNTY :CBSA :CSA :NECTA :CNECTA
:NAME :POP100 :HU100 :POP100.2000 :HU100.2000 :P035001
:P035001.2000]
[5100148 160 51 "" "" "" "" "" "Abingdon town" 8191
4271 7780 3788 2056 2091]
[5101528 160 51 "" "" "" "" "" "Altavista town" 3450
1669 3425 1650 928 940]
[5101640 160 51 "" "" "" "" "" "Amelia Court House CDP"
1099 419 "" "" 273 ""]
[5101672 160 51 "" "" "" "" "" "Amherst town" 2231 1032
2251 1000 550 569]
```

Incanter's query language is more powerful than this, but these examples should show us the basic structure and give us an idea of the possibilities.

## How it works...

To a better understand how to use $where, let's pick apart the last example:

```
($where {:POP100 {:gt 1000 :lt 40000}} va-data)
```

The query is expressed as a hash-map from fields (highlighted) to values. As we saw in the first example, the value can be a raw value, either a literal or an expression. This tests for equality.

```
($where {:POP100 {:gt 1000 :lt 40000}} va-data)
```

It can also be another map as it is here (highlighted). The keys of this map are tests, and the values are parameters to those tests. All of the tests in this map are *and*ed together, so that the field's values have to pass all predicates.

Incanter supports a number of test operators. Basic Boolean tests are :$gt (greater than), :$lt (less than), :$gte (greater than or equal to), :$lte (less than or equal to), :$eq (equal to), and :$ne (not equal to). There are also some operators that take sets as parameters: :$in (in) and :$nin (not in).

The last operator—:$fn—is interesting. It allows us to use any predicate function. For example, this would randomly select approximately half of the dataset.

```
(def random-half
  ($where {:GEOID {:$fn (fn [_] (< (rand) 0.5))}} va-data))
```

All of these tests are *and*ed together to produce the final result set.

*Working with Incanter Datasets*

### There's more...

For full details of the query language, see the documentation for incanter.core/query-dataset (http://liebke.github.com/incanter/core-api.html#incanter.core/query-dataset).

## Grouping data with $group-by

Datasets often come with inherent structure. Two or more rows may have the same value in one column, and we may want to leverage that by grouping those rows together in our analysis.

### Getting ready

First, we'll need to declare a dependency on Incanter in the `project.clj` file:

```
:dependencies [[org.clojure/clojure "1.4.0"]
               [incanter "1.4.1"]]
```

Next, we'll include Incanter `core` and `io` in our script or REPL.

```
(use '(incanter core io))
```

For data, we'll use the census race data for all states. We first saw this in the *Selecting columns with $* recipe, and we can download it from http://www.ericrochester.com/clj-data-analysis/data/all_160.P3.csv.

```
(def data-file "data/all_160.P3.csv")
(def race-data (read-dataset data-file :header true))
```

### How to do it...

Incanter lets us group rows for further analysis or summarizing with the `$group-by` function. All we need to do is pass the data to `$group-by` with the column or function to group on.

```
(def by-state ($group-by :STATE race-data))
```

### How it works...

This function returns a map where each key is a map of the fields and values represented by that grouping. For example, the keys look like this:

```
user=> (take 5 (keys by-state))
```

```
({:STATE 29} {:STATE 28} {:STATE 31} {:STATE 30} {:STATE 25})
We can get the data for Virginia back out by querying the
group map for state 51.
user=> ($ [0 1 2 3] :all (by-state {:STATE 51}))
[:P003005 :SUMLEV :P003008.2000 :HU100.2000 :P003002.2000
:HU100 :P003007.2000 :NAME :GEOID :NECTA :P003006.2000
:P003001.2000 :CBSA :P003001 :P003002 :CSA :P003005.2000
:POP100.2000 :CNECTA :POP100 :COUNTY :P003007 :P003008
:P003004.2000 :P003003.2000 :STATE :P003004 :P003003 :P003006]
[86 160 49 3788 7390 4271 15 "Abingdon town" 5100148 ""
1 7780 "" 8191 7681 "" 50 7780 "" 8191 ""
64 82 10 265 51 15 257 6]
[3 160 4 235 389 229 5 "Accomac town" 5100180 "" 0 547 "
" 519 389 "" 14 547 "" 519 "" 17 3 0 135 51 0 106 1]
[0 160 0 158 183 163 1 "Alberta town" 5100724 "
" 0 306 "" 298 177 "" 1 306 "" 298 "" 2 3 0 121 51 4 112 0]
[8432 160 5483 64251 76702 72376 9467 "Alexandria city"
5101000 "" 112 128283 "" 139966 85186 "" 7249 128283 "
" 139966 "" 9902 5225 355 28915 51 589 30491 141]
```

# Saving datasets to CSV and JSON

Once we've gone to the work of slicing, dicing, cleaning, and aggregating our datasets, we might want to save them. Incanter by itself doesn't have a good way to do that. However, with the help of some Clojure libraries, it's not difficult at all.

## Getting ready

We'll need to include a number of dependencies in our `project.clj` file.

```
:dependencies [[org.clojure/clojure "1.4.0"]
               [incanter "1.4.1"]
               [org.clojure/data.json "0.2.1"]
               [org.clojure/data.csv "0.1.2"]]
```

We'll also need to include those libraries in our script or REPL.

```
(use '(incanter core io))
(require '[clojure.data.csv :as csv]
         '[clojure.data.json :as json]
         '[clojure.java.io :as io])
```

We'll be using the same data file that we introduced in the *Selecting columns with $* recipe.

*Working with Incanter Datasets*

## How to do it...

This process is really as simple as getting the data and saving it. We'll pull out the state, name of the location, and the population and race data from the larger dataset. We'll use this subset of the data in both formats.

```
(def census2010 ($ [:STATE :NAME :POP100 :P003002 :P003003
  :P003004 :P003005 :P003006 :P003007
  :P003008]
  race-data))
```

### Saving data as CSV

To save a dataset as CSV, all in one statement, we open a file and use `clojure.data.csv/write-csv` to write the column names and data to it.

```
(with-open [f-out (io/writer "data/census-2010.csv")]
  (csv/write-csv f-out [(map name (col-names census2010))])
  (csv/write-csv f-out (to-list census2010)))
```

### Saving data as JSON

To save a dataset as JSON, we open a file and use `clojure.data.json/write` to serialize the file.

```
(with-open [f-out (io/writer "data/census-2010.json")]
  (json/write (:rows census2010) f-out))
```

## How it works...

For CSV and JSON, as well as many other data formats, the process is very similar. Get the data, open the file, and serialize data into it. There will be differences in how the output function wants the data (`to-list` or `:rows`), and there will be differences in how the output function is called. (For instance, is the file handle the first argument or the second?) But generally, outputting datasets will be very similar and relatively simple.

## See also

- The *Reading CSV data into Incanter datasets* recipe in *Chapter 1, Importing Data for Analysis*
- The *Reading JSON data into Incanter datasets* recipe in *Chapter 1, Importing Data for Analysis*

# Projecting from multiple datasets with $join

So far we've been focusing on splitting datasets up, on dividing them into groups of rows or groups of columns with functions and macros such as `$` or `$where`. However, sometimes we'd like to move in the other direction. We may have two, related datasets, and we'd like to join them together to make a larger one.

## Getting ready

First, we'll need to include these dependencies in our `project.clj` file.

```
:dependencies [[org.clojure/clojure "1.4.0"]
               [incanter "1.4.1"]]
```

We'll use the following statements for includes:

```
(use '(incanter core io charts)
     '[clojure.set :only (union)])
```

For our data file, we'll use the census data that we used in the *Converting datasets to matrices* recipe. You can download this from http://www.ericrochester.com/clj-data-analysis/data/all_160_in_51.P35.csv. Save it to `data/all_160_in_51.P35.csv`.

We'll also use a new data file, `data/all_160_in_51.P3.csv`. This contains the race questions from the census for Virginia. I downloaded this also from http://census.ire.org/. You can query it from there or download it directly at http://censusdata.ire.org/51/all_160_in_51.P3.csv or http://www.ericrochester.com/clj-data-analysis/data/all_160_in_51.P3.csv.

## How to do it...

In this recipe, we'll look at how to join two datasets using Incanter.

1. Once all the data is in place, we first need to load both files into separate datasets.

   ```
   (def family-data (read-dataset
                       "data/all_160_in_51.P35.csv" :header
                       true))
   (def racial-data (read-dataset
                       "data/all_160_in_51.P3.csv" :header
                       true))
   ```

*Working with Incanter Datasets*

2. Looking at the columns, we can see that there's a fair amount of overlap between them.

   ```
   user=> (set/intersection (set (col-names family-data))
     #_=>                   (set (col-names racial-data)))
   #{:SUMLEV :HU100.2000 :HU100 :NAME :GEOID :NECTA :CBSA
    :CSA :POP100.2000 :CNECTA :POP100 :COUNTY :STATE}
   ```

3. We can project from the `racial-data` dataset to get rid of all of the duplicate columns from it. Any duplicates not listed in the join will get silently dropped. The values kept will be those from the last dataset listed. To make this easier, we'll create a function that returns the columns of the second dataset, minus those found in the first dataset, plus the index column.

   ```
   (defn dedup-second
     [a b id-col]
     (let [a-cols (set (col-names a))]
       (conj (filter #(not (contains? a-cols %))
                     (col-names b))
             id-col)))
   ```

4. We apply that to the `racial-data` dataset to get a copy of it without the duplicate fields.

   ```
   (def racial-short ($ (vec (dedup-second family-data
   racial-data :GEOID))
                        racial-data))
   ```

5. Once it's in place, we merge the full family dataset with the `race` data subset using `$join`.

   ```
   user=> (def all-data
     #_=>   ($join [:GEOID :GEOID] family-data racial-short))
   #'user/all-data
   user=> (col-names all-data)
   [:P003005 :SUMLEV :P003008.2000 :P035001 :HU100.2000 :P003002.2000
   :HU100 :P003007.2000 :NAME :GEOID :NECTA :P003006.2000
   :P003001.2000 :CBSA :P003001 :P003002 :CSA :P003005.2000
   :P035001.2000 :POP100.2000 :CNECTA :POP100 :COUNTY :P003007
   :P003008 :P003004.2000 :P003003.2000 :STATE :P003004 :P003003
   :P003006]
   ```

6. We can also see that all rows from both input datasets were merged into the final dataset.

   ```
   user=> (= (nrow family-data) (nrow racial-short) (nrow all-data))
   true
   ```

From this point on, we can use `all-data` just as we would use any other Incanter dataset.

## How it works...

Let's look at this in more detail.

```
($join [:GEOID :GEOID] family-data racial-short)
```

The pair of column keywords in a vector (`[:GEOID :GEOID]`) are the keys that the datasets will be joined on. In this case, the `:GEOID` column from both datasets are used, but the keys could be different for the two datasets. The first column listed will be from the first dataset (`family-data`). The second column listed will be from the second dataset (`racial-short`).

This returns a new dataset. As I mentioned, in the output, duplicate columns contain only the values from the second dataset. But otherwise, each row is the superset of the corresponding rows from the two input datasets.

# 7
# Preparing for and Performing Statistical Data Analysis with Incanter

In this chapter, we will cover:

- Generating summary statistics with $rollup
- Differencing variables to show changes
- Scaling variables to simplify variable relationships
- Working with time series data with Incanter Zoo
- Smoothing variables to decrease noise
- Validating sample statistics with bootstrapping
- Modeling linear relationships
- Modeling non-linear relationships
- Modeling multimodal Bayesian distributions
- Finding data errors with Benford's law

# Introduction

So far, we've focused on data and process. We've seen how to get data and how to get it ready to analyze. We've also looked at how to organize and partition our processing to keep things simple and to get the best performance.

Now, we'll look at how to leverage statistics to gain insights into our data. This is a subject that is both deep and broad, and covering statistics in any meaningful way is far beyond the scope of this chapter. For more information about some of the procedures and functions described here, you should refer to a textbook, class, your local statistician, or another resource. For instance, **Coursera** has an online statistics course (https://www.coursera.org/course/stats1), and **Harvard** has a course on probability on iTunes (https://itunes.apple.com/us/course/statistics-110-probability/id502492375).

Some of the recipes in this chapter will involve generating simple summary statistics. Some will involve further massaging our data to make trends and relationships more clear. Then we'll look at different ways to model the relationships in our data. Finally, we'll look at Benford's law, a curious observation about the behavior of naturally occurring sequences of numbers, which we can leverage to discover problems with our data.

# Generating summary statistics with $rollup

One of the basic ways of getting a grip on a dataset is to look at some summary statistics: measures of centrality and variance, such as mean and standard deviation. These provide useful insights into our data and help us know what questions to ask next and how best to proceed.

## Getting ready

First, we'll need to make sure Incanter is listed in the dependencies of our Leiningen `project.clj` file.

```
:dependencies [[org.clojure/clojure "1.4.0"]
               [incanter "1.4.1"]]
```

And we'll need to require these libraries in our script or REPL.

```
(require
  '[incanter.core :as i]
  'incanter.io
  '[incanter.stats :as s])
```

Finally, we'll use the dataset of census race data that we compiled for the *Grouping data with $group-by* recipe in *Chapter 6, Working with Incanter Datasets*. We'll bind the file name to the name `data-file`. You can download this from `http://www.ericrochester.com/clj-data-analysis/data/all_160.P3.csv`.

```
(def data-file "data/all_160.P3.csv")
```

## How to do it...

To generate summary statistics in Incanter, we use the `$rollup` function.

1. First, we'll load the dataset and bind it to the name `census`.

   ```
   (def census (incanter.io/read-dataset data-file :header true))
   ```

2. Then, we use `$rollup` to get the statistics for groups of data.

   ```
   user=> (i/$rollup :mean :POP100 :STATE census)
   [:STATE :POP100]
   [29 695433/172]
   [28 812159/181]
   [31 70836/29]
   [30 341847/182]
   ...
   user=> (i/$rollup s/sd :POP100 :STATE census)
   [:STATE :POP100]
   [29 20135.43888222624]
   [28 11948.001546221063]
   [31 20443.062360819255]
   [30 7846.878660629906]
   ...
   ```

## How it works...

The $rollup function takes the dataset (the fourth parameter) and groups the rows by the values of the grouping field (the third parameter). It takes the group subsets of the data and extracts the values from the field to aggregate (the second parameter). It passes those values to the aggregate function (the first parameter) to get the final table of values. That's a lot for one small function. The following diagram makes it more clear:

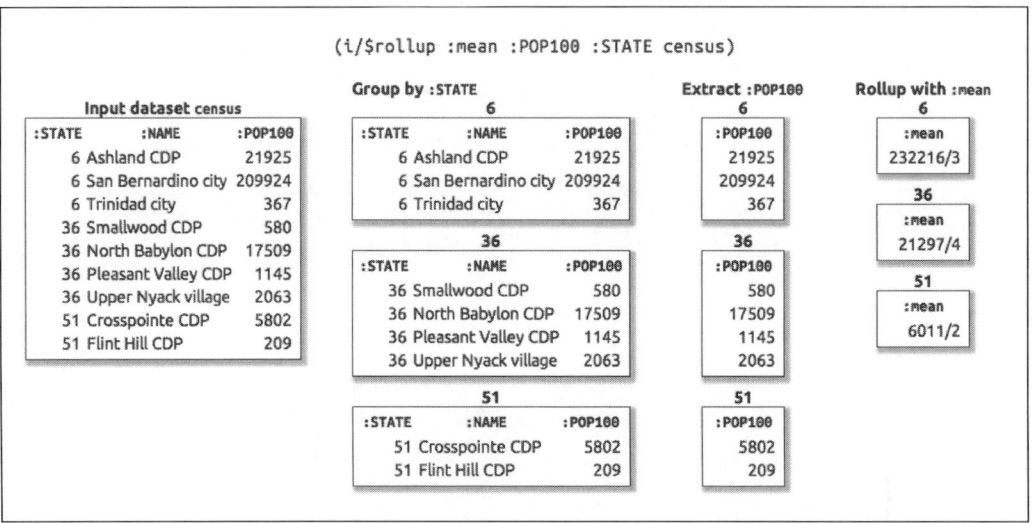

$rollup defines some standard aggregation functions—:count, :sum, :min, :max, and :mean—but we can also use any other function that takes a collection of values and returns a single value. This is what we did with incanter.stats/sd. For complete details of the $rollup function and the aggregate keyword functions it provides, see the documentation at http://liebke.github.com/incanter/core-api.html#incanter.core/$rollup.

As an aside, the numbers in the first example, which calculated the mean, are expressed as rational numbers. These are real numbers that are more precise than IEEE floating point numbers, which is what Clojure uses for its doubles. When Clojure divides two integers, we get rational numbers. If you want to see floating point numbers, you convert them by passing the values to float.

```
user=> (/ 695433 172)
695433/172
user=> (float 695433/172)
4043.215
```

## Differencing variables to show changes

Sometimes, we're more interested in how values change than we are in the values themselves. This information is latent in the data, but making it explicit makes it easier to work with and visualize.

### Getting ready

First, we'll use the following dependencies in our `project.clj` file.

```
:dependencies [[org.clojure/clojure "1.4.0"]
               [incanter "1.4.1"]]
```

We also need to require Incanter in our script or REPL.

```
(require
  '[incanter.core :as i]
  'incanter.io)
```

Finally, we'll use the Virginia census data. You can download the file from http://www.ericrochester.com/clj-data-analysis/data/all_160_in_51.P3.csv.

```
(def data-file "data/all_160_in_51.P3.csv")
```

### How to do it...

For this recipe, we'll take some census data and add a column to show the change in population between the 2000 and 2010 censuses.

1. We need to read in the data.

   ```
   (def data (incanter.io/read-dataset data-file
   :header true))
   ```

2. If we look at the values in the field for the year 2000 census population, some of them are empty. This will cause errors, so we'll replace those with zeros. The following is the function to do that:

   ```
   (defn replace-empty [x] (if (empty? x) 0 x))
   ```

3. Now we can get the difference in population between the two censuses.

   ```
   (def growth-rates
     (->> data
       (i/$map replace-empty :POP100.2000)
       (i/minus (i/sel data :cols :POP100))
       (i/dataset [:POP.DELTA])
       (i/conj-cols data)))
   ```

4. And as we might expect, some places have grown and some have shrunk.

```
user=> (i/sel growth-rates
         :cols [:NAME :POP100 :POP100.2000 :POP.DELTA]
         :rows (range 5))
[:NAME :POP100 :POP100.2000 :POP.DELTA]
["Abingdon town" 8191 7780 411]
["Accomac town" 519 547 -28]
["Alberta town" 298 306 -8]
["Alexandria city" 139966 128283 11683]
["Allisonia CDP" 117 "" 117]
```

## How it works...

This was a pretty straightforward process, but let's look at it line by line to make sure everything's clear. We'll follow the steps of the `->>` macro.

1. We map the values in the year 2000 census population column over the `replace-empty` function we defined earlier to get rid of empty values.

   ```
   (->> data
        (i/$map replace-empty :POP100.2000)
   ```

2. We select the 2010 census population and subtract the year 2000 values from it.

   ```
   (i/minus (i/sel data :cols :POP100))
   ```

3. We take the differences and create a new dataset with one column named `:POP.DELTA`.

   ```
   (i/dataset [:POP.DELTA])
   ```

4. And we merge it back into the original dataset with `incanter.core/conj-cols`. This function takes two datasets with the same number of rows, and it returns a new dataset with the columns from both of the input datasets.

   ```
   (i/conj-cols data))
   ```

## Scaling variables to simplify variable relationships

We don't always work with numbers as they are. For example, population is often given in thousands. In this recipe, we'll scale some values to make them easier to work with. In fact, some algorithms work better with scaled data. For instance, linear regression models are sometimes able to fit the data better after it has been scaled logarithmically.

## Getting ready

We'll use the following dependencies in our `project.clj` file:

```
:dependencies [[org.clojure/clojure "1.4.0"]
               [incanter "1.4.1"]]
```

And we'll use the following namespaces in our script or REPL:

```
(require
  '[incanter.core :asi]
  'incanter.io
  '[incanter.charts :as c])
```

For data, we'll use the census data that we did in the *Differencing variables to show changes* recipe.

```
(def data-file "data/all_160_in_51.P3.csv")
```

## How to do it...

In this recipe, we'll scale the data in two ways.

1. Before we start scaling anything, we'll read in the data and sort it.

   ```
   (def data
     (i/$order :POP100 :asc
         (incanter.io/read-dataset data-file :header true)))
   ```

2. We'll first scale the population by thousands. To do this, we'll pull out the column's data, scale it, wrap it in a new dataset, and join that with the original dataset.

   ```
   (def data
     (->> (i/div (i/sel data :cols :POP100) 1000.0)
       (i/dataset [:POP100.1000])
       (i/conj-cols data)))
   ```

3. Another useful scaling method is to scale logarithmically. In this case, we'll scale by a base-10 log.

   ```
   (def data
     (->> (i/sel data :cols :POP100)
   i/log10
       (i/dataset [:POP100.LOG10])
       (i/conj-cols data)))
   ```

## How it works...

Let's take a look at these transformations. In the original data, we can see that most locations are fairly small—less than 50,000—but the populations climb quickly from there.

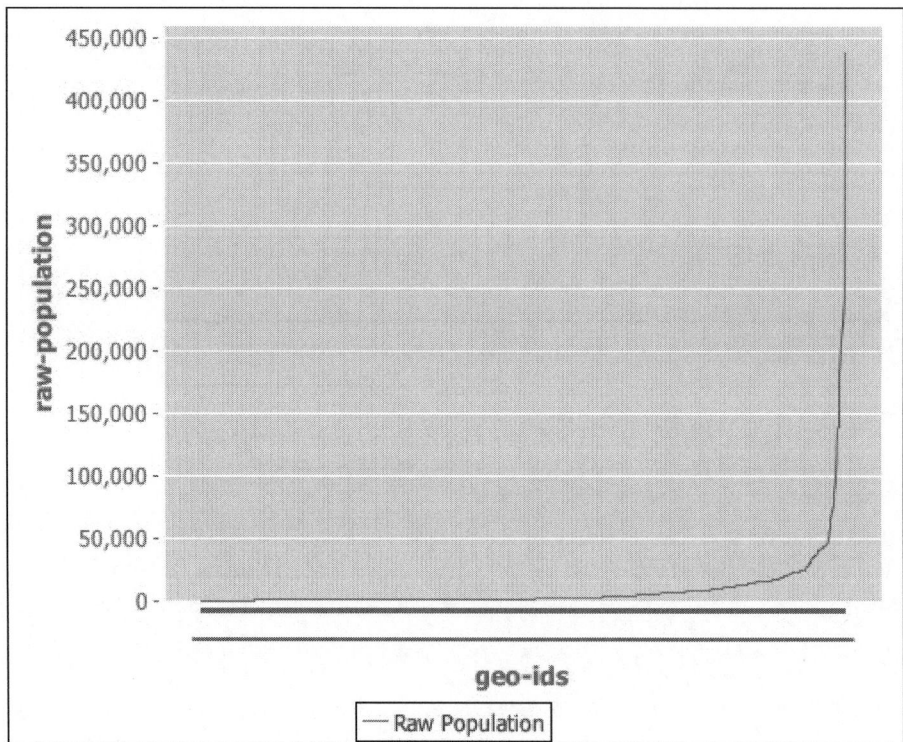

We don't need to see a graph of the second, linear scaling. The shape of the graph is the same, and the only difference is the scale on the left-hand side. Instead of going up to 450,000, it would only go up to 450.

However, the graph for the logarithmic transformation is a bit different. We can see that the values aren't quite on a straight-line log scale, but they're pretty close. Instead of climbing steeply, much of the line is a gentle rise. Given a logarithmic scale, this is what we'd expect. After this transformation, we could model this dataset with a linear regression, whereas with the original data, we could not.

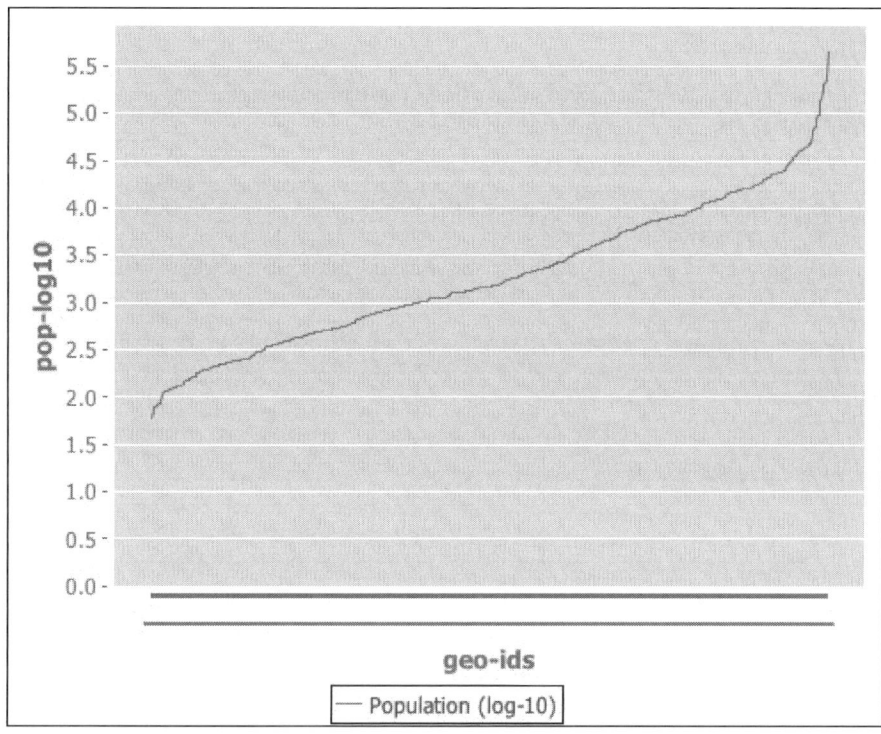

# Working with time series data with Incanter Zoo

Data that includes a regular timestamp is very common. Stock prices and weather are time series data, tracking values that change over the course of seconds, hours, days, weeks, months, or even years.

Incanter includes a namespace—`incanter.zoo`—that makes working with time series data very easy. We can use that to compute running averages and to map other functions over a moving window of the data.

For this, we'll take a look at some stock data for IBM. You can get this from a number of sources, but I downloaded a decade's worth of data from Google Finance (http://www.google.com/finance). You can download the same data from http://www.ericrochester.com/clj-data-analysis/data/ibm.csv.

*Preparing for and Performing Statistical Data Analysis with Incanter*

## Getting ready

First, we need to list the dependencies we'll need in our Leiningen `project.clj` file. Notice that we have to include `incanter-zoo` as a separate dependency, since it's not distributed with the core Incanter packages.

```
:dependencies [[org.clojure/clojure "1.4.0"]
               [incanter "1.4.1"]
               [incanter/incanter-zoo "1.4.1"]
               [clj-time "0.4.4"]]
```

Also, we'll need to require those namespaces in our script or REPL.

```
(require
  '[incanter.core :as i]
  '[incanter.zoo :as zoo]
  '[clj-time.format :as tf])
```

And we'll need the data I mentioned in the introduction to this recipe. I've downloaded mine to a file named `data/ibm.csv`, and I'll bind that to the name `data-file`.

```
(def data-file "data/ibm.csv")
```

## How to do it...

Unfortunately, Incanter doesn't convert the dates in the data file, so we'll need to do this ourselves. This isn't difficult to do, but it will take a few lines. Once that's done, we can calculate the rolling averages.

1. First, we'll write a function to parse the dates.

    ```
    (def ^:dynamic *formatter* (tf/formatter "dd-MMM-yy"))
    (defn parse-date [date] (tf/parse *formatter* date))
    ```

2. Now we can open the data file, convert the appropriate rows to dates, and merge the results back into the original dataset.

    ```
    (def data
      (i/with-data
        (i/col-names
          (incanter.io/read-dataset data-file)
          [:date-str :open :high :low :close :volume])
        (->>
          (i/$map parse-date :date-str)
          (i/dataset [:date])
          (i/conj-cols i/$data))))
    ```

3. To use this with `incanter.zoo`, we have to convert the dataset to a Zoo object. When we do this, we'll tell it which column contains the time data (`:date`). From this point on, we'll need to refer to this column with the key `:index`.

    ```
    (def data-zoo (zoo/zoo data :date))
    ```

4. Now, to compute a rolling 5-day average, we just call the `incanter.zoo/roll-mean` function. This will merge the five-day rolling average back into the dataset as the `:five-day` column.

   ```
   (def data-roll5
     (->>
       (i/sel data-zoo :cols :close)
       (zoo/roll-mean 5)
       (i/dataset [:five-day])
       (i/conj-cols data-zoo)))
   ```

## There's more...

If we look at a graph of the observations for approximately the last year of data using `incanter.core/sel`, we can see how much the rolling dates smoothed the input. Especially looking at the line for the 30-day average, it's clear that the data is capturing a larger trend, not the day-to-day fluctuations of the raw data.

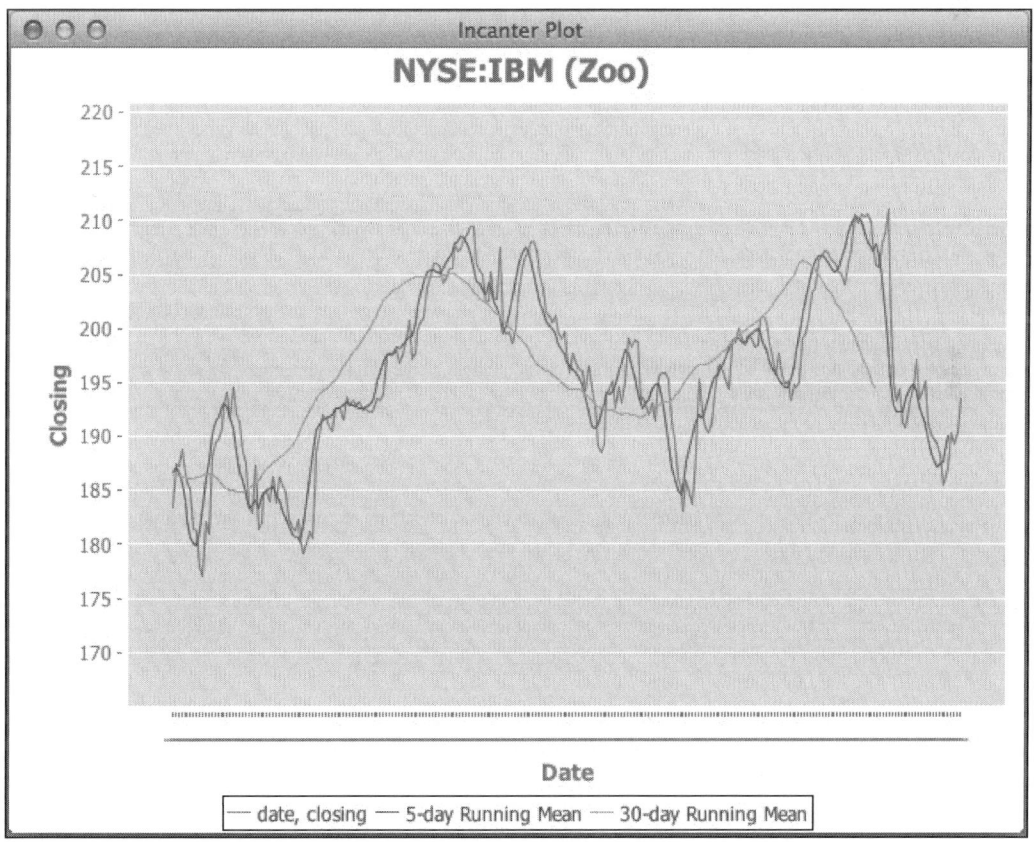

## Smoothing variables to decrease noise

We saw in the last recipe how to use Incanter Zoo to work with time series data and how to smooth values using a running mean. But sometimes we'll want to smooth data that doesn't have a time component. For instance, we may want to track the usage of a word throughout a larger document or set of documents. This would show us places where the word is more important within the larger body of text.

### Getting ready

For this we'll need the usual dependencies.

```
:dependencies [[org.clojure/clojure "1.4.0"]
               [incanter "1.4.1"]]
```

And we'll require those in our script or REPL.

```
(require
  '[incanter.core :as i]
  '[incanter.stats :as s]
  '[incanter.charts :as c]
  '[clojure.string :as str])
```

For this recipe, we'll look at Sir Arthur Conan Doyle's Sherlock Holmes stories. You can download this from Project Gutenberg at http://www.gutenberg.org/cache/epub/1661/pg1661.txt or http://www.ericrochester.com/clj-data-analysis/data/pg1661.txt.

### How to do it...

We'll look at the distribution of *baker* over the course of the book. This may give some indication of how important Holmes' residence at 221B Baker Street is for a given story.

1. First, we'll define a function that takes a text string and pulls the words out of it, or tokenizes it.

    ```
    (defn tokenize
      [text]
      (map str/lower-case (re-seq #"\w+" text)))
    ```

2. Next, we'll write a function that takes an item and a collection and returns how many times the item appears in the collection.

    ```
    (defn count-hits
      [x coll]
      (get (frequencies coll) x 0))
    ```

3. Now we can read the file, tokenize it, and break it into overlapping windows of 500 tokens.

   ```
   (def data-file "data/pg1661.txt")
   (def windows
     (partition 500 250 (tokenize (slurp data-file))))
   ```

4. We use `count-hits` to get the number of times that *baker* appears in each window of tokens.

   ```
   (def baker-hits
     (map (partial count-hits "baker") windows))
   ```

5. At this point, we have the frequency of *baker* across the document. This doesn't really show trends, however. To get the rolling average, we'll define a function that maps a function to a rolling window of *n* items from a collection.

   ```
   (defn rolling-fn
     [f n coll]
     (map f (partition n 1 coll)))
   ```

6. We'll apply the `mean` function to the sequence of frequencies for the term *baker* to get the rolling average for sets of ten windows.

   ```
   (def baker-avgs (rolling-fn s/mean 10 baker-hits))
   ```

7. This graphs easily over the raw frequencies.

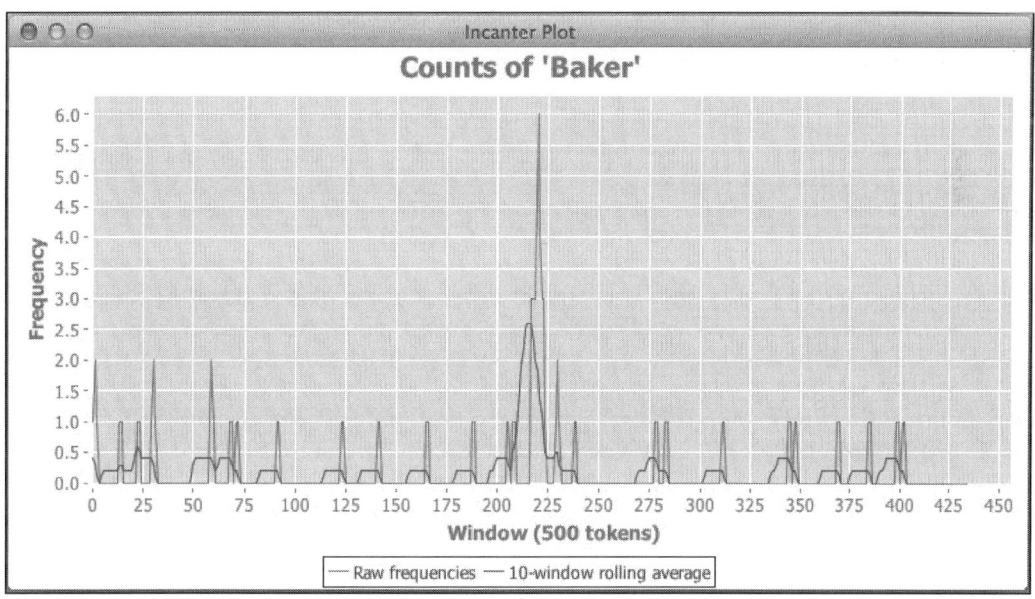

## How it works...

This recipe processes a document through a number of stages to get the results.

1. We read in the file and pull out the words.
2. We partition the tokens into a chunks of 500 tokens, each overlapping by 250 tokens. This allows us to deal with localized parts of the document. Each partition is large enough to be interesting, but small enough to be narrowly focused.
3. For each window, we get the frequency of the term *baker*. This data is kind of spiky. This is fine for some applications, but we may want to smooth it out to make the data less noisy and to show the trends better.
4. So we break the sequence of frequencies of *baker* into a rolling set of ten windows. Each set is offset from the previous set by one.
5. We get the average frequency for each set of frequencies. This removes much of the noise and spikiness from the raw data, but it maintains the general shape of the data. We can still see the spike around 220.

And by the way, that spike is from the short story, *The Adventure of the Blue Carbuncle*. A character in that story is *Henry Baker*, so the spike is not just from references to Baker Street, but to the street and to the character.

# Validating sample statistics with bootstrapping

When working with sampled data, we need to produce the same descriptive statistics that we do when working with populations of data. Of course, these will just be estimates, and there is error inherent in those estimations.

**Bootstrapping** is a way to estimate the distribution of a population. Bootstrapping works by taking a sample from the population and repeatedly resampling with replacement from the original sample. *With replacement* means that the same observation is allowed in the sample more than once. After each re-sampling, the statistic is computed from the new sample. From this we estimate the shape of the distribution of a value in the population.

We can use bootstrapping when the sample we're working with is small, or even when we don't know the distribution of the sample's population.

## Getting ready

For this recipe, we'll use the following dependencies in our `project.clj` file:

```
:dependencies [[org.clojure/clojure "1.4.0"]
               [incanter "1.4.1"]]
```

And we'll use the following namespaces in our script or REPL:

```
(require
  '[incanter.core :as i]
  '[incanter.stats :as s]
  'incanter.io
  '[incanter.charts :as c])
```

For data, we'll use the same census data that we did in the *Differencing variables to show changes* recipe.

```
(def data-file "data/all_160_in_51.P3.csv")
```

## How to do it...

This is a simple recipe. In it, we'll use Incanter's bootstrapping functions to estimate the median of the census population.

1. First, we read in the data.

   ```
   (def data (incanter.io/read-dataset data-file :header true))
   ```

2. Then we'll pull out the population column and resample it for the median using the `incanter.stats/bootstrap` function.

   ```
   (def pop100 (i/sel data :cols :POP100))
   (def samples (s/bootstrap pop100 s/median :size 2000))
   ```

3. Now let's look at a histogram of the samples to see what the distribution of the median looks like.

   ```
   (i/view (c/histogram samples))
   ```

The following diagram shows the histogram:

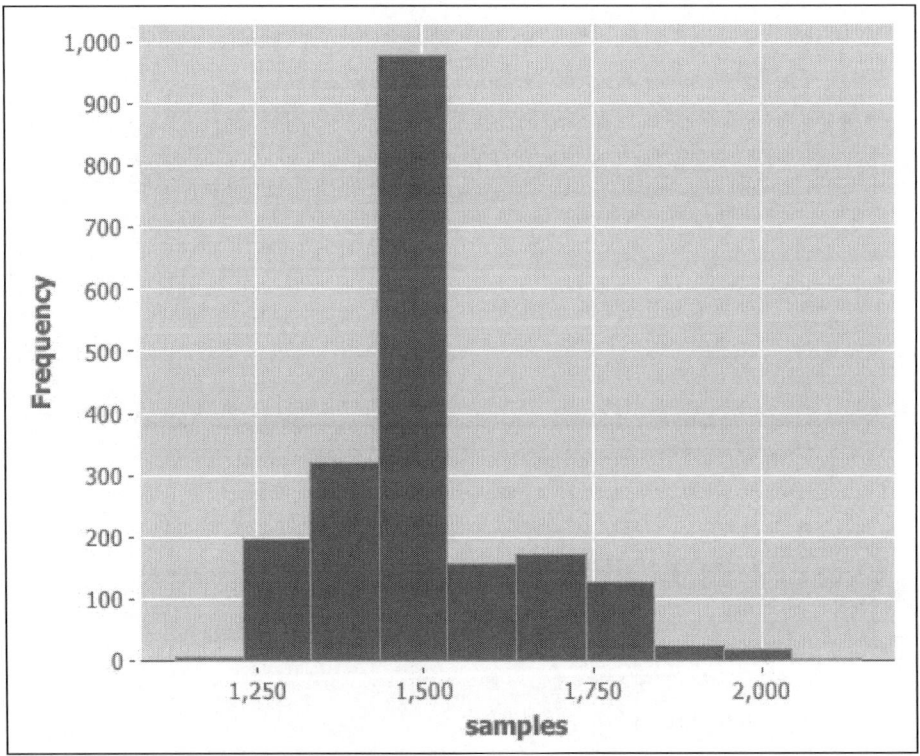

So we can see that the median clusters pretty closely around the sample's median (1480).

### How it works...

Bootstrapping validates whether the output of a function over a data sample represents that value in the population by repeatedly resampling from the original sample of inputs to the function. But there's a twist. When the original sample was created, it was done without replacement, that is, without duplicates. The same observation cannot be included in the sample twice.

However, the resampling is done with replacements, which means that duplicates are permitted. Actually, since the resample is of the same size as the original sample that it's drawn from, some observations must be included multiple times in the resample.

Each resample is then fed to the function being validated, and its outputs are used to estimate the distribution of the population.

## There's more...

For more about bootstrapping, *Bootstrap: A Statistical Method* by Kesar Singh and Minge Xie gives a good, general introduction. You can find this paper at `http://www.stat.rutgers.edu/home/mxie/rcpapers/bootstrap.pdf`.

# Modeling linear relationships

When doing data analysis, often we look for relationships in our data. Does one variable affect another? If we have more of one thing, do we have less of something else? Does, say, a person's body mass index (BMI) have a relationship to his/her longevity? This isn't always obvious just by looking at a graph. A relationship that seems obvious to our eyes may not be significant.

**Linear regression** is a way of finding a linear formula that matches the relationship between an independent variable (the BMI) and a dependent variable (longevity). It also tells us how well that formula explains the variance in the data and how significant that relationship is.

## Getting ready

For this, we'll need the following dependencies:

```
:dependencies [[org.clojure/clojure "1.4.0"]
               [incanter "1.4.1"]]
```

We'll use the following set of requirements:

```
(require
  '[incanter.core :as i]
  'incanter.io
  '[incanter.stats :as s]
  '[incanter.charts :as c])
```

And we'll use the Virginia census race data file that we can download from `http://www.ericrochester.com/clj-data-analysis/data/all_160_in_51.P35.csv`.

```
(def data-file "data/all_160_in_51.P35.csv")
```

*Preparing for and Performing Statistical Data Analysis with Incanter*

## How to do it...

In this recipe, we'll use the Virginia census family data to examine the relationship between the number of families and the number of housing units. Does having more families imply more housing units? We probably expect these two variables to have a fairly tight linear relationship, so this should be a nice, clear test.

1. First, let's load the data and pull out the two fields we're interested in.

   ```
   (def family-data
     (incanter.io/read-dataset "data/all_160_in_51.P35.csv"
                               :header true))
   (def housing (i/sel family-data :cols [:HU100]))
   (def families (i/sel family-data :cols [:P035001]))
   ```

2. Computing the linear regression takes just one line.

   ```
   (def families-lm (s/linear-model housing families :intercept false))
   ```

3. The output of `s/linear-model` is a mapping that contains a lot of useful information. We can get the *r2* value (roughly, how well the model explains the variance in the data) and the *F* test (how significant the relationship is). High *F* values are associated with lower *p*-values, which is to say that high *F* values imply a lower probability that the relationship is the result of chance.

   ```
   user=> (:r-square families-lm)
   0.9594579287744827
   user=> (:f-prob families-lm)
   0.9999999999999999
   ```

4. The *F* test looks good, as does the *r2* value. Our expectation that more families means more housing units was probably right. Let's look at a graph of the data, too, though.

   ```
   (def housing-chart
     (doto
       (c/scatter-plot families housing
                       :title "Relationship of Housing to Families"
                       :x-label "Families"
                       :y-label "Housing"
                       :legend true)
       (c/add-lines families (:fitted families-lm)
                    :series-label "Linear Model")
       (i/view)))
   ```

Our graph looks like the following:

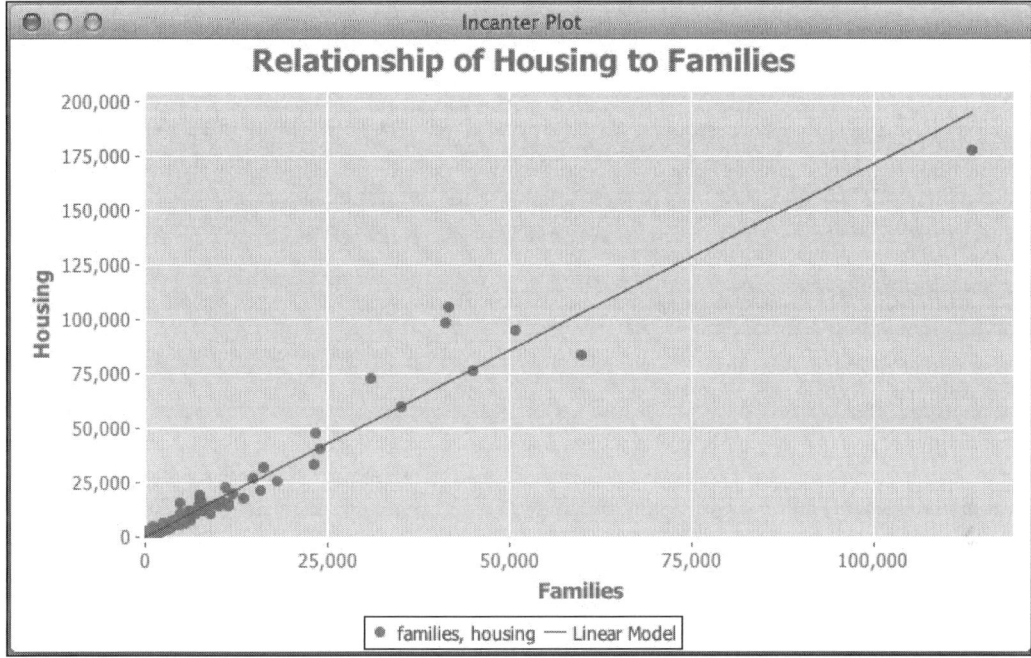

## How it works...

To perform the linear regression, Incanter uses **least squares linear regression**. This measures the distance between each data point (x, y) and the corresponding value from the linear function (f(x)). The method returns a line that minimizes the sum of the squares of those distances.

## There's more...

For more information, Stat Trek has a nice overview of this method at http://stattrek.com/regression/linear-regression.aspx.

## Modeling non-linear relationships

Non-linear models are similar to linear regression models, except that the lines aren't straight.

Well, that's overly simplistic and a little tongue-in-cheek, but it does have a grain of truth. We're looking to find a formula that best fits the data, but without the restriction that the formula be linear. This introduces a lot of complications and makes the problem significantly more difficult. Unlike linear regressions, fitting non-linear models typically involves a lot more guessing and trial-and-error.

### Getting ready

We'll need to declare Incanter as a dependency in the Leiningen `project.clj` file.

```
:dependencies [[org.clojure/clojure "1.4.0"]
               [incanter "1.4.1"]]
```

We'll also need to require a number of Incanter's namespaces in our script or REPL.

```
(require
  '[incanter.core :as i]
  'incanter.io
  '[incanter.optimize :as o]
  '[incanter.stats :as s]
  '[incanter.charts :as c])
(import [java.lang Math])
```

And for data, we'll visit the website of the National Highway Traffic Safety Administration (http://www-fars.nhtsa.dot.gov/QueryTool/QuerySection/selectyear.aspx). This organization publishes data on all fatal accidents on US roads. For this recipe, we'll download data for 2010, including the speed limit. You can also download the data file I'm working with directly from http://www.ericrochester.com/clj-data-analysis/data/accident-fatalities.tsv.

```
(def data-file "data/accident-fatalities.tsv")
```

## How to do it...

For this recipe, we'll see how to fit a formula to a set of data points. In this case, we'll look for a relationship between the speed limit and the number of fatal accidents that occur over a year.

1. First, we need to load the data from the tab-delimited files.

   ```
   (def data
     (incanter.io/read-dataset data-file
   :header true
   :delim \tab))
   ```

2. From this data, we'll use the `$rollup` function to calculate the number of fatalities per speed limit, and then filter out any invalid speed limits (empty values). We then sort it by the speed limit and create a new dataset. That seems like a mouthful, but it's really quite simple.

   ```
   (def fatalities
     (->> data
       (i/$rollup :count :Obs. :spdlim)
       (i/$where {:spdlim {:$ne "."}})
       (i/$where {:spdlim {:$ne 0}})
       (i/$order :spdlim :asc)
       (i/to-list)
       (i/dataset [:speed-limit :fatalities])))
   ```

3. Now, we'll pull out the columns to make them easier to refer to later.

   ```
   (def speed-limit (i/sel fatalities :cols :speed-limit))
   (def fatality-count (i/sel fatalities :cols :fatalities))
   ```

4. The first difficult part of non-linear models is that the general shape of the formula isn't pre-decided. We have to figure out what type of formula might best fit the data. To do that, let's graph it and try to think of a class of functions that roughly matches the shape of the data.

   ```
   (def chart
     (doto
       (c/scatter-plot speed-limit fatality-count
                       :title "Fatalities by Speed Limit (2010)"
                       :x-label "Speed Limit"
                       :y-label "Fatality Count"
                       :legend true)
       i/view))
   ```

The graph is as follows:

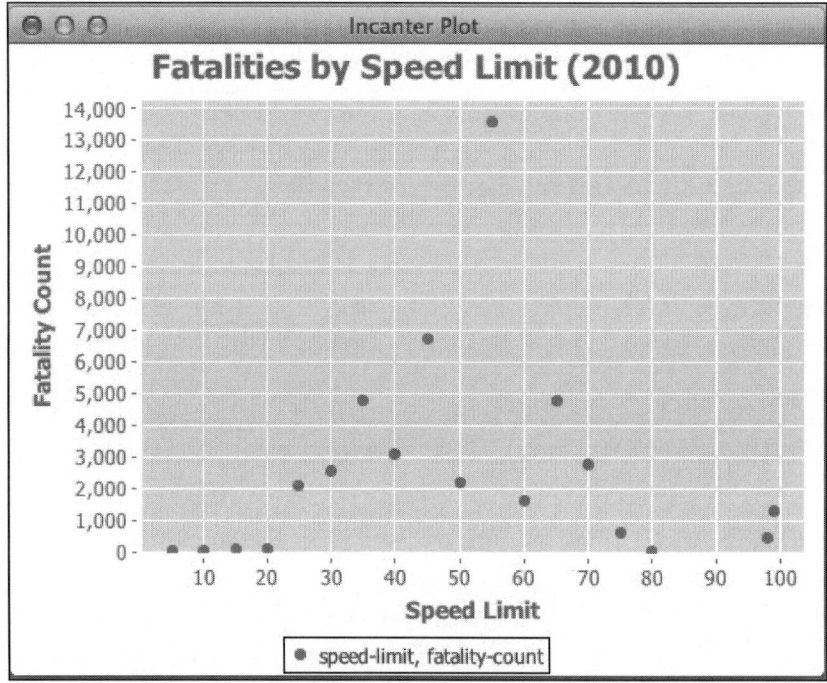

5. Eye-balling this graph, I decided to go with a simple, but very general, sine wave formula: $y(t) = A \cdot \sin(\omega t + \phi)$. This may not be the best fitting function, but it should do well enough for this demonstration.

```
(defn sine-wave
  [theta x]
  (let [[amp ang-freq phase shift] theta]
    (i/plus
      (i/mult amp (i/sin (i/plus (i/mult ang-freq x) phase))) shift)))
```

6. The non-linear modeling function then determines the parameters that make the function fit the data best. But before that can happen, we need to pick some starting parameters. This involves a lot of guess work. After playing around some and trying out different values until I got something in the neighborhood of the data, here's what I came up with:

```
(def start [3500.0 0.07 Math/PI 2500.0])
```

7. Now, we find the parameter that best fit the function to the data using the non-linear-model function.

```
(def nlm (o/non-linear-model sine-wave fatality-count speed-limit start))
```

8. Let's add the function with the starting parameters and the function with the final fitted parameters to the graph.

   ```
   (-> chart
     (c/add-lines speed-limit (sine-wave start speed-limit))
     (c/add-lines speed-limit (:fitted nlm)))
   ```

   The graph is as follows:

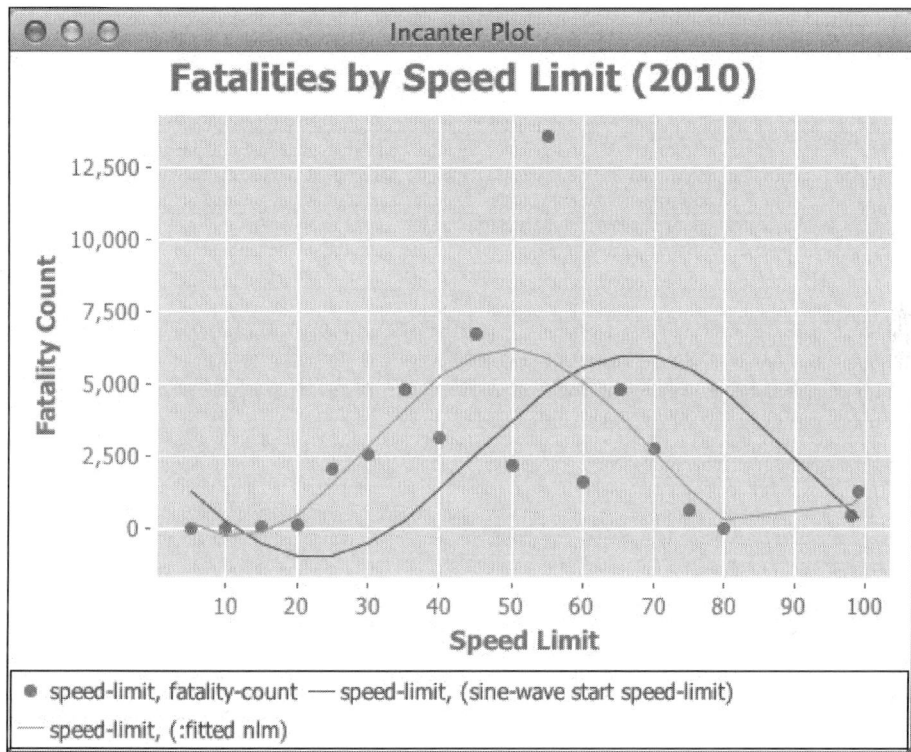

## How it works...

We can see that the function fits all right, but not great. The fatalities for 55-miles-per-hour seem like an outlier, too. The amount of road mileage may be skewing the data: since there are so many miles of road with a speed limit of 55 MPH, it stands to reason that there will also be more accidents for that speed limit. If we could get even an approximation of how many miles of roads are marked for various speed limits, we could compare the ratio of fatalities by the miles of road for that speed. This might return more interesting, useful results.

We should also say a few words about the parameters for the sine wave function.

*A* is the amplitude. This is the peak of the wave.

ω is the angular frequency. This is the slope of the wave, measured in radians per second.

Ø is the phase. This is the point of the waves' oscillation where *t=0*.

*t* is the time along the x axis.

## Modeling multimodal Bayesian distributions

A **multimodal distribution** is one where every observation in the dataset is taken from one of the limited number of options. For example, in the race census data, *race* is a multimodal parameter: it can be one of the seven options. If the census were a sample, how good of an estimate of the population would the ratios of the race observations be?

Bayesian methods work by updating a prior assumption with more data. In this example, we assume a prior probability distribution. For multivariate data, the Dirichlet distribution is commonly used. The Bayesian process observes how many times each option is seen and returns an estimate of the ratios of the different options from the multimodal distribution.

So in the case of the census race data, this algorithm looks at the ratios from a sample and updates the prior distribution from those values. The output is a belief about the probabilities of those ratios in the population.

### Getting ready

We'll need the following dependencies:

```
:dependencies [[org.clojure/clojure "1.4.0"]
               [incanter "1.4.1"]]
```

And we'll use the following requirements:

```
(require
  '[incanter.core :as i]
  'incanter.io
  '[incanter.bayes :as b]
  '[incanter.stats :as s])
```

For data, we'll use the census race table for Virginia, just as we did in the *Differencing variables to show changes* recipe.

## How to do it...

For this recipe, we'll first load the data, then we'll perform the Bayesian analysis, and finally we'll summarize the values from the distribution returned, getting the median, standard deviation, and confidence interval.

1. First, we need to load the data. When we do so, we'll rename the fields to make them easier to work with. We'll also pull out a sample to work with, so we can compare our results against the population when we're done processing.

   ```
   (def census-race
     (i/col-names
       (incanter.io/read-dataset
         "data/all_160_in_51.P3.csv"
         :header true)
       [:geoid :sumlev :state :county :cbsa :csa :necta
        :cnecta :name :pop :pop2k :housing :housing2k :total
        :total2k :white :white2k :black :black2k :indian
        :indian2k :asian :asian2k :hawaiian :hawaiian2k
        :other :other2k :multiple :multiple2k]))

   (def census-sample
     (->> census-race
       i/to-list
       shuffle
       (take 60)
       (i/dataset (i/col-names census-race))))
   ```

2. We'll now pull out the race columns and total them.

   ```
   (def race-keys
     [:white :black :indian :asian :hawaiian :other :multiple])
   (def race-totals
     (into {}
           (map #(vector % (i/sum (i/$ % census-sample)))
                race-keys)))
   ```

3. Next, we'll pull out just the sums from the totals map.

   ```
   (def y (map second (sort race-totals)))
   ```

4. And then we will draw samples for this from the Dirichlet distribution, using `sample-multinomial-params`, and put those into a new map associated with their original key.

   ```
   (def theta (b/sample-multinomial-params 2000 y))
   (def theta-params
     (into {}
           (map #(vector %1 (i/sel theta :cols %2))
                (sort race-keys)
                (range))))
   ```

5. Now we can summarize these by calling basic statistical functions on the distributions returned. In this case, we're curious about the distribution of these summary statistics in the population of which our data is a sample. For example, in this case, African-Americans are almost 24 percent.

```
user=> (s/mean (:black theta-params))
0.2391651213115365
user=> (s/sd (:black theta-params))
4.205486396994371E-4
user=> (s/quantile (:black theta-params) :probs [0.025 0.975])
(0.2383275589805636 0.23999025580193575)
```

6. A histogram of the proportions can also be helpful.

```
(i/view (c/histogram (:black theta-params)))
```

The histogram looks like the following:

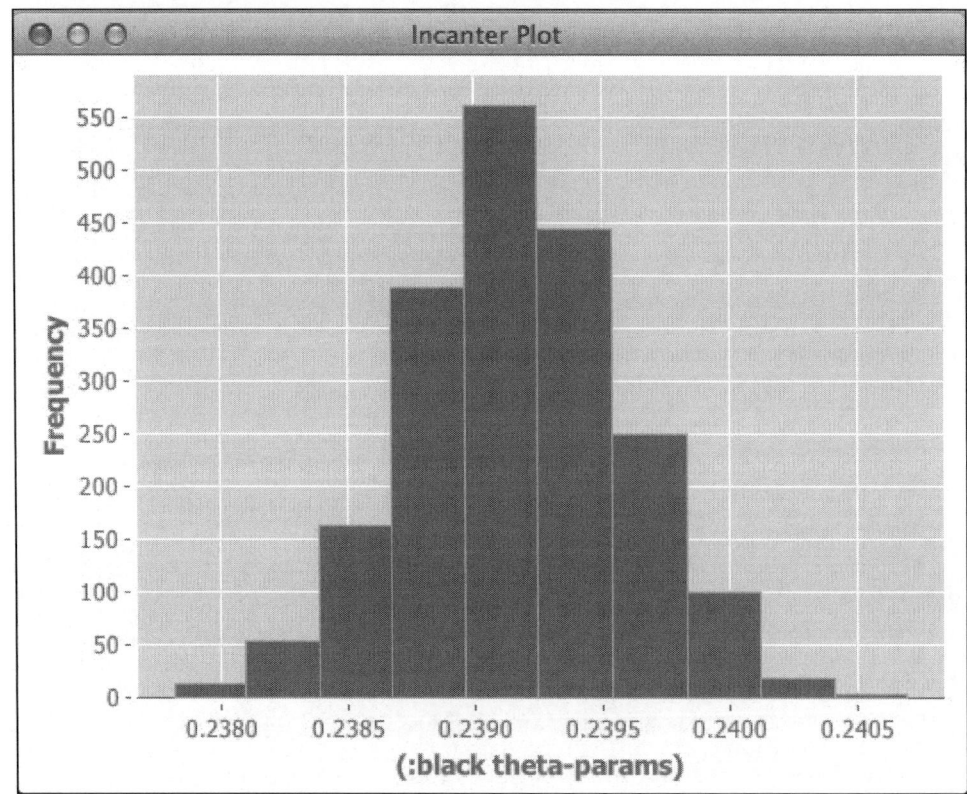

## How it works...

However, the real test of this system is how well it modeled the population. We can find that out easily by dividing the total African-American population by the total population.

```
user=> (/ (i/sum (i/sel census-race :cols :black))
          (i/sum (i/sel census-race :cols :total)))
0.21676297226785196
user=> (- *1 (s/mean (:black theta-params)))
-0.02240214904368454
```

So in fact, the results were close, but not very close.

So, to reiterate what we we've learned about the Bayesian analysis, what has this process done? It starts out with a standard distribution (the Dirichlet distribution) and based upon the input data from the sample, updates its estimate of the probability distribution of the population that the sample was drawn from.

Often Bayesian methods provide better results than alternative methods, and they're a powerful addition to any data worker's tool set.

## There's more...

Incanter includes functions that sample from a number of Bayesian distributions. They can be found at http://liebke.github.com/incanter/bayes-api.html.

For more on Bayesian approaches to data analysis, and life in general, see http://bayes.bgsu.edu/nsf_web/tutorial/a_brief_tutorial.htm and http://dartthrowingchimp.wordpress.com/2012/12/31/dr-bayes-or-how-i-learned-to-stop-worrying-and-love-updating/.

# Finding data errors with Benford's law

Benford's law is a curious observation about the distribution of the first digits of numbers in many naturally occurring datasets. In sequences that conform to Benford's law, the first digit will be *1* about a third of the time, and higher digits will occur progressively less often. However, manually-constructed data rarely looks like this. Because of that, lack of a Benford's law distribution is evidence that a dataset is not manually constructed.

This has been shown to hold true in financial data, for example. And investigators leverage this for fraud detection. The US Internal Revenue Service reportedly uses it for identifying potential tax fraud, and financial auditors also use it.

*Preparing for and Performing Statistical Data Analysis with Incanter*

## Getting ready

We'll need the following dependencies:

```
:dependencies [[org.clojure/clojure "1.4.0"]
               [incanter "1.4.1"]]
```

And we'll use the following requirements:

```
(require
  '[incanter.core :as i]
  'incanter.io
  '[incanter.stats :as s])
```

For data, we'll use the Virginia census race data file that we can download from http://www.ericrochester.com/clj-data-analysis/data/all_160_in_51.P35.csv.

## How to do it...

Bendford's law has been observed in many other places, including population numbers. In this recipe, we'll look at using it on the Virginia census data.

1. First, of course, we'll load the data.

    ```
    (def data-file "data/all_160_in_51.P35.csv")
    (def data (incanter.io/read-dataset data-file :header true))
    ```

2. Now we perform the analysis using the `incanter.stats/benford-test` function. It returns a map containing some interesting tests and values for determining whether the collection conforms to Benford's test, and we can also use it to view a bar chart of the distribution.

    ```
    (def bt (s/benford-test (i/sel data :cols :POP100)))
    ```

3. In the map that's returned, `:X-sq` is the value for the $X^2$ test, `:df` is the degrees of freedom for the test, and `:p-value` is the *p* value for the test statistic.

    ```
    user=> (:X-sq bt)
    15.74894048668777
    user=> (:df bt)
    8
    user=> (:p-value bt)
    0.046117795289705776
    ```

4. A histogram can help us visualize the distribution of the digits.

    ```
    (def chart
      (let [digits (map inc (:row-levels bt))
            frequency (:table bt)]
        (doto (c/bar-chart digits frequency)
          (i/view))))
    ```

The histogram looks like the following:

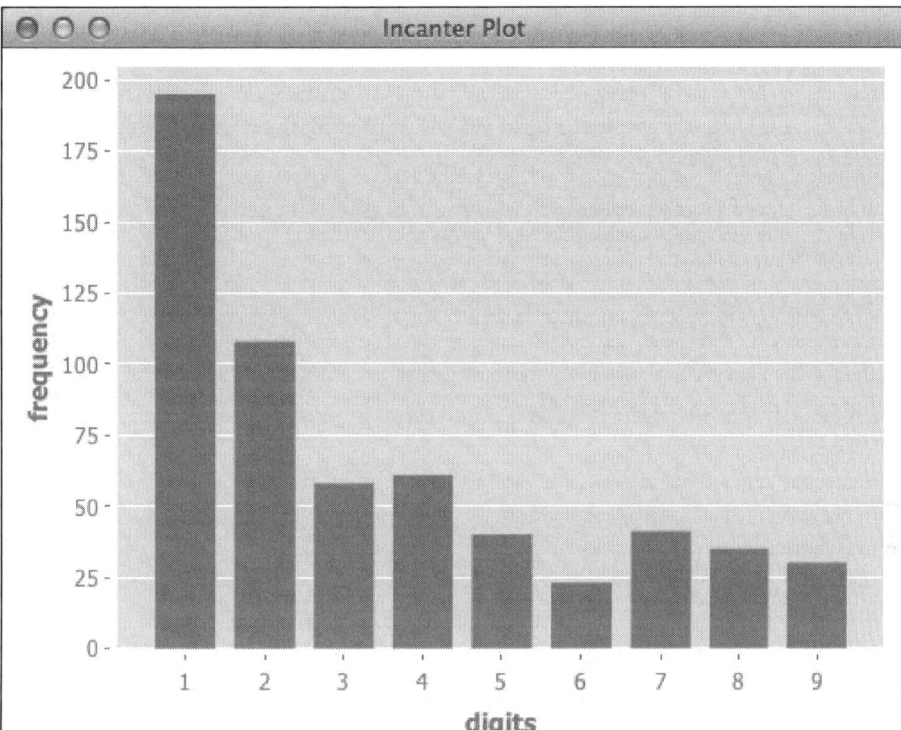

So the distribution just graphed appears to naturally follow Benford's law.

## How it works...

Benford's law states that the initial digits in a naturally occurring dataset should display a logarithmic probability. So for $d \in \{1, \ldots, 9\}$, $P(d) = \log(1 + 1/d)$.

The `benford-test` function calculates the frequencies of the initial digits from the input and performs an $X^2$ test, based upon the frequencies expected by Benford's law.

## There's more...

For more about Benford's law, see the Wikipedia article at http://en.wikipedia.org/wiki/Benford%27s_law or the article on Wolfram MathWorld at http://mathworld.wolfram.com/BenfordsLaw.html.

Finally, Testing Benford's Law (http://testingbenfordslaw.com/) is a fun site that applies Benford's law to various large, publicly available datasets.

# 8
# Working with Mathematica and R

In this chapter, we will learn about:

- Setting up Mathematica to talk to Clojuratica for Mac OS X and Linux
- Setting up Mathematica to talk to Clojuratica for Windows
- Calling Mathematica functions from Clojuratica
- Sending matrices to Mathematica from Clojuratica
- Evaluating Mathematica scripts from Clojuratica
- Creating functions from Mathematica
- Processing functions in parallel in Mathematica
- Setting up R to talk to Clojure
- Calling R functions from Clojure
- Passing vectors into R
- Evaluating R files from Clojure
- Plotting in R from Clojure

# Introduction

Clojure and Incanter are powerful, flexible tools, but they're not the only ones we have. We may have some analyses already implemented in another system, for instance, and we'd like to use them even though we're using Clojure everywhere else.

**Mathematica** (http://www.wolfram.com/mathematica/) is one of those tools. It's a software environment produced by Wolfram Research. It does complex mathematics and graphing, among many other things. It's a powerful tool made more powerful and customizable, thanks to its programming language.

**R** (http://www.r-project.org/) is another such tool. It's an open source system that specializes in statistical computing. It is also a programming language, and thanks to an active user community, there are a lot of contributed packages for almost any statistical task.

Both of these systems are powerful and complex in their own right, and we won't be able to go into how to use them or their features in this chapter. However, if you already have some analyses implemented in either Mathematica or R, or you want to learn one of these, and you wish to incorporate them into a Clojure-dominated workflow, this chapter should help show you the way.

Unfortunately, interoperability—interfacing directly between different computer systems, such as Clojure and Mathematica or R—is a difficult, often tricky task. We could fall back on shuffling data back and forth using CSV files; however, for more power and flexibility, having a direct connection between the two systems is unmatched, and it's often worth the effort and frustration. In this chapter, we'll talk about how to set up this interoperability and how to use each system from Clojure to do simple tasks.

# Setting up Mathematica to talk to Clojuratica for Mac OS X and Linux

Before we start interfacing with Mathematica, we have to download the libraries and set up our system to do so. This is a little complicated. We'll need to download the library to handle the interoperability and move a few files around.

Part of what makes this task so difficult is that several things vary, depending on your operating system. Moreover, in order to work with Leiningen, this recipe uses some features of the underlying operating system that aren't available for Windows (symbolic links), so this recipe won't work for the Windows platform. However, Windows users can refer to the next recipe, *Setting up Mathematica to talk to Clojuratica for Windows*.

## Getting ready

We'll need to have Mathematica installed. You can get an evaluation copy from http://www.wolfram.com/mathematica/trial/, but if you're looking at this recipe, you probably already have it and are just looking for a way to connect to it from Clojure.

You'll also need to have **Ant** (http://ant.apache.org/) and **Maven** (http://maven.apache.org/) installed. These are Java development tools that are used to build and install the libraries for accessing Mathematica.

## How to do it...

For this recipe, we'll get the Clojuratica library, incorporate it into our project, and place the dependencies where they should be.

1. First, we'll install Clojuratica. Download the library from https://github.com/stuarthalloway/Clojuratica/archive/master.zip. Unzip it inside of your project directory. Then change into that directory and build the JAR file.

   ```
   $ cd Clojuratica/
   $ ant jar
   …
   BUILD SUCCESSFUL
   Total time: 0 seconds
   ```

2. Second, we'll add the Clojuratica source code to our project. In our Leiningen project.clj file, add the following line of code:

   ```
   :source-paths ["src" "Clojuratica/src/clj"]
   ```

3. Third, in a Mathematica notebook evaluate $Path to see the list of places where Mathematica looks for code to load automatically. Pick one to copy some files into. It shouldn't matter which, except you probably want to use a directory under your home directory, not in the Mathematica installation directory. I'll use ~/Library/Mathematica/Autoload. A good choice for Linux might be ~/.Mathematica/Autoload.

## Working with Mathematica and R

By the way, also make a note about where Mathematica appears to be installed. We'll need that information in a few steps.

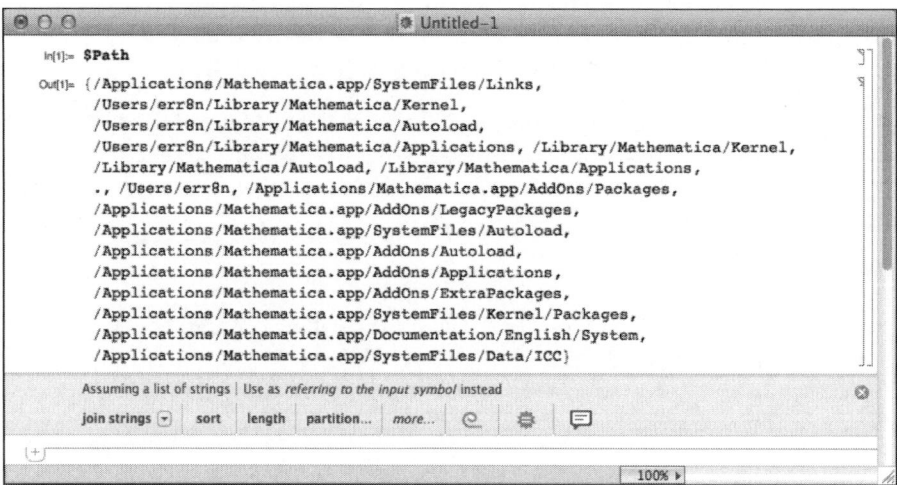

4. We'll copy some files from Clojuratica into one of these directories. (In the following command, substitute the destination with whichever directory from Mathematica's load path you selected).

   ```
   $ cp src/mma/*.m ~/Library/Mathematica/Autoload/
   ```

5. We need to install Mathematica's Java Interface library, JLink, where Maven knows how to find it. To do that, we need to find it inside the Mathematica directory. On my machine (a Mac), it's in `/Applications/Mathematica.app/SystemFiles/Links/JLink`. Under Linux, look in `/usr/local/Wolfram/Mathematica/9.0/SystemFiles/Links/JLink`. Once you find it, change into that directory and use Maven to install it. I used Version 9.0, since that's the version of Mathematica that I'm using.

   ```
   $ cd /Applications/Mathematica.app/SystemFiles/Links/JLink/
   $ mvn install:install-file -Dfile=./JLink.jar -DartifactId=JLink \
        -Dversion=9.0 -DgroupId=local.repo -Dpackaging=jar...
   [INFO] BUILD SUCCESS...
   ```

6. Unfortunately, the JLink library, which we just installed, expects to be called from within the Mathematica directory tree, not from within the Maven repository directory. To make it happy, we'll need to go into the local Maven repository, remove the installed JAR file, and add a symbolic link to the original one.

   ```
   $ cd ~/.m2/repository/local/repo/JLink/9.0/
   $ rm JLink-9.0.jar
   remove JLink-9.0.jar? y
   ```

```
$ ln -s \
  /Applications/Mathematica.app/SystemFiles/Links/JLink/JLink.jar \
  JLink-9.0.jar
```

7. We can now include the JLink library in our `project.clj` file.

   ```
   :dependencies [[org.clojure/clojure "1.5.0-alpha3"]
                  [local.repo/JLink "9.0"]]
   ```

8. We can import the libraries we've just installed and define a few utility functions that we'll need to run whenever we want to interface with Mathematica.

   ```
   (use 'clojuratica)
   (import [com.wolfram.jlink MathLinkFactory])
   (defn init-mma
     ([mma-command]
      (defonce math-evaluate
        (math-evaluator
          (doto
            (MathLinkFactory/createKernelLink mma-command)
            (.discardAnswer))))))
   (init-mma
     (str "-linkmode launch -linkname "
          "/Applications/Mathematica.app/Contents/MacOS/MathKernel"))
   (def-math-macro math math-evaluate)
   ```

Notice that the call to `init-mma` includes the full path to `MathKernel` (I've highlighted this). This will change depending on your system. For example, under Linux, the program will be `/usr/local/Wolfram/Mathematica/9.0/Executables/math`. Substitute the path and name of the executable so that it works on your system.

### How it works...

This is fairly typical for setting up a rough-around-the-edges complex computer system. There are lots of things that may vary from computer to computer and lots of things that could go wrong. Just have patience and grab some coffee. The Mathematica **StackExchange** is an excellent resource for problems (http://mathematica.stackexchange.com/).

One thing that I would point out is the last line from the final code block.

   ```
   (def-math-macro math math-evaluate)
   ```

This defines a macro, which we've named `math`, that has to wrap every call to Mathematica. We'll see examples of this in all of the following recipes that use Mathematica.

*Working with Mathematica and R*

## There's more...

I originally got the steps for this from a blog post by David Cabana (http://drcabana.org/2012/10/23/installation-and-configuration-of-clojuratica/). Although in the end I needed to do a few things slightly differently, this was my original source. If the steps I outline previously don't work for you, you may want to refer to it.

Also, as I mentioned previously, the Mathematica is a good resource if you run into issues (http://mathematica.stackexchange.com/).

# Setting up Mathematica to talk to Clojuratica for Windows

Getting Clojure and Mathematica to communicate under Windows is perhaps slightly easier to get set up than it is under Mac and Clojure; but it comes at a price. Because we can't create symbolic links, we can't use Maven to manage the `JLink.jar` file. And because of that, we can't use Leiningen to manage our project and its dependencies. Instead, we'll need to download everything and manage the dependencies and classpath ourselves.

## Getting ready

To prepare for this, we need to download the following resources:

- The Java Development Kit (http://www.oracle.com/technetwork/java/javase/downloads/index.html)
- Clojuratica (https://github.com/stuarthalloway/Clojuratica/archive/master.zip)
- Apache Ant (http://ant.apache.org/bindownload.cgi)
- Clojure (http://clojure.org/downloads)

Unzip each of these as subdirectories of your project directory. For example, my project directory is named `clj-interop`, and it contains the subdirectories `apache-ant-1.8.4`, `Clojuratica-master`, and `clojure-1.4.0`.

Of course, you'll also need to have Mathematica (http://www.wolfram.com/mathematica/) installed.

*Chapter 8*

## How to do it...

We first need to get Clojuratica built, and then we'll worry about running Clojure in the right environment to be able to talk to Mathematica.

1. In the Windows console or PowerShell terminal, change to the `Clojuratica-master` directory and use Ant to build the Clojuratica JAR file.

    ```
    PS C:\clj-interop> cd .\Clojuratica-master
    PS C:\clj-interop\Clojuratica-master> ..\apache-ant-1.8.4\bin\ant jar
    ...
    BUILD SUCCESSFUL
    ```

2. Go back up a directory and start Clojure. When we do, we'll pass Java a classpath with Clojure, Clojuratica, and JLink, which is the library that handles the communication between Clojure and Mathematica.

    ```
    PS C:\clj-interop\Clojuratica-master> cd ..
    PS C:\clj-interop> java -cp ".\clojure-1.4.0\clojure-1.4.0.jar;.\Clojuratica-master\clojuratica.jar;C:\Program Files\Wolfram Research\Mathematica\9.0\SystemFiles\Links\JLink\JLink.jar;." clojure.main
    Clojure 1.4.0
    user=>
    ```

3. We'll also need a module containing the code to start the system and define the `math` macro. Create a file named `mma.clj` with the following content:

    ```
    (ns mma)

    (use 'clojuratica)
    (import [com.wolfram.jlink MathLinkFactory])
    (defn init-mma
      ([mma-command]
        (defonce math-evaluate
          (math-evaluator
            (doto
              (MathLinkFactory/createKernelLink mma-command)
              (.discardAnswer))))))
    (init-mma
      (str "-linkmode launch -linkname "
           "\"C:/Program Files/Wolfram Research/Mathematica/9.0/MathKernel.exe\""))
    (def-math-macro math math-evaluate)
    ```

4. Now, in the Clojure REPL interpreter, we simply use the following namespace:

    ```
    user=> (use 'mma)
    nil
    ```

*Working with Mathematica and R*

## How it works...

Just as in the last recipe, this uses Clojuratica to provide a Clojure-friendly layer between the rest of Clojure and Mathematica's JLink library. You'll need to use the mma namespace in every script or REPL session that you want to communicate with Mathematica in.

# Calling Mathematica functions from Clojuratica

No matter what data we're working on with Mathematica, we'll want to call Mathematica functions from Clojure. The Clojuratica library makes this almost as easy as calling Clojure functions. Let's see how to do it.

## Getting ready

We must first have Clojuratica and Mathematica talking to each other. Either complete the *Setting up Mathematica to talk to Clojuratica for Mac OS X and Linux* recipe or the *Setting up Mathematica to Talk to Clojuratica for Windows* recipe. Also, you must first call the `init-mma` function.

Also, make sure that the `clojuratica` namespace is imported into our script or REPL.

```
(use 'clojuratica)
```

## How to do it...

To call a function, we just use Mathematica's name for it with Clojure's function-calling syntax. For this example, we'll solve a non-linear system of equations. In Mathematica, it would look like the following:

```
FindRoot[{Exp[x-2] == y, y^2 == x}, {{x, 1}, {y, 1}}]
```

In Clojure, it looks like the following:

```
user=> (math (FindRoot [(== (Exp (- x 2)) y) (== (Power y 2) x)] [[x 1] [y 1]]))
[(-> x 0.019026016103714054) (-> y 0.13793482556524314)]
```

## How it works...

This recipe was very simple, but it doesn't hurt to break it down a little.

```
(FindRoot [(== (Exp (- x 2)) y) (== (Power y 2) x)] [[x 1] [y 1]])
```

This is just Mathematica's `FindRoot` function. That's right. All we need to do is call the function just as we would any Clojure function, but using the same name that we do in Mathematica. The arguments to `FindRoot` are a sequence of `Equals` expressions and a sequence of starting points for each variable in the system of equations. These are also the same as the Mathematica expression, but Clojuratica, in good lisp fashion, requires that the operator always goes first. It does define some aliases to Mathematica functions, such as the `==` and `-` in this expression, which are changed to `Equals` and `Subtract`.

```
(math ...)
```

Any calls that we make to Mathematica must be wrapped in the `math` macro. We briefly discussed this macro at the end of the *Setting up Mathematica to talk to Clojuratica for Mac OS X and Linux* recipe. It takes the function name and parameters that we just talked about, sends those to Mathematica, and returns the answer.

## Sending matrices to Mathematica from Clojuratica

After the last recipe, we should be able to execute Mathematica functions from Clojure. We'll also need to send data to Mathematica so that there's something to call those functions on.

### Getting ready

We must first have Clojuratica and Mathematica talking to each other. Either complete the *Setting up Mathematica to talk to Clojuratica for Mac OS X and Linux* recipe or the *Setting up Mathematica to talk to Clojuratica for Windows* recipe. Also, you'll need to have called the `init-mma` function.

We'll also need to have Incanter listed in the dependencies in our `project.clj` file.

```
:dependencies [[org.clojure/clojure "1.4.0"]
               [local.repo/JLink "9.0"]
               [incanter "1.4.1"]
```

And we'll require those namespaces in our script or REPL.

```
(use 'clojuratica)
(require '[incanter.core :as i]
         'incanter.io)
```

Finally, we'll use the dataset of racial census data that we compiled for the *Grouping Data with $group-by* recipe in *Chapter 6, Working with Incanter Datasets*. We'll bind the filename to the name `data-file`. You can download this from http://www.ericrochester.com/clj-data-analysis/data/all_160.P3.csv.

```
(def data-file "data/all_160.P3.csv")
```

# Working with Mathematica and R

## How to do it...

In this recipe, we'll load some data into Clojure, define a couple of wrapper functions that call functions defined in Mathematica, and then we'll apply those functions to our Incanter dataset.

1. First, we'll load the data.

   ```
   (def data (incanter.io/read-dataset data-file :header true))
   ```

2. Next, we'll define some wrapper functions to call Mathematica's `Mean` and `Median` functions.

   ```
   (defn mma-mean
     ([dataset col]
       (math (Mean ~(i/sel dataset :cols col)))))
   (defn mma-median
     ([dataset col]
       (math (Median ~(i/sel dataset :cols col)))))
   ```

3. Now, we can call those functions just as we would any other Clojure function.

   ```
   user=> (mma-mean data :POP100)
   230766493/29439
   user=> (mma-median data :POP100)
   1081
   ```

## How it works...

There's one important point to note about this recipe.

```
~(i/sel dataset :cols col)
```

The code that calls Mathematica can't call back out to evaluate expressions that you pass it, so we have to do it ourselves first. If we stick a quasi-quote expander on expressions, then Clojure makes the `i/sel` call and interpolates the results into the body of the function.

# Evaluating Mathematica scripts from Clojuratica

Calling single functions is nice and very useful, but sometimes we may have a number of operations in a file that we want to call from Clojure. Clojuratica allow us to do that also.

## Getting ready

We must first have Clojuratica and Mathematica talking to each other. Either complete the *Setting up Mathematica to talk to Clojuratica for Mac OS X and Linux* recipe or the *Setting up Mathematica to talk to Clojuratica for Windows* recipe. Also, you'll need to have the `init-mma` function called.

Also, make sure that the `clojuratica` namespace is imported into our script or REPL.

```
(use 'clojuratica)
```

And we need a Mathematica file to run. I created one called `line-integral.m`, and it just contains the following lines:

```
SyntaxInformation[
    lineIntegrate] = {"LocalVariables" -> {"Plot", {3, 3}},
    "ArgumentsPattern" -> {_, _, _}};

lineIntegrate[r_?VectorQ, f_Function, {t_, tMin_, tMax_}] :=
 Module[{param, localR}, localR = r /. t -> param;
   Integrate[(f[localR, #] Sqrt[#.#]) &@@D[localR, param], {param, tMin,
      tMax}]]

lineIntegrate[{Cos[t], Sin[t]}, 1 &, {t, 0, 2 Pi}]
```

## How to do it...

In Mathematica we execute a file using the `Get` function. Here, we just use Clojuratica to call that on the appropriate filename.

```
user=> (math (Get "line-integral.m"))(* 2 Pi)
```

## How it works...

This uses the Mathematica function `Get`, which takes the name of a file that contains one or more Mathematica commands. It executes those, and it returns the value of the last command.

# Creating functions from Mathematica

We can use Mathematica to create functions that we can pass around and call from Clojure just like other functions. Moreover, we can also call them from within Mathematica and pass them around in Mathematica.

*Working with Mathematica and R*

## Getting ready

We must first have Clojuratica and Mathematica talking to each other. Either complete the *Setting up Mathematica to talk to Clojuratica for Mac OS X and Linux* recipe or the *Setting up Mathematica to talk to Clojuratica for Windows* recipe. Also, you'll need to have the `init-mma` function called.

Also, make sure that the `clojuratica` namespace is imported into our script or REPL.

```
(use 'clojuratica)
```

## How to do it...

Here, we'll create a function that simply wraps the Mathematica function `FactorInteger`.

```
(def factor-int
  (math
    (Function [x] (FactorInteger x))))
```

We can call it like a regular function.

```
user=> (factor-int 1234567890)
[[2 1] [3 2] [5 1] [3607 1] [3803 1]]
```

## How it works...

The key here is that we used the Mathematica keyword `Function` to create the function and return it. We assigned this to `factor-int`, and from that point on, we could treat that value like a regular function value.

# Processing functions in parallel in Mathematica

One of the benefits of using Mathematica is its speed. This can be augmented by adding parallelization. It's not difficult, but there are a few things to remember.

## Getting ready

We must first have Clojuratica and Mathematica talking to each other. Either complete the *Setting up Mathematica to talk to Clojuratica for Mac OS X and Linux* recipe or the *Setting up Mathematica to talk to Clojuratica for Windows* recipe. Also, you'll need to have the `init-mma` function called.

Also, make sure that the `clojuratica` namespace is imported into our script or REPL.

```
(use 'clojuratica)
```

## How to do it...

Executing functions in Mathematica isn't as straightforward as doing it in Clojure is.

1. Before we parallelize any task, we have to initialize Mathematica for this by calling its `LaunchKernels` function.

   ```
   (math (LaunchKernels))
   ```

2. Now, for simple parallelization, we can use some functions that are designed specifically for this, such as `ParallelMap`. This is similar to Clojure's `pmap`.

   ```
   user=> (math (ParallelMap #'(Plus % 1) [1 2 3 4 5]))
   [2 3 4 5 6]
   ```

3. For more control and flexibility, we'll kick off each parallel task in a separate thread using Clojure's agents. Each agent will wait for Mathematica to finish and return the results. As part of the output, we'll explicitly call `$KernelID` so we can see that the functions are executing on different CPUs. The CPU number is what each agent will return.

   ```
   user=> (let [f (math :parallel (Function [x] (Fibonacci x)
                                             $KernelID))
                agents (map (fn [_] (agent nil)) (range 10))]
           (dorun (map #(send-off % f) agents))
           (dorun (map await agents))
           (map deref agents))
   (2 1 5 7 8 8 7 3 6 4)
   ```

## How it works...

We have to do a couple of things to get this function to run in different threads.

First, we have to call the `math` macro with the `:parallel` keyword.

Also, we have to call it from different threads to get the function to run on different CPUs. We use agents to do that.

Finally, for this recipe we return the kernel the function runs on so we can see that they were in fact run in separate threads.

*Working with Mathematica and R*

# Setting up R to talk to Clojure

Another major statistical processing environment is R (http://www.r-project.org/). It's an open source programming language and environment designed for statistical analysis. It's widely used with an active community and a growing body of useful add-on packages.

While there's no Clojure-specific interoperability library, there is one for Java, and we can use that to pass calls to R and to get results back. In this recipe, we'll set up this system.

## Getting ready

We'll need to have R installed. We can download it from http://www.r-project.org/ by following the link to **CRAN**, picking a mirror, and downloading the correct version of R for your platform.

You'll also need to have Maven (http://maven.apache.org/) installed to build and install the libraries for accessing R.

## How to do it...

There are two parts to setting up this system. We'll get the R-side working, and then we'll see what Clojure needs to have in place.

### Setting up R

To set up the system, we first have to configure R to talk to Clojure.

1. Once R is installed, we'll download the interoperability package, `Rserve`. In my case, I went to http://www.rforge.net/Rserve/files/, and I downloaded `Rserver_1.7-0.tar.gz`, but you may have a more recent version available.

2. You'll need to extract the files from the tarball that you've downloaded. On Windows, **7-Zip** (http://www.7-zip.org/) can help here.

   ```
   $ tar xfzv Rserve_1.7-0.tar.gz
   x Rserve/
   x Rserve/configure.win
   x Rserve/cleanup
   ...
   ```

3. Change into the `src/client/java-new` subdirectory of the `Rserve` directory.

   ```
   $ cd Rserve/src/client/java-new/
   ```

4. Use Maven to install the two JAR files in that directory into your local Maven repository.

   ```
   $ mvn install:install-file -Dfile=./REngine.jar \
     -DartifactId=REngine -Dversion=1.7.0 -DgroupId=local.repo \
     -Dpackaging=jar
   ...
   $ mvn install:install-file -Dfile=./Rserve.jar \
     -DartifactId=Rserve -Dversion=1.7.0 -DgroupId=local.repo \
     -Dpackaging=jar
   ...
   ```

5. Start R and install the package.

   ```
   > install.packages("Rserve")
   --- Please select a CRAN mirror for use in this session ---
   ```

   At this point, R will pop up a dialog window with a list of mirrors. Select one near you, and R will download the package and install it.

6. While still in R, load and start the Rserver. The code for this chapter has a shell script, `start-rserve.sh`, that starts the Rserver. You can also download that script from `https://gist.github.com/erochest/4974005`.

   ```
   $ ./start-rserve.sh
   R version 2.15.2 (2012-10-26) -- "Trick or Treat"
   ...
   Rserv started in daemon mode.
   ```

## Setting up Clojure

Now we need to turn our attention to Clojure.

1. First, we must declare the two JAR files that we just installed as dependencies in our Leiningen `project.clj` file.

   ```
   :dependencies [[org.clojure/clojure "1.4.0"]
                  [local.repo/REngine "1.7.0"]
                  [local.repo/Rserve "1.7.0"]]
   ```

2. Then, we'll import a couple of namespaces from them into our script or REPL.

   ```
   (import '[org.rosuda.REngine REngine]
           '[org.rosuda.REngine.Rserve RConnection])
   ```

3. Finally, we create a connection to the R server. This will be a dynamic variable so we can swap it out easily later. If the Rserve isn't running, this step will fail. So make sure you have the Rserver running before you execute this (see the step 6 of the previous section), and if this succeeds, you successfully have R and Clojure communicating.

   ```
   (def ^:dynamic *r-cxn* (RConnection.))
   ```

*Working with Mathematica and R*

### How it works...

The Rserve package runs a server in the background that the Java library communicates with. From Clojure, we can now feed data to the Rserver and get results back. We'll see examples of this in the following recipes.

Because Rserve has to be running, step 6 of the previous section (load and start the Rserver) has to be done every session you want to call R from Clojure in.

## Calling R functions from Clojure

R, and the packages that have been developed for it, provide a rich environment for doing statistical computing. To access any of that, however, we'll need to be able to call functions from Clojure. We do this by constructing R expressions as strings, sending them to the R server, and getting the results back. The Rserve Java library helps us convert the results to Java objects that we can access.

### Getting ready

We must first complete the *Setting up R to talk to Clojure* recipe, and have Rserve running. We must also have the Clojure-specific parts of that recipe done and the connection to Rserve made.

### How to do it...

Once we have a connection to the Rserver, we can call functions by passing the complete call—function and arguments—to the server as a string and evaluating it. Then we have to pull the results back out.

```
user=> (map #(.asDouble %) (.. *r-cxn* (eval "qr(c(1,2,3,4,5,6,7))") asList))
(-11.832159566199232 1.0 1.0845154254728517 1.0)
```

### How it works...

To call an R function, we make a series of method calls on the RConnection object that we created in the *Setting up R to talk to Clojure* recipe. The first call, `eval`, takes the code to evaluate as a string and passes it to R.

Next we have to convert the output to a Clojure data structure. We first call `asList` on the result, which converts it to a type that implements `java.lag.Iterable`. This can be passed to `map`, which is used to convert the list's members to doubles.

## There's more...

The example in this recipe called the R `qr` function. This calculates the QR decomposition of a matrix. For more on this function, see http://www.math.montana.edu/Rweb/Rhelp/qr.html.

# Passing vectors into R

In order to do any very complex or meaningful analysis, we'll need to be able to pass vector or matrix data into R to operate on and analyze.

Let's see how to do this.

## Getting ready

We must first complete the *Setting up R to talk to Clojure* recipe, and have Rserve running. We must also have the Clojure-specific parts of that recipe done and the connection to Rserve made.

We'll also need access to the `clojure.string` namespace.

```
(require '[clojure.string :as str])
```

## How to do it...

To make passing values into R easier, we'll first define a protocol, and then we'll use it to pass a matrix to R.

1. In order to handle converting all the datatypes into a string that R can read, we'll define a protocol, ToR. Any datatypes that we want to marshal into R must implement this.

   ```
   (defprotocol ToR
     (->r [x] "Convert an item to R."))
   ```

2. Now, we'll implement this protocol for sequences, vectors, and numeric types.

   ```
   (extend-protocol ToR
     clojure.lang.ISeq
     (->r [coll] (str "c(" (str/join \, (map ->r coll)) ")"))
     clojure.lang.PersistentVector
     (->r [coll] (->r (seq coll)))
     java.lang.Integer
     (->r [i] (str i))
     java.lang.Long
     (->r [l] (str l))
   ```

```
        java.lang.Float
        (->r [f] (str f))
        java.lang.Double
        (->r [d] (str d)))
```

3.  We create a wrapper function for calling R's `mean` function.

    ```
    (defn r-mean
      ([coll] (r-mean coll *r-cxn*))
      ([coll r-cxn]
       (.. r-cxn
         (eval (str "mean(" (->r coll) ")"))
         asDouble)))
    ```

4.  With these in place, we can call them just as we would any other function.

    ```
    user=> (r-mean [1.0 2.0 3.0])
    2.0
    user=> (r-mean (map (fn [_] (rand)) (range 5)))
    0.3966653617356786
    ```

## How it works...

For most datatypes, marshaling to R simply means converting it to a string. However, for sequences and vectors, it's a little more complicated. Clojure has to convert all of the sequence's items to R strings, join the items with a comma, and wrap it in a call to R's `c` constructor.

This is a perfect place to use protocols. Defining methods to marshal more datatypes to R is simple. For example, we could define a naïve method for working with strings like the following:

```
(extend-protocol ToR
  java.lang.String
  (->r [s] (str \' s \')))
```

Of course, this method isn't without its problems. If a string has a quote within it, for instance, it must be escaped. Also, having to marshal datatypes back and forth like this can be computationally expensive, especially for large or complex datatypes.

## Evaluating R files from Clojure

We may not always want to feed R code from Clojure directly into R. Many times we may have files containing R expressions, and we want to evaluate the whole file.

We can do that quite easily. Let's see how.

## Getting ready

We must first complete the *Setting up R to talk to Clojure* recipe, and have Rserve running. We must also have the Clojure-specific parts of that recipe done and the connection to Rserve made.

And we'll need access to the `java.io.File` class.

```
(import '[java.io File])
```

## How to do it...

We'll first define a function to make evaluating a file in R easier, and then we'll find a file and execute it.

1. The function to evaluate a file of R code takes a filename and (optionally) a connection to the R server. It feeds the file to R using R's `source` function, and it returns whatever R does.

   ```
   (defn r-source
     ([filename] (r-source filename *r-cxn*))
     ([filename r-cxn]
       (.eval r-cxn (str "source(\""
                         (.getAbsolutePath (File. filename))
                         "\")"))))
   ```

2. For example, suppose we have a file named `chrsqr-example.R` that creates a random data table and performs a $X^2$ test on it:

   ```
   dat <- data.frame(q1=sample(c("A","B","C"),size=1000,replace=TRUE),
          sex=sample(c("M","F"),size=1000,replace=TRUE))
   dtab <- with(dat,table(q1,sex))

   (Xsq <- chisq.test(dtab))
   ```

3. The results that come back from it are a little complicated, but with some trial and error, we can tease the answers back out.

   ```
   user=> (def x-sqr (.asList (r-source "chisqr-example.R")))
   #'user/x-sqr
   ;; X-square
   user=> (.. x-sqr (at 0) asList (at "statistic") asDouble)
   0.2166086470268894
   ;; degrees of freedon
   user=> (.. x-sqr (at 0) asList (at "parameter") asInteger)
   2
   ;; p-value
   user=> (.. x-sqr (at 0) asList (at "p.value") asDouble)
   0.897354468808211
   ```

*Working with Mathematica and R*

### How it works...

The most difficult part of this really is dealing with the return value. After calling `r-source`, we convert the output to an R list. We pull the `statistic` item from that and convert it to a double. That's the $X^2$ value. The `parameter` item is the degrees of freedom. And the `p.value` item is the p-value for the test.

Generally, when I'm picking the results out of their Java data structures, the REPL and the documentation are the biggest helps. For example, the value `x-sqr`, when printed on the REPL, displays the following:

```
user=> x-sqr
#<RList RList[org.rosuda.REngine.REXPGenericVector@61df092e+[9]named,
org.rosuda.REngine.REXPLogical@79d3dd34[1]]{named,2}>
```

This tells me that the list's first item is a generic R vector, and the second is an R logical structure. Diving further into the first item shows the names of the members it contains.

```
user=> (.. rl (at 0) asList names)
#<Vector [statistic, parameter, p.value, method, data.name, observed,
expected, residuals, stdres]>
```

This helps me pick out the values I'm looking for, and by using some test data and referring to the documentation for the datatypes, I can pretty easily write the code necessary to dig down to the results.

### There's more...

The documentation for R's Java datatypes can be found at http://rforge.net/org/docs/index.html?org/rosuda/REngine/package-tree.html.

## Plotting in R from Clojure

One of R's strengths is its plotting ability. In this recipe, we'll see how to take some data and plot it on a graph. We won't really exercise R's graphic abilities, but this should be enough to get started.

### Getting ready

We must first complete the, *Setting up R to talk to Clojure* recipe, and have Rserve running. We must also have the Clojure-specific parts of that recipe done and the connection to Rserve made.

We'll need the ToR protocol and implementations that we defined in the *Passing vectors into R* recipe.

And we'll need access to the `java.io.File` class.

```
(import '[java.io File])
```

## How to do it...

This recipe will look a lot like a number of the other R-related recipes. We'll create a function that assembles the string with the R expression, and then we'll see it in action.

1. First, we'll define a function to initialize a PNG file for output, plot some data, and save the file, all from R.

    ```
    (defn r-plot
      ([data filename] (r-plot data filename *r-cxn*))
      ([data filename r-cxn]
       (.. r-cxn
         (eval (str "png(filename=\""
                    (.getAbsolutePath (File. filename))
                    "\", height=300, width=250, bg=\"white\")\n"
                    "plot(" (->r data) ")\n"
                    "dev.off()\n")))))
    ```

2. Now let's test it out on the start of the Fibonacci sequence.

    ```
    user=> (r-plot [1.0 1.0 2.0 3.0 5.0 8.0 11.0] "fib.png")
    #<REXPInteger org.rosuda.REngine.REXPInteger@7342054+[1]>
    ```

    If we open up the `fib.png` file and look at it, we can see the results of the simple graphing call that we made.

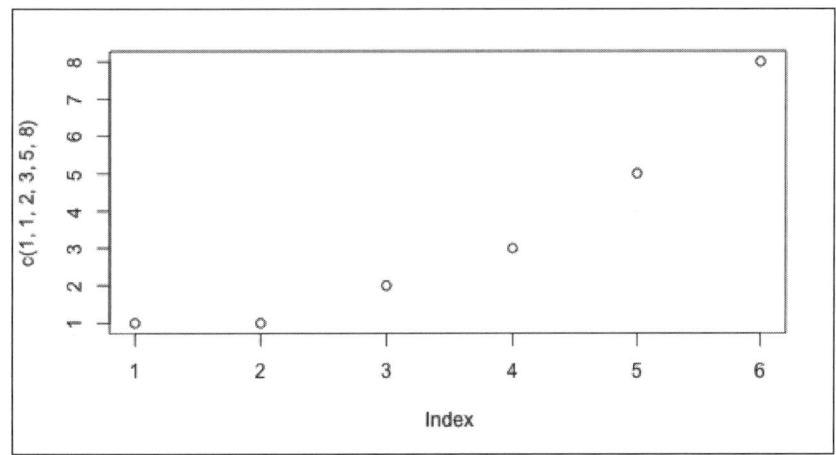

## How it works...

The body of this function is in the string that gets passed to R to evaluate. It's composed of three function calls. First, it initializes the PNG output with the `png` function.

```
"png(filename=\""
(.getAbsolutePath (File. filename))
"\", height=300, width=500, bg=\"white\")\n"
```

Then, we actually plot the data.

```
"plot(" (->r data) ")\n"
```

Finally, save the plot to the file.

```
"dev.off()\n"
```

## There's more...

A scatterplot is a very basic plot, which Incanter can do as well. However, R's graphing features are more sophisticated than what Incanter can currently do. To get a taste of what R's capable of, browse through the R gallery at http://gallery.r-enthusiasts.com/.

# 9
# Clustering, Classifying, and Working with Weka

In this chapter, we will cover:

- Loading CSV and ARFF files into Weka
- Filtering and renaming columns in Weka datasets
- Discovering groups of data using K-means clustering
- Finding hierarchical clusters in Weka
- Clustering with SOMs in Incanter
- Classifying data with decision trees
- Classifying data with the Naive Bayesian classifier
- Classifying data with support vector machines
- Finding associations in data with the Apriori algorithm

## Introduction

A large part of data analysis is looking for patterns in our dataset. Of course, a dataset of any complexity is too much for the human mind to see patterns in, so we rely on computers, statistics, and machine learning to augment our insights.

In this chapter, we'll take a look at a number of methods for clustering and classifying data. Depending on the nature of the data and the question we're trying to answer, different algorithms will be more or less useful. For instance, K-means clustering is great for clustering numeric datasets, it's poorly suited for working with nominal data.

Most of the recipes in this chapter will use the Weka machine learning and data mining library (http://www.cs.waikato.ac.nz/ml/weka/). This is a full-featured library for analyzing data using many different procedures and algorithms. It includes a more complete set of these algorithms than Incanter, which we've been using a lot so far. We'll start by seeing how to load CSV files into Weka and work with Weka datasets, but we'll spend most of the rest of this chapter examining how to perform different analyses using this powerful library.

Weka's interface to the classes implementing these algorithms is very consistent, so for the first recipe in which we use one of these algorithms, *Discovering groups of data using K-means clustering*, we'll define a macro that will facilitate creating wrapper functions for Weka algorithms. This is a great example of using macros, and of how easy it is to create a wrapper over an external Java library to make it more natural to use from Clojure.

# Loading CSV and ARFF files into Weka

Weka is most comfortable using its own file format, ARFF. This format includes the types of data in the columns and other information that allows it to be loaded incrementally. However, Weka can still import CSV files, and when it does, it attempts to guess the type of data in the columns.

In this recipe, we'll see what's necessary to load data from a CSV file and an ARFF file.

## Getting ready

First, we'll need to add Weka to the dependencies in our Leiningen `project.clj` file:

```
:dependencies [[org.clojure/clojure "1.4.0"]
               [nz.ac.waikato.cms.weka/weka-dev "3.7.7"]]
```

Then, we'll import the right classes into our script or REPL.

```
(import [weka.core.converters ArffLoader CSVLoader]
        [java.io File])
```

Finally, we'll need to have a CSV file to import. In this recipe, I'll use the dataset of racial census data that we compiled for the *Grouping data with $group-by* recipe in *Chapter 6, Working with Incanter Datasets*. It's in the file named `data/all_160.P3.csv`. You can also download this file from http://www.ericrochester.com/clj-data-analysis/data/all_160.P3.csv.

## How to do it...

For this recipe, we'll write several utility functions and then use them to load the data.

1. First, we'll need a utility function to convert options into an array of strings.

   ```
   (defn ->options
     [& opts]
     (into-array String
                 (map str (flatten (remove nil? opts)))))
   ```

2. Next, we'll create a function that takes a filename and an optional `:header` keyword argument and returns the Weka dataset of instances.

   ```
   (defn load-csv
     ([filename & {:keys [header]
                   :or {header true}}]
      (let [options (->options (when-not header "-H"))
            loader (doto (CSVLoader.)
                     (.setOptions options)
                     (.setSource (File. filename)))]
        (.getDataSet loader))))
   ```

3. Finally, we can use the following to load CSV files:

   ```
   (def data (load-csv "data/all_160.P3.csv"))
   ```

4. Or, if we have a file without a header row, we can do the following:

   ```
   (def data (load-csv "data/all_160.P3.csv" :header false))
   ```

5. We can use a similar function for loading ARFF files shown as follows:

   ```
   (defn load-arff
     ([filename]
      (.getDataSet (doto (ArffLoader.)
                     (.setFile (File. filename))))))
   ```

There are pre-prepared ARFF files of standard datasets available to download from http://weka.wikispaces.com/Datasets. We'll use some of these in later recipes.

## How it works...

Weka is fundamentally set up to work as a command-line application. Whether used from a GUI or programmatically, at some point we're setting options using a command-line-style string array.

The `->options` function takes care of converting and cleaning up a list of these options. `into-array` converts the sequence into a string array.

For all the later recipes that use Weka, this function will be a template. Essentially, each time we'll create an object, set the options as a string array, and perform the operation. In the recipe, *Discovering groups of data using K-means clustering*, we'll reify the process with the macro defanalysis.

The **ARFF** format that we created a function for in Step 5 is a Weka-specific data file format. The name stands for **Attribute-Relation File Format**. CSV files don't include information about the types of data stored in the columns. Weka tries to be smart and figure out what they are, but it isn't always successful. However, ARFF files do contain information about the columns' datatype, and that's what makes this Weka's preferred file format.

### There's more...

The columns may need filtering or renaming, especially if the CSV file doesn't have a header row. We'll see how to do that in the next recipe, *Filtering and renaming columns in Weka datasets*.

### See also

For more about Weka, visit its website at http://www.cs.waikato.ac.nz/ml/weka/.

## Filtering and renaming columns in Weka datasets

Generally, the data won't be quite in the form we'll need for our analyses. Weka contains several methods for renaming columns and filtering which ones will make it into the dataset.

Most datasets have one or more columns that will throw off clustering—row identifiers or name fields, for instance—so we must filter the columns in the datasets before we perform any analysis. We'll see a lot of examples of this in the recipes to come.

### Getting ready

We'll use the dependencies, imports, and data files that we did in the *Loading CSV and ARFF files into Weka* recipe. We'll also use the dataset that we loaded in that recipe.

We'll need to access a different set of Weka classes as well as to the `clojure.string` library.

```
(import [weka.filters Filter]
        [weka.filters.unsupervised.attribute Remove])
(require '[clojure.string :as str])
```

## How to do it...

In this recipe, we'll first rename the columns from the dataset, and then we'll look at two different ways to remove columns, one destructively and one not.

### Renaming columns

We'll create a function to rename the attributes with a sequence of keywords, and then we'll see this function in action.

1. First, we'll define a function that takes a dataset and a sequence of field names, and it renames the columns in the dataset to match those passed in.

    ```
    (defn set-fields
      ([instances field-seq]
        (doseq [n (range (.numAttributes instances))]
          (.renameAttribute instances (.attribute instances n)
                            (name (nth field-seq n))))))
    ```

2. Now, let's look at the dataset's current column names.

    ```
    user=> (map #(.. data (attribute %) name)
                (range (.numAttributes data)))
    ("GEOID" "SUMLEV" "STATE" "COUNTY" "CBSA" "CSA" "NECTA" "CNECTA"
    "NAME" "POP100" "HU100" "POP100.2000"
    "HU100.2000" "P003001" "P003001.2000" "P003002"
    "P003002.2000" "P003003" "P003003.2000" "P003004"
    "P003004.2000" "P003005" "P003005.2000" "P003006"
    "P003006.2000" "P003007" "P003007.2000" "P003008"
    "P003008.2000")
    ```

3. These are the names that the US Census gives these fields, but we can change the field names to something more obvious. Note that the -2000 suffixes on some attribute names mark a field containing numbers from the 2000 census.

    ```
    (set-fields
      data
      [:geoid :sumlev :state :county :cbsa :csa :necta
       :cnecta :name
       :pop100 :housing-units-100 :pop100-2000
       :housing-units-100-2000
       :race-total :race-total-2000 :race-white
       :race-white-2000
       :race-black :race-black-2000 :race-indian
       :race-indian-2000
       :race-asian :race-asian-2000 :race-hawaiian
       :race-hawaiian-2000
       :race-other :race-other-2000 :race-two-more
       :race-two-more-2000])
    ```

## Removing columns

This dataset contains a number of columns that we'll never use. These include the `sumlev`, `county`, `cbsa`, and other fields. Since these won't ever be used, we'll destructively remove them from the dataset using the following steps:

1. Weka allows us to delete attributes by index, but we want to specify them by name. We'll write a function that takes an attribute name and returns the index.

   ```
   (defn attr-n
     [instances attr-name]
     (->> instances
       (.numAttributes)
       range
       (map #(vector % (.. instances (attribute %) name)))
       (filter #(= (second %) (name attr-name)))
       ffirst))
   ```

2. We can use that function to call `reduce` on the instances and remove the attributes as we go.

   ```
   (defn delete-attrs
     [instances attr-names]
     (reduce (fn [is n] (.deleteAttributeAt is
   (attr-n is n)) is)
           instances
           attr-names))
   ```

3. Finally, we can use the following to delete the attributes I mentioned earlier:

   ```
   (delete-attrs data [:sumlev :county :cbsa :csa :necta :cnecta])
   ```

## Hiding columns

Finally, there are a few attributes that we'll hide. Instead of destructively deleting attributes from one set of instances, filtering them creates a new dataset without the hidden attributes. This can be useful to have one dataset for clustering and another with the complete information for the dataset, including a name or ID attribute, for instance. For this example, I'll take out all of the fields representing the census from 2000 using the following steps:

1. Weka does this by applying a `filter` class to a dataset to create a new dataset. We'll use the `Remove` filter in this function. This also uses the `attr-n` function from earlier in this recipe.

   ```
   (defn filter-attributes
     ([dataset remove-attrs]
      (let [attrs (map inc (map attr-n remove-attrs))
            options (->options "-R"
                     (str/join \, (map str attrs)))
   ```

```
          rm (doto (Remove.)
               (.setOptions options)
               (.setInputFormat dataset))]
      (Filter/useFilter dataset rm))))
```

2. We can call this function with the attribute names that we want to filter out.

   ```
   (def data-2010
     (filter-attributes data [[:pop100-2000
     :housing-units-100-2000
        :race-total-2000  :race-white-2000
        :race-black-2000  :race-indian-2000
        :race-asian-2000  :race-hawaiian-2000
        :race-other-2000  :race-two-more-2000]]))
   ```

3. We can now see the following results:

   ```
   user=> (map #(.. data-2010 (attribute %) name)
               (range (.numAttributes data-2010)))
   ("geoid" "state" "name" "pop100"
   "housing-units-100" "race-total" "race-white"
   "race-black" "race-indian" "race-asian"
   "race-hawaiian" "race-other" "race-two-more")
   ```

### How it works...

Weka's attributes are an integral part of its data model. Moreover, later algorithms that we'll see can be sensitive to which columns are in the dataset. In order to work with only the attributes that are important, we can hide them or delete them altogether using the functions in this recipe.

## Discovering groups of data using K-means clustering

One of the most popular and well-known clustering methods is **K-means clustering**. It's conceptually simple. It's also easy to implement and computationally cheap. We can get decent results quickly for many different datasets.

On the downside, it sometimes gets stuck in local optima and misses a better solution altogether.

Generally, K-means clustering works best when groups in the data are spatially distinct. This means that if the natural groups in the data overlap, the clusters that K-means generates will not properly distinguish the natural groups in the data.

*Clustering, Classifying, and Working with Weka*

## Getting ready

For this recipe, we'll need the same dependencies in our `project.clj` file that we used in the *Loading CSV and ARFF files into Weka* recipe.

We'll need a slightly different set of imports in our script or REPL, however.

```
(import [weka.core EuclideanDistance]
        [weka.clusterers SimpleKMeans])
```

For data, we'll use the Iris dataset, which is often used for learning about and testing clustering algorithms. You can download this dataset from the Weka wiki at `http://weka.wikispaces.com/Datasets` or from `http://www.ericrochester.com/clj-data-analysis/UCI/iris.arff`. We will load it using `load-arff` from the *Loading CSV and ARFF data into Weka* recipe.

## How to do it...

For this recipe, we'll first define a function and macro that will greatly facilitate writing wrapper functions around Weka classes and processes. Then we'll use that macro for the first time to wrap the `weka.clusters.SimpleKMeans` class.

1. First, we'll define a function to generate a random seed from the current time. By default, Weka always uses `1` as the random seed. This function will allow us to use the current time by specifying `nil` as the seed.

   ```
   (defn random-seed
     [seed]
     (if (nil? seed)
       (.intValue (.getTime (java.util.Date.)))
       seed))
   ```

2. Most of the Weka analyses follow the same pattern. We'll take keyword parameters, turn them into a command-line-style string array. We'll create a Weka object and pass it the options array. This is the kind of boilerplate that lisp and lisp macros are particularly good at abstracting away.

   The most complicated part of this will involve parsing a sequence of vectors into the wrapper function's parameter list and into the options array. Each vector will list the option, a variable name for it, and a default value. Optionally, they may also contain a keyword indicating how the value is converted to an option and under what circumstances it's included. The highlighted comments in the code show some examples of these near where they're passed. Here's the function to parse an options vector into the code to pass to `->` options.

   ```
   (defn analysis-parameter
     [parameter]
   ```

```
(condp = (count parameter)
  ;; [option-string variable-name default-value]
  ;; ["-N" k 2]
  `[~(first parameter) ~(second parameter)]

  ;; [option-string variable-name default-value flag]
  ;; ["-V" verbose false :flag-true]
  (condp = (last parameter)
     :flag-true `[(when ~(second parameter)
                    ~(first parameter))]
     :flag-false `[(when-not ~(second parameter)
                    ~(first parameter))]
     :not-nil `[(when-not (nil?
  ~(second parameter))
                [~(first parameter)
                 ~(second parameter)])]
     :seq (let [name (second parameter)]
            (apply concat
                   (map-indexed (fn [i flag] `
                     [~flag (nth ~name ~i)])
                    (first parameter))))

     `[~(first parameter)
       (~(last parameter)
        ~(second parameter))])

  ;; [option-string variable-name default-value
  ;; flag option]
  ;; ["-B" distance-of :node-length :flag-equal
  ;;:branch-length]
  (condp = (nth parameter 3)
     :flag-equal `[(when (= ~(second parameter)
  ~(last parameter))
                     ~(first parameter))]

     :predicate `[(when ~(last parameter)
                   [~(first parameter) ~(second
  parameter)])])))))
```

3. With that, we can create a macro that takes a name for the wrapper function, a class, and a method for it, and a sequence of parameter vectors. It then defines the analysis as a function.

```
(defmacro defanalysis
  ([a-name a-class a-method parameters]
   `(defn ~a-name
```

```
      [dataset# &
       ;; The variable-names and
       ;; default-values are used here
       ;; to build the function's parameter list.
       {:keys ~(mapv second parameters)
        :or ~(into {}
                   (map #(vector (second %) (nth % 2))
                        parameters))}]
       ;; The options, flags, and predicats are used to
       ;; construct the options list.
       (let [options# (->options
       ~@(mapcat analysis-parameter
                                            parameters))]
         ;; The algorithm's class and invocation function
         ;; are used here to actually perform the
         ;; processing.
         (doto (new ~a-class)
           (.setOptions options#)
           (. ~a-method dataset#))))))
```

4. Now, we can define a wrapper for K-means clustering (as well as the other algorithms we'll introduce later in the chapter), very briefly. This also makes clear how the macro has helped us. It's allowed us to **DRY**-up (**Don't Repeat Yourself**) the options list. Now we can clearly see what options an algorithm takes and how it uses them.

```
(defanalysis
  k-means SimpleKMeans buildClusterer
  [["-N" k 2]
   ["-I" max-iterations 100]
   ["-V" verbose false :flag-true]
   ["-S" seed 1 random-seed]
   ["-A" distance EuclideanDistance .getName]])
```

5. We can also call this wrapper function and get the results easily just as if we're using any other function, which we are. We'll first load the dataset and then filter it into a new dataset that only includes the columns related to the petal size. Our clustering will be based upon those attributes.

```
user=> (def iris (load-arff "data/UCI/iris.arff"))
user=> (def iris-petal (filter-attributes iris [:sepallength
:sepalwidth :class]))
#'user/iris-petal
user=> (def km (k-means iris-petal :k 3))
#'user/km
user=> km
```

```
#<SimpleKMeans
kMeans
======

Number of iterations: 8
Within cluster sum of squared errors: 1.7050986081225123
...
```

## How it works...

There are several interesting things to talk about in this recipe.

### Clustering with K-means

As far as clustering algorithms go—as far as any algorithms go, really—K-means is simple. To group the input data into *K* clusters, initially pick *K* random points in the data's domain space. Now, follow the steps listed here:

1. Assign each of the data points to the nearest cluster
2. Move the cluster's position to the centroid of the data assigned to that cluster
3. Repeat

We keep following these steps until either the maximum number of iterations have been reached or until the clusters are stable, when the set of data points assigned to each cluster doesn't change. We see this in the example in this recipe. The maximum number of iterations was set to `100`, but the clusters stabilized after eight iterations.

K-means clustering does have a number of quirks to be aware of. First, it must be used with measurement data. After all, what would be the distance between two species in the Iris dataset? What's the distance between Virginica and Setosa?

Another factor is that it won't work well if the natural classifications within the data (for example, the species in the Iris dataset) aren't spatially separated. If the data points for each class tend to run into each other, then K-means won't be able to distinguish between the classifications reliably.

## Analyzing the results

This following chart graphs petal dimensions of the items in the Iris dataset and distinguishes each point by species (shape) and classification (color). Generally, the results are good, but I've highlighted a half dozen points that the algorithm puts into the wrong category (some green crosses or yellow diamonds).

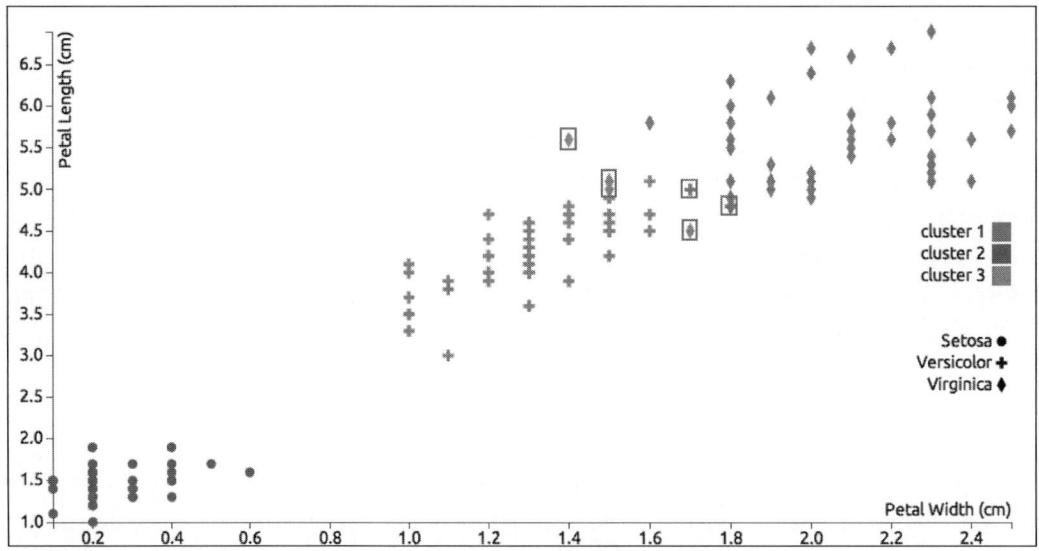

This chart helps us visually verify the results, but probably the most important part of the algorithm's output is the **within-cluster sum of squared errors** (**WCSS**). This should be as low as possible. In the example, this value is approximately 1.71, which is good.

## Building macros

Another interesting aspect of this recipe is using a macro to create a wrapper function for the cluster analysis. Because Clojure, like other lisps, is written in its own data structures, it's common to write programs to manipulate programs. In fact, it's so common that Clojure provides a stage of compilation dedicated to letting the user manipulate the input program. Those meta-programs are macros. The Clojure compiler reads in forms, uses macros to manipulate those forms, and finally compiles the output of the macros. Macros are a powerful tool that allow users to define their own control structures and other forms far beyond what programmers of other languages have available to them.

We can easily see how the macro is turned into a function using `macroexpand-1` as follows:

```
(macroexpand-1 '(defanalysis
                  k-means SimpleKMeans buildClusterer
                  [["-N" k 2]
                   ["-I" iterations 100]
```

```
                    ["-V" verbose false :flag-true]
                    ["-S" seed 1 random-seed]
                    ["-A" distance EuclideanDistance .getName]]))
```

I cleaned up the output of this to make it look more like something we'd type, but the function that the macro creates is listed as follows:

```
(defn k-means
  ([dataset__1079__auto__ &
    {:or {k 2, iterations 100, verbose false, seed 1,
          distance EuclideanDistance},
     :keys [k iterations verbose seed distance]}]
   (let [options__1080__auto__
         (->options ""
                    "-N" k
                    "-I" iterations
                    (when verbose "-V")
                    "-S" (random-seed seed)
                    "-A" (.getName distance))]
     (doto (new SimpleKMeans)
       (.setOptions options__1080__auto__)
       (. buildClusterer dataset__1079__auto__)))))
```

## See also

- For information about K-means clustering, Wikipedia provides a good introduction at http://en.wikipedia.org/wiki/K-means_clustering
- For information about Weka's SimpleKMeans class, including an explanation of its options, visit http://weka.sourceforge.net/doc.dev/weka/clusterers/SimpleKMeans.html
- For more about macros in Clojure, visit http://clojure.org/macros, and I've also written a longer tutorial on macros that is available at http://writingcoding.blogspot.com/2008/07/stemming-part-8-macros.html

## Finding hierarchical clusters in Weka

Another common way to cluster data is hierarchically. This involves either splitting the dataset down to pairs or building the clusters up by pairing the data or clusters that are closest to each other.

Weka has a class—HierarchicalClusterer—for performing hierarchical clustering. We'll use the defanalysis macro that we created in the *Discovering groups of data using K-means clustering* recipe to create a wrapper function for this analysis also.

## Getting ready

We'll use the same `project.clj` dependencies that we did in the *Loading CSV and ARFF data into Weka* recipe. And we'll use the following set of imports:

```
(import [weka.core EuclideanDistance]
        [weka.clusterers HierarchicalClusterer])
(require '[clojure.string :as str])
```

Because hierarchical clustering can be memory-intensive, we'll use the Iris dataset, which is fairly small. The easiest way to get this dataset is to download it from http://www.ericrochester.com/clj-data-analysis/data/UCI/iris.arff. You can also download it and other datasets in a JAR file from http://weka.wikispaces.com/Datasets. I loaded it using the `load-arff` function from the *Loading CSV and ARFF Data into Weka* recipe.

```
(def iris (load-arff "data/UCI/iris.arff"))
```

We'll also use the `defanalysis` macro that we defined in the *Discovering groups of data using K-means clustering* recipe.

## How to do it...

Now we see some return on having defined the `defanalysis` macro. We can create a wrapper function for Weka's `HierarchicalClusterer` in just a few lines.

1. We define the wrapper function as follows:

    ```
    (defanalysis
      hierarchical HierarchicalClusterer buildClusterer
      [["-A" distance EuclideanDistance .getName]
       ["-L" link-type :centroid
        #(str/upper-case (str/replace (name %) \- \_))]
       ["-N" k nil :not-nil]
       ["-D" verbose false :flag-true]
       ["-B" distance-of :node-length :flag-equal
        :branch-length]
       ["-P" print-newick false :flag-true]])
    ```

2. Using this, we can filter the petal dimensions fields and perform the analysis.

    ```
    (def iris-petal (filter-attributes iris [:sepallength :sepalwidth :class]))
    (def hc (hierarchical iris-petal :k 3 :print-newick true))
    ```

3. To see which cluster an instance falls in, we use `clusterInstance`, and we can check the same index in the full dataset to see all attributes for the instance.

```
user=> (.clusterInstance hc (.get iris-petal 2))
0
user=> (.get iris 2)
#<DenseInstance 4.7,3.2,1.3,0.2,Iris-setosa>
```

## How it works...

Hierarchical clustering usually works in a bottom-up manner. It's process is fairly simple.

1. Identify the two data points or clusters that are closest to each other.
2. Group them into a new cluster positioned at the centroid of the pair.
3. In the population, replace the pair with the new group in the population.
4. Repeat until we're left with only the number of clusters we expect (the -N option we saw earlier).

If we look at a graph of the results, we can see that the results are very similar to what K-means clustering produced. Actually, there's only one data point that was classified differently, which I've highlighted in the following graph. In this case, hierarchical clustering grouped that data point incorrectly, possibly pairing it with one of the points to its right.

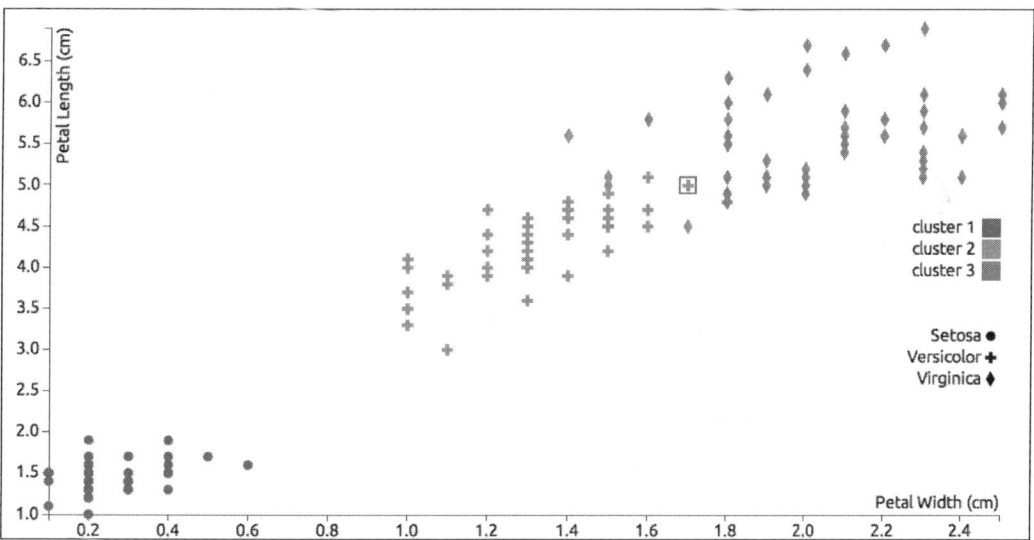

Like K-means clustering, hierarchical clustering is based on a distance measurement, so it will also have trouble correctly classifying data points along the margins between two groups with close, non-distinct data points.

*Clustering, Classifying, and Working with Weka*

## There's more...

- The documentation for the `HierarchicalClusterer` class has more information about the options available for this algorithm at http://weka.sourceforge.net/doc.dev/weka/clusterers/HierarchicalClusterer.html.

- Wikipedia has a good introduction to hierarchical clustering at http://en.wikipedia.org/wiki/Hierarchical_clustering.

- David Blei has a set of slides that provides another excellent summary of this algorithm at http://www.cs.princeton.edu/courses/archive/spr08/cos424/slides/clustering-2.pdf.

- The book *Introduction to Information Retrieval* also has a more in-depth look at hierarchical clustering. You can find this online at http://nlp.stanford.edu/IR-book/html/htmledition/hierarchical-clustering-1.html.

# Clustering with SOMs in Incanter

**Self-organizing maps** (**SOM**s) are a type of neural network that clusters and categorizes the data without supervision. It starts from a random set of groupings and competitively updates the values in the network to eventually match those in the distribution of the training data. In this way, it learns the clusters in the data by looking at the attributes of the data.

Incanter has an easy-to-use implementation of SOMs. We'll use it here to look for clusters in the Iris dataset.

## Getting ready

First, we'll need to have these dependencies in our `project.clj` file.

```
:dependencies [[org.clojure/clojure "1.4.0"]
               [incanter "1.4.1"]]
```

We'll need to have these libraries loaded into our script or REPL.

```
(require '[incanter.core :as i]
         '[incanter.som :as som]
         'incanter.datasets)
```

And, we'll use the Iris dataset.

```
(def iris (incanter.datasets/get-dataset :iris))
```

## How to do it...

Incanter includes the SOM algorithm in its core library. We'll use it from there.

1. To cluster this dataset, we'll use the `incanter.som/som-batch-train` function on a matrix of our data. This time, we'll use all measurement attributes, so the SOM will map the four dimensional attribute vectors onto two dimensions.

   ```
   (def iris-clusters
     (som/som-batch-train
       (i/to-matrix
         (i/sel iris
                :cols [:Sepal.Length :Sepal.Width
                       :Petal.Length :Petal.Width]))))
   ```

2. Now, we can get the indices of the rows in each cluster by looking at the `:sets` key of `iris-clusters`. We can also pull the species to look at the frequency of each species in each cluster.

   ```
   user=> (doseq [[pos rws] (:sets iris-clusters)]
            (println pos \:
                     (frequencies
                       (i/sel iris :cols :Species :rows rws))))
   [4 1] : {virginica 23}
   [8 1] : {virginica 27, versicolor 50}
   [9 0] : {setosa 50}
   ```

Now we can see that `setosa` and `versicolor` are each put into their own clusters and half of the `virginica` are in their own cluster and half are in with `versicolors`.

## How it works...

Self-organizing maps use a neural network to map data points onto a grid. As the neural network is trained, the data points converge into cells in the grid, based upon the similarities between the items.

We can get the size of the output map using the `:dims` key as follows:

```
user=> (:dims iris-clusters)
[10.0 2.0]
```

We can use this information, combined with the cell frequencies we saw earlier, to graph the clustering of data in the SOM.

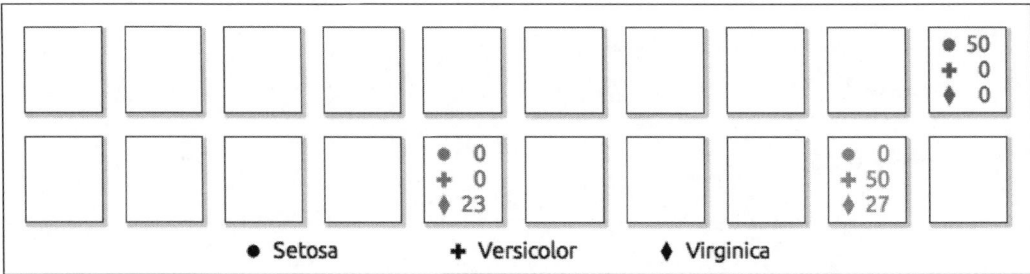

One of the downsides of SOMs is that the network's weights are largely opaque. We can see the groupings, but figuring out why the algorithm grouped them the way it did is difficult to divine.

## There's more...

- The Incanter documentation has more information about the `som/som-batch-train` function and its parameters at http://clojuredocs.org/incanter/incanter.som/som-batch-train
- Tom Germano has a more in-depth discussion of self-organizing maps at http://davis.wpi.edu/~matt/courses/soms/

# Classifying data with decision trees

One way to classify documents is to follow a set of rules down through a tree finally to place an instance into a bucket. This is essentially what decision trees do. They are especially good at classifying nominal data (discrete categories of data, such as the `species` attribute of the Iris dataset), where statistics designed for working with numerical data—such as K-means clustering—don't work as well.

Decision trees have another handy feature. Unlike many types of data mining where the analysis is somewhat of a black box, decision trees are very intelligible. We can examine them easily and readily tell how and why they classify our data the way they do.

In this recipe, we'll look at a dataset of mushrooms and create a decision tree to tell us if an instance is edible or poisonous.

## Getting ready

First, we'll need to use the dependencies that we specified in the `project.clj` file in the *Loading CSV and ARFF data into Weka* recipe.

We'll also need this import in our script or REPL:

```
(import [weka.classifiers.trees J48])
```

For data, we'll use one of the UCI data sets that Weka provides. You can download this from `http://www.cs.waikato.ac.nz/ml/weka/datasets.html` or more directly from `http://www.ericrochester.com/clj-data-analysis/data/UCI/mushroom.arff`. We can load the data file using the `load-arff` function from the *Loading CSV and ARFF data into Weka* recipe.

We'll also use the `defanalysis` macro from the *Discovering groups of data using K-means clustering* recipe in Weka.

As an added bonus, if you have Graphviz installed (`http://www.graphviz.org/`), you can use it to generate a graph of the decision tree. Wikipedia lists other programs that can display DOT or GV files at `http://en.wikipedia.org/wiki/DOT_language#Layout_programs`.

## How to do it...

We'll build a wrapper for the J48 class. This is Weka's implementation of the C4.5 algorithm for building decision trees.

1. First, we create the wrapper function for this algorithm.

    ```
    (defanalysis
      j48 J48 buildClassifier
      [["-U" pruned true :flag-false]
       ["-C" confidence 0.25]
       ["-M" min-instances 2]
       ["-R" reduced-error false :flag-true]
       ["-N" folds 3 :predicate reduced-error]
       ["-B" binary-only false :flag-true]
       ["-S" subtree-raising true :flag-false]
       ["-L" clean true :flag-false]
       ["-A" smoothing true :flag-true]
       ["-J" mdl-correction true :flag-false]
       ["-Q" seed 1 random-seed]])
    ```

*Clustering, Classifying, and Working with Weka*

2. We can use this function to create a decision tree of the mushroom data. But before that, we have to load the file and tell which field contains the classification for each one. In this case, it's the last field that tells whether the mushroom is poisonous or edible.

   ```
   (def shrooms (doto (load-arff "data/UCI/mushroom.arff")
                      (.setClassIndex 22)))
   (def d-tree (j48 shrooms :pruned true))
   ```

3. The decision tree outputs graphviz dot data, so we can write the data to a file and generate an image from that.

   ```
   (with-open [w (io/writer "decision-tree.gv")]
     (.write w (.graph d-tree)))
   ```

4. Now, from the command line, process `decision-tree.gv` with dot. If you're using another program to process the Graphviz file, substitute that here.

   ```
   $ dot -O -Tpng decision-tree.gv
   ```

### How it works...

The graphic created by Graphviz is illuminating, seen in the following diagram:

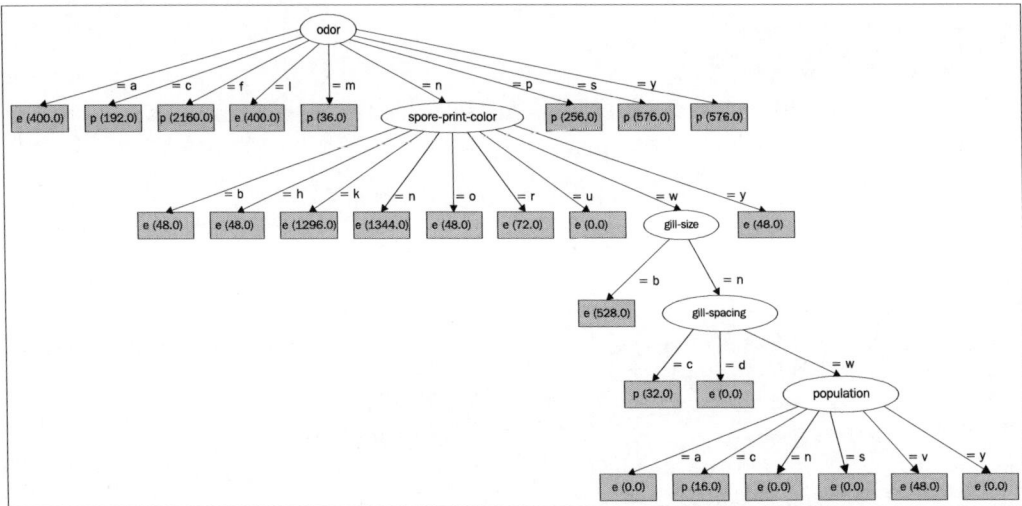

The decision tree starts from the root looking at the `odor` attribute. Instances that have a value of *a* (almond) go to the left-most node, which is marked *e* (edible). Instances that have a value of *c* (creosote) go to the next node, which is marked *p* (poisonous).

However, instances with an `odor` value of *n* (none) go to the oval child, which looks at the `spore-print-color` attribute. If that value is *b* (buff), then the instance is edible. Other sequences of attributes and values end in different categories of mushrooms.

## There's more...

- Giorgio Ingargiola of Temple University has a tutorial page for a class that breaks down the C4.5 algorithm and the ID3 algorithm it's based on at `http://www.cis.temple.edu/~giorgio/cis587/readings/id3-c45.html`
- The overview page for the mushroom dataset at `http://archive.ics.uci.edu/ml/datasets/Mushroom` has information about the attributes used

# Classifying data with the Naive Bayesian classifier

Bayesian classification is a way of updating your estimate of the probability that an item is in a given category, depending on what you already know about that item. In the case of a Naïve Bayesian system, we assume that all features are independent. This algorithm has been useful in a number of interesting areas, for example, spam detection in e-mails, automatic language detection, and document classification.

In this recipe, we'll apply it to the mushroom dataset that we looked at in the *Classifying data with decision trees* recipe.

## Getting ready

First, we'll need to use the dependencies that we specified in the `project.clj` file in the *Loading CSV and ARFF data into Weka* recipe. We'll also need the following import in our script or REPL:

```
(import [weka.classifiers.bayes NaiveBayes])
```

For data, we'll use the mushroom dataset that we did in the *Classifying data with decision trees* recipe. You can download it from `http://www.ericrochester.com/clj-data-analysis/data/UCI/mushroom.arff`. We'll also need to make sure the class attribute is marked, just as we did in that recipe.

```
(def shrooms (doto (load-arff "data/UCI/mushroom.arff")
               (.setClassIndex 22)))
```

We'll also use the `defanalysis` macro from the *Discovering groups of data using K-means clustering* recipe.

*Clustering, Classifying, and Working with Weka*

## How to do it...

In order to test the classifier, we'll take a sample of the data and train the classifier on that. Then, we'll see how well it classifies the entire dataset.

1. The following function takes a dataset of instances and a sample size, and it returns a sample of the dataset:

   ```
   (defn sample-instances
     [instances size]
     (let [inst-count (.numInstances instances)]
       (if (<= inst-count size)
         instances
         (let [indexes (loop [sample #{}]
                         (if (= (count sample) size)
                           (sort sample)
                           (recur (conj sample
                                        (rand-int inst-count)))))
               sample (Instances. instances size)]
           (doall
             (map #(.add sample (.get instances %)) indexes))
           sample))))
   ```

2. We also need to create the wrapper function for the Bayesian analyzer.

   ```
   (defanalysis
     naive-bayes NaiveBayes buildClassifier
     [["-K" kernel-density false :flag-true]
      ["-D" discretization false :flag-true]])
   ```

3. Now, we can create a sample of the mushroom data and apply the analyzer to the sample.

   ```
   (def shroom-sample (sample-instances shrooms 2000))
   (def bayes (naive-bayes shroom-sample))
   ```

4. We can pull an instance from the original dataset and use the Bayesian model to classify it. In this dataset, edible (e) is 0, and poisonous (p) is 1, so the model correctly classified this data.

   ```
   user=> (.get shrooms 2)
   #<DenseInstance b,s,w,t,l,f,c,b,n,e,c,s,s,w,w,p,w,o,p,n,n,m,e>
   user=> (.classifyInstance bayes (.get shrooms 2))
   0.0
   ```

## How it works...

Bayesian models work by initially assuming that there's a 50-50 chance that a mushroom is edible or poisonous. For each item in the training set, it uses the values of each mushroom's attributes to nudge this 50-50 chance in the direction of the classification for that mushroom. So, if a mushroom has a bell-shaped cap, smells of anise, and is edible, the model will assume that if it sees another mushroom with a bell-shaped cap that smells of anise, it's slightly more likely to be edible than poisonous.

By classifying each instance in the mushroom dataset, we can evaluate how well the model has done. The following code snippet will do this:

```
user=> (frequencies
         (map #(vector (.classValue (.get shrooms %))
                       (.classifyInstance bayes (.get shrooms %)))
              (range (.numInstances shrooms))))
{[1.0 0.0] 459, [0.0 0.0] 4182, [1.0 1.0] 3457, [0.0 1.0] 26}
```

So, it classified approximately 94 percent of data correctly (4182 + 3457). It thought that 459 poisonous mushrooms were edible, and 26 edible mushrooms were poisonous. This isn't a bad result, although we might wish that it erred on the side of caution!

## There's more...

- Weka's documentation for the `NaiveBayes` class at http://weka.sourceforge.net/doc.dev/weka/classifiers/bayes/NaiveBayes.html has information about the options available
- Alexandru Nedelcu has a good introduction to Bayesian modeling and classifiers at https://www.bionicspirit.com/blog/2012/02/09/howto-build-naive-bayes-classifier.html

# Classifying data with support vector machines

**Support vector machines** (**SVM**s) transform the input data into a higher dimension. This is called a kernel trick, and it means that often a non-linear classification of the input data becomes linear and therefore much easier to compute efficiently. So, while other clustering or classification algorithms work well with defined clusters of data, SVMs may work fine with data that isn't in well-defined and -delineated groupings. They are also not affected by local minima. Algorithms such as K-means or SOMs—which begin from a random starting point—can get caught in solutions that aren't bad for the area around the solution, but aren't the best for the entire space, but this isn't a problem for SVMs.

*Clustering, Classifying, and Working with Weka*

## Getting ready

First, we'll need these dependencies in our `project.clj` file.

```
:dependencies [[org.clojure/clojure "1.4.0"]
               [nz.ac.waikato.cms.weka/weka-dev "3.7.7"]
               [nz.ac.waikato.cms.weka/LibSVM "1.0.5"]]
```

In the script or REPL, we'll import the SVM library.

```
(import [weka.classifiers.functions LibSVM])
```

We'll also use the ionosphere dataset from the Weka datasets. (You can download this from http://www.ericrochester.com/clj-data-analysis/data/UCI/ionosphere.arff.) This data is taken from a phased-array antenna system in Goose Bay, Labrador. For each observation, the first 34 attributes are from 17 pulse numbers for the system, two attributes per pulse number. The 35th attribute indicates whether the reading is good or bad. Good readings show evidence of some kind of structure in the ionosphere. Bad readings do not; their signals pass through the ionosphere. We'll load this and set the last column, the "good" or "bad" column as the class index.

```
(def ion (doto (load-arff "data/UCI/ionosphere.arff")
           (.setClassIndex 34)))
```

Finally, we'll also use the `defanalysis` macro from the *Discovering groups of data using K-means clustering* recipe and the `sample-instances` function from the *Classifying data with the Naive Bayesian Classifiers* recipe.

## How to do it...

For this recipe, we'll define some utility functions and the analysis algorithm wrapper. Then, we'll put it through its paces.

1. A number of the options to the SVM analysis have to be converted from Clojure-friendly values. For example, we want to pass `true` to one option and a mnemonic keyword to another, but Weka wants both of these as integers. So, to make the parameter values more natural to Clojure, we'll use several functions that convert the Clojure parameters to the integer strings that Weka wants.

    ```
    (defn bool->int [b] (if b 1 0))
    (def svm-types
      {:c-svc 0, :nu-svc 1, :one-class-svm 2, :epsilon-svr 3,
       :nu-svr 4})
    (def svm-fns
      {:linear 0, :polynomial 1, :radial-basis 2, :sigmoid 3})
    ```

256

2. We'll use these to define the wrapper function for the LibSVM class.

   ```
   (defanalysis
     svm LibSVM buildClassifier
     [["-S" svm-type :c-svc svm-types]
      ["-K" kernel-fn :radial-basis svm-fns]
      ["-D" degree 3]
      ["-G" gamma nil :not-nil]
      ["-R" coef0 0]
      ["-C" c 1]
      ["-N" nu 0.5]
      ["-Z" normalize false bool->int]
      ["-P" epsilon 0.1]
      ["-M" cache-size 40]
      ["-E" tolerance 0.001]
      ["-H" shrinking true bool->int]
      ["-W" weights nil :not-nil]])
   ```

3. Before we use this, let's also write a function to test the algorithm's accuracy by re-classifying each instance and tracking whether the SVM identified the class values correctly or not. We'll use the following code snippet to see how well the trained SVM did:

   ```
   (defn eval-instance
     ([] {:correct 0, :incorrect 0})
     ([_] {:correct 0, :incorrect 0})
     ([classifier sums instance]
       (if (= (.classValue instance)
              (.classifyInstance classifier instance))
         (assoc sums :correct (inc (sums :correct)))
         (assoc sums :incorrect (inc (sums :incorrect))))))
   ```

4. Now, let's get a sample of 35 of the observations (about 10 percent of the total) and train the SVM on them.

   ```
   (def ion-sample (sample-instances ion 35))
   (def ion-svm (svm ion-sample))
   ```

5. It'll output some information about the optimizations, and then it will be ready to use. We'll use `eval-instance` to see how it did.

   ```
   user=> (reduce (partial eval-instance ion-svm)
                  (eval-instance) ion)
   {:incorrect 70, :correct 281}
   ```

   This gives us a total correct of 80 percent.

*Clustering, Classifying, and Working with Weka*

## How it works...

Support vector machines are a method to find the optimal hyperplane to separate data linearly. Of course, this isn't really any better than a linear regression. SVMs improve on this by first transforming the data using a kernel function. This makes many non-linear datasets linear, and therefore much easier to work with.

## There's more...

- The Weka website's documentation has a good page on the `LibSVM` class at http://weka.wikispaces.com/LibSVM.
- R. Berwick has written *An Idiot's guide to Support vector machines (SVMs)*, which is an excellent introduction to the history and theoretical background of SVMs. You can find it at http://www.cs.ucf.edu/courses/cap6412/fall2009/papers/Berwick2003.pdf.
- For more information on the ionosphere dataset is available at http://archive.ics.uci.edu/ml/datasets/Ionosphere.

# Finding associations in data with the Apriori algorithm

One of the main goals of data mining and clustering is to learn the relationships implicit in the data. The Apriori algorithm helps to do this by teasing out those relationships into an explicit set of association rules.

In this recipe, we'll use this algorithm to extract the relationships from the mushroom dataset that we've seen several times earlier in this chapter.

## Getting ready

First, we'll use the same dependencies that we did in the *Loading CSV and ARFF data into Weka* recipe.

We'll use just one import in our script or REPL.

```
(import [weka.associations Apriori])
```

We'll use the mushroom dataset that we introduced in the *Classifying data with decision trees* recipe. We'll also set the `class` attribute to the column indicating whether the mushroom is edible or poisonous.

```
(def shrooms (doto (load-arff "data/UCI/mushroom.arff")
               (.setClassIndex 22)))
```

Finally, we'll use the `defanalysis` macro from the *Discovering groups of data using K-means clustering in Weka* recipe.

## How to do it...

For this, we'll train an instance of the `Apriori` class, extract the classification rules, and use it to classify the instances.

1. First, we need to define the wrapper function for the `Apriori` class.

   ```
   (defanalysis
     apriori Apriori buildAssociations
     [["-N" rules 10]
      ["-T" rank-metric :confidence rank-metrics]
      ["-C" min-metric 0.9]
      ["-D" min-support-delta 0.05]
      [["-M" "-U"] min-support-bounds [0.1 1.0] :seq]
      ["-S" significance nil :not-nil]
      ["-I" output-itemsets false :flag-true]
      ["-R" remove-missing-value-columns false :flag-true]
      ["-V" progress false :flag-true]
      ["-A" mine-class-rules false :flag-true]
      ["-c" class-index nil :not-nil]])
   ```

2. With this in place, we can use it the way we have the other wrapper functions.

   ```
   (def a (apriori shrooms))
   ```

3. Afterwards, we can print out the association rules.

   ```
   user=> (doseq [r (.. a getAssociationRules getRules)]
            (println
              (format "%s => %s %s = %.4f"
                      (mapv str (.getPremise r))
                      (mapv str (.getConsequence r))
                      (.getPrimaryMetricName r)
                      (.getPrimaryMetricValue r))))
   ["veil-color=w"] => ["veil-type=p"] Confidence = 1.0000
   ["gill-attachment=f"] => ["veil-type=p"] Confidence = 1.0000
   ...
   ```

## How it works...

The Apriori algorithm looks for items that are often associated together within a transaction. This is often used for things such as analyzing shopping patterns. In this case, we're viewing the constellation of attributes related to each mushroom as a transaction, and we're using the Apriori algorithm to see which traits are associated with which other traits.

The algorithm attempts to find the premises that imply a set of consequences. For instance, white veil colors (the premise) imply a partial veil type with a confidence of 1.0, so whenever the premise is found, the consequence is also. A white veil color also implies a free gill attachment, but the confidence is 99 percent, so we know that these two aren't associated quite all the time.

The abbreviated data dump of the traits above isn't particularly legible, so here's the same information as a table:

| Premise | Consequence | Confidence |
| --- | --- | --- |
| veil-color=w | veil-type=p | 1.0000 |
| gill-attachment=f | veil-type=p | 1.0000 |
| gill-attachment=f, veil-color=w | veil-type=p | 1.0000 |
| gill-attachment=f | veil-color=w | 0.9990 |
| gill-attachment=f, veil-type=p | veil-color=w | 0.9990 |
| gill-attachment=f | veil-type=p, veil-color=w | 0.9990 |
| veil-color=w | gill-attachment=f | 0.9977 |
| veil-type=p, veil-color=w | gill-attachment=f | 0.9977 |
| veil-color=w | gill-attachment=f, veil-type=p | 0.9977 |
| veil-type=p | veil-color=w | 0.9754 |

From this we can see that a white veil is associated with a partial veil type; a free gill attachment is associated with a partial, white veil; and so on. If we want more information, we can request more rules using the `rules` parameter.

## There's more...

- The Weka documentation has more information about the `Apriori` class and its options at http://weka.sourceforge.net/doc.dev/weka/associations/Apriori.html
- For more about the algorithm itself, see Wikipedia's page on the Apriori algorithm at http://en.wikipedia.org/wiki/Apriori_algorithm

# 10
# Graphing in Incanter

In this chapter, we will cover:

- Creating scatter plots with Incanter
- Creating bar charts with Incanter
- Graphing non-numeric data in bar charts
- Creating histograms with Incanter
- Creating function plots with Incanter
- Adding equations to Incanter charts
- Adding lines to scatter charts
- Customizing charts with JFreeChart
- Saving Incanter graphs to PNG
- Using PCA to graph multi-dimensional data
- Creating dynamic charts with Incanter

## Introduction

Graphs serve a couple of important functions in data analysis. First, while exploring data, they can help us understand our data and the relationships in it.

But data analysis isn't all about wrangling data and crunching numbers. We also must communicate our findings and convey evidence for our arguments. Graphs serve an important role in succinctly communicating complex relationships. While there's always the danger of creating graphs that aren't clear or that don't really have much informational content, well-done graphs can clarify concepts and relationships that are difficult to explain verbally.

*Graphing in Incanter*

Designing good, informative, and beautiful charts is difficult, and if you want to dive into that topic, and there's a lot of good information out there. Anything by Edward Tufte (http://www.edwardtufte.com/tufte/) is a good place to start, and his book, *The Visual Display of Quantitative Information*, is considered a classic in the field of data visualization design.

For creating charts and graphs, there are a number of options. There are a lot of solutions for graphing. In the next chapter, we'll look at some involving ClojureScript (https://github.com/clojure/clojurescript), d3 (http://d3js.org/), and Kevin Lynagh's C2 (http://keminglabs.com/c2/). R (http://www.r-project.org/) and Mathematica (http://www.wolfram.com/mathematica/), which we worked with in *Chapter 8, Working with Mathematica and R*, both have strong graphing libraries, and R also has the ggplot2 library (http://ggplot2.org/), which makes creating charts easier.

But in this chapter, we'll focus on Incanter charts. They are built on the JFreeChart library (http://www.jfree.org/jfreechart/), which provides a powerful set of functions for graphing data. In this chapter, we'll use these to create a variety of types of graphs. We'll also look at how to save graphs as PNG images. We'll use **principal component analysis** (**PCA**) to project multi-dimensional data down to two dimensions so they can be graphed easily. Finally, we'll create an interactive, dynamic graph.

## Creating scatter plots with Incanter

One of the most common types of charts is a scatter plot. This helps us visualize the relationship between two numeric variables.

### Getting ready

We'll need to list Incanter as a dependency in our Leiningen `project.clj` file.

```
:dependencies [[org.clojure/clojure "1.4.0"]
               [incanter "1.4.1"]]
```

We'll also need to enter several of Incanter's namespaces into our script or REPL.

```
(require '[incanter.core :as i]
         '[incanter.charts :as c]
         'incanter.datasets)
```

Finally, we'll use the Iris dataset, which we saw in several recipes in *Chapter 9, Clustering, Classifying, and Working with Weka*.

```
(def iris (incanter.datasets/get-dataset :iris))
```

## How to do it...

For this recipe, we'll do a chart graphing the dimensions of the Iris' petals.

1. We'll create the chart, but hang on to the object created so we can do things with the chart later, like display it.

   ```
   (def iris-petal-scatter
     (c/scatter-plot (i/sel iris :cols :Petal.Width)
                     (i/sel iris :cols :Petal.Length)
                     :title "Irises: Petal Width by
                     Petal Length"
                     :x-label "Width (cm)"
                     :y-label "Length (cm)"))
   ```

2. To actually display it, we pass this chart to the `incanter.core/view` function.

   ```
   (i/view iris-petal-scatter)
   ```

3. The output looks as follows:

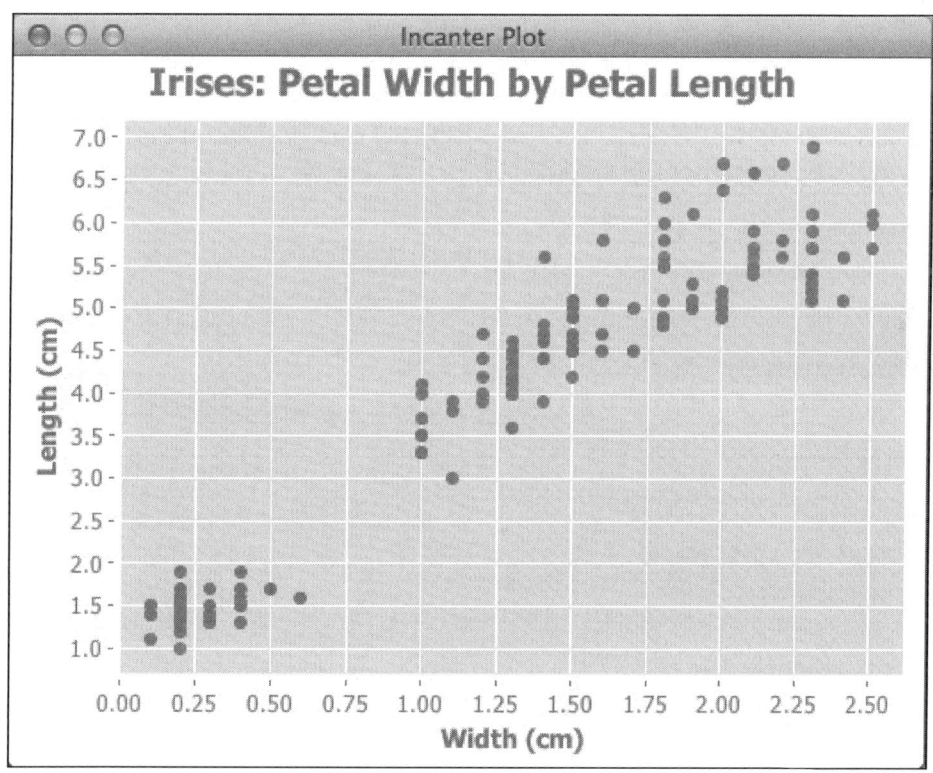

## How it works...

The function `incanter.charts/scatter-plot` takes two sequences, one of the points' *x* coordinates and one of their *y* coordinates.

By default, Incanter labels the x and y axes from the expressions we use in the call to `scatter-plot`. In this case, that would be `(i/sel race-data :cols :Petal.Width)` for the x axis and `(i/sel race-data :cols :Petal.Length)` for the y axis. That's not very readable, so we specify the axes' labels with the `:x-label` and `:y-label` parameters.

However, the `scatter-plot` function only creates the chart object. To view it, we have to pass it to the `incanter.core/view` function.

If we right-click on a displayed graph, there are several other options as well. From the context menu, we can zoom in and out, print the chart, and change the labels. The charts are also interactive. Clicking and dragging on the graph zooms the view in to focus on the area we selected.

## There's more...

- The Incanter API documentation lists the supported charts and the options for each. This is available at `http://liebke.github.com/incanter/charts-api.html`.
- The Incanter Wiki on Github also has a gallery of sample charts at `https://github.com/liebke/incanter/wiki/sample-plots-in-incanter`.

## See also

- The *Saving Incanter graphs to PNG* recipe

# Creating bar charts with Incanter

Another common type of chart is a bar chart. These are good for comparing the sums or the counts of a few categories in the data.

## Getting ready

We'll use the same dependencies in our `project.clj` file as we did in the *Creating scatter plots with Incanter* recipe.

We'll use the following set of imports in our script or REPL:

```
(require '[incanter.core :as i]
         '[incanter.charts :as c]
         'incanter.datasets)
```

*Chapter 10*

For this recipe, we'll use a standard dataset of chick weights. This comes with Incanter, so it's simple to load.

```
(def chick-weight (incanter.datasets/get-dataset :chick-weight))
```

## How to do it...

In this example, we'll chart the weight of the chicks by their diets.

1. We get the total weights for the chicks eating each diet with the `incanter.core/$rollup` function.

   ```
   (def chick-weight-bar
     (i/with-data
       (i/$order :Diet :asc
         (i/$rollup :sum :weight :Diet chick-weight))
       (c/bar-chart (i/$map int :Diet)
                    :weight
                    :title "Chick Weight"
                    :x-label "Diet"
                    :y-label "Weight")))
   ```

2. When we pass this to `incanter.core/view`, like follows:

   ```
   (i/view chick-weight-bar)
   ```

3. We get a chart that looks as follows:

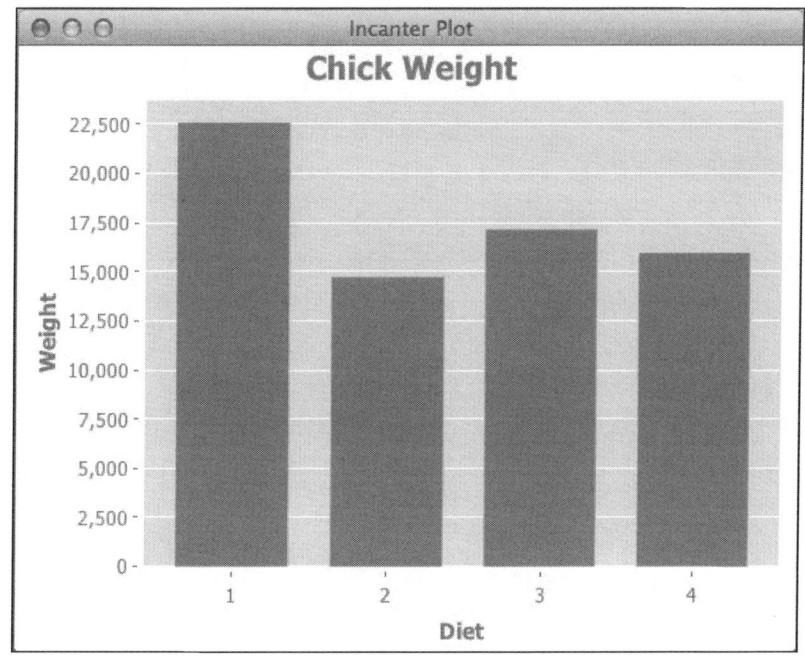

265

*Graphing in Incanter*

## How it works...

In this recipe, we used the `incanter.core/with-data` macro to temporarily create and sort a dataset on the fly and use it as our default dataset. This temporary dataset summarized the weight values for each diet, and this was the default dataset that we used to create the chart.

```
(i/with-data
  (i/$order :Diet :asc
    (i/$rollup :sum :weight :Diet chick-weight))
  ...
```

However, the main wrinkle is that we had to convert the values in the `Diet` column to integers. We did this by mapping `int` over the values in the `Diet` column before we passed these values to the chart, using this function.

```
(i/$map int :Diet)
```

# Graphing non-numeric data in bar charts

Not everything is numeric, and often non-numeric data has to be handled differently, as we saw in the chapter on statistics and the one on data mining. For example, a scatter plot doesn't make much sense unless the data is naturally ordered in some way.

In this recipe, we'll use a bar chart to display how many items have each possible value for a field of categorical data.

## Getting ready

We'll use the same dependencies in our `project.clj` file as we did in the *Creating scatter plots with Incanter* recipe.

We'll use this set of imports in our script or REPL.

```
(require '[incanter.core :as i]
         '[incanter.charts :as c]
         '[incanter.io :as iio])
```

For this chart, we'll use the mushroom dataset from the UCI machine learning archive. The web page with information about this dataset is at http://archive.ics.uci.edu/ml/datasets/Mushroom, and we can download a copy of it with header names directly from http://www.ericrochester.com/clj-data-analysis/data/agaricus-lepiota.data. I've downloaded it into a data directory, so I can load it with the following expression:

```
(def shrooms (iio/read-dataset "data/agaricus-lepiota.data" :header true))
```

*Chapter 10*

## How to do it...

In order to graph this, we need to summarize the data in some way. This can be done using the following steps:

1. Here, we'll get the number of mushrooms with each cap shape and create a bar chart with that data.

   ```
   (def shroom-cap-bar
     (i/with-data
       (->> shrooms
         (i/$group-by :cap-shape)
         (map (fn [[k v]] (assoc k :count (i/nrow v))))
         (sort-by :cap-shape)
         i/to-dataset)
       (c/bar-chart :cap-shape :count)))
   ```

2. Now, we view it.

   ```
   (i/view shroom-cap-bar)
   ```

3. For output we have the following:

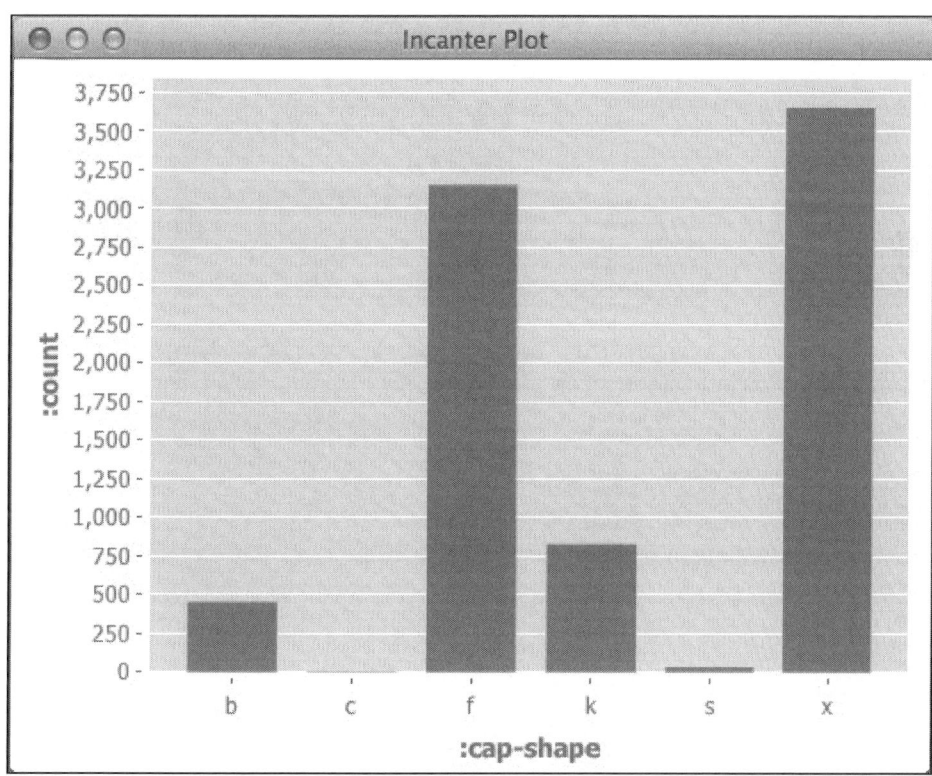

*Graphing in Incanter*

## How it works…

The most complicated part of this is transforming the data to get the counts. Let's break that apart line-by-line.

1. We start with the dataset we loaded from the CSV file.

   ```
   (->> shrooms
   ```

2. We group that by the `:cap-shape` field. This produces a hash map going from a map like `{:cap-shape 0.0}` to a dataset.

   ```
   (i/$group-by :cap-shape)
   ```

3. We take each key-value pair in the group hash map and add the number of rows in the dataset to the key. The output of this operation is a sequence of maps like `{:cap-shape 0.0, :count 452}`.

   ```
   (map (fn [[k v]] (assoc k :count (i/nrow v))))
   ```

4. We sort that by the cap shape.

   ```
   (sort-by :cap-shape)
   ```

5. And convert it to a new dataset.

   ```
   i/to-dataset)
   ```

We implicitly pass the output of that expression to `incanter.charts/bar-chart` using `incanter.core/with-data`, and we have our chart.

# Creating histograms with Incanter

Histograms are useful for seeing the distribution of data. It's even effective with continuous data. In a histogram, the data is divided into a limited number of buckets—10 is common—and the number of items in each bucket is counted. Histograms are especially useful for finding how much data are available for various percentiles. For instance, these charts can clearly show how much of your data was in the 90th percentile or lower.

## Getting ready

We'll use the same dependencies in our `project.clj` file as we did in the *Creating scatter plots with Incanter* recipe.

We'll use the following set of imports in our script or REPL:

```
(require '[incanter.core :as i]
         '[incanter.charts :as c]
         '[incanter.io :as iio])
```

For this recipe, we'll use the iris dataset that we used in the *Creating scatter plots with Incanter* recipe.

```
(def iris (incanter.datasets/get-dataset :iris))
```

## How to do it...

As we have in the previous recipes, we just create the graph and display it with `incanter.core/view`.

1. We create a histogram of the Iris' petal length.

   ```
   (def iris-petal-length-hist
     (c/histogram (i/sel iris :cols :Petal.Length)
                  :title "Iris Petal Lengths"
                  :x-label "cm"
                  :nbins 20))
   ```

2. View it using the following.

   ```
   (i/view iris-petal-length-hist).
   ```

3. We get the following graph:

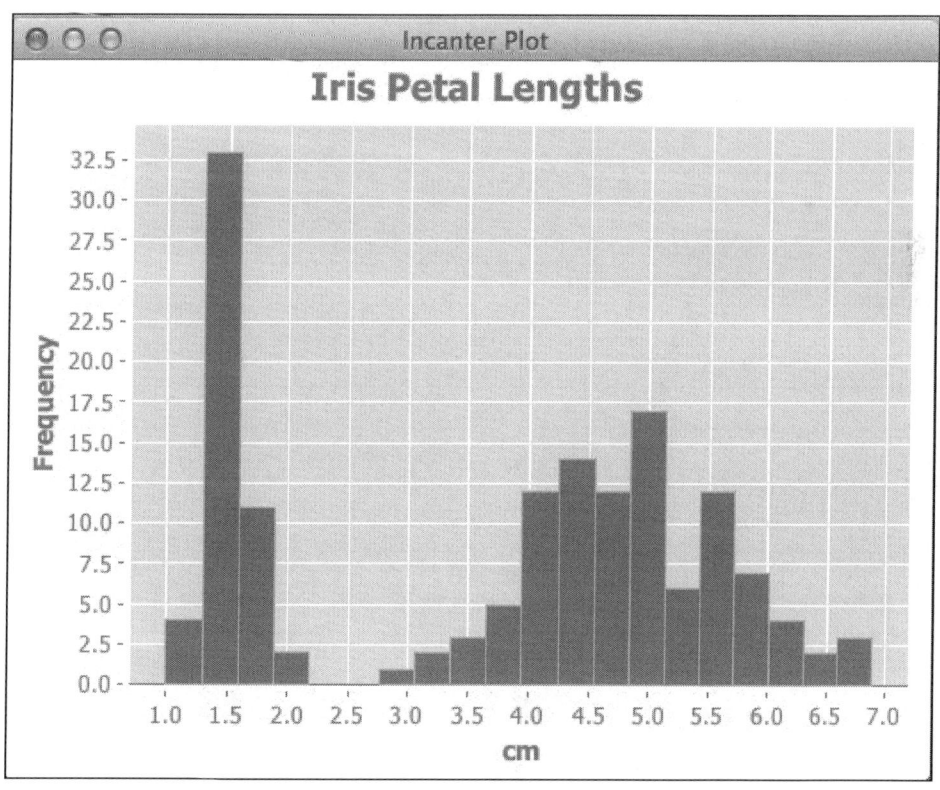

*Graphing in Incanter*

## How it works...

Looking at the graph just created, the distribution of the data becomes clear. We can observe that the data does not fit a normal distribution, and in fact the distribution has two spikes. If we compare this to the the graph from the *Creating scatter plots with Incanter* recipe, we can also see the cluster of smaller petals there. Looking into the data, this seems to be the data for Iris Setosa. Versicolor, and Virginica are grouped in the upper distribution.

By default, Incanter creates histograms with 10 bins. When we made this graph, we wanted more detail and more resolution, so we doubled the number of bins by adding the option `:nbins 20` when we created the graph.

## Creating function plots with Incanter

Sometimes we don't want to graph data directly, but instead, plot the values of a function over a given domain. In this recipe, we'll see how to graph an inverse log function.

## Getting ready

We'll use the same dependencies in our `project.clj` file as we did in the *Creating scatter plots with Incanter* recipe.

We'll use the following set of imports in our script or REPL:

```
(require '[incanter.core :as i]
         '[incanter.charts :as c])
```

## How to do it...

We just create and display a `function-plot` object.

```
(def f-plot
  (c/function-plot
    #(/ 1.0 (Math/log %)) 0.0 1.0
    :title "Inverse log function."
    :y-label "Inverse log"))
(i/view f-plot)
```

The graph is as we would expect:

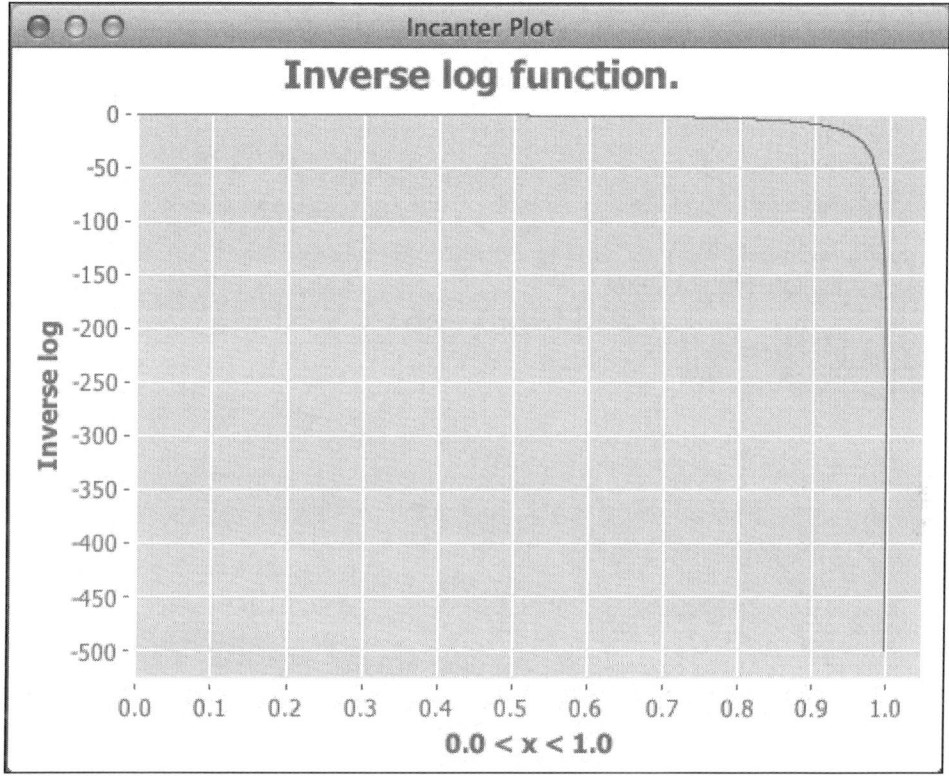

## How it works...

The incanter.charts/function-plot function takes the function to plot and the range of the domain (in this case, from 0.0 to 1.0). We've added some labels to make things more clear, but overall, this is a very straightforward function. Not having to worry about messy data simplifies a lot of things!

## See also

- The *Adding lines to scatter charts* recipe

*Graphing in Incanter*

# Adding equations to Incanter charts

We've seen how to add a title to the charts and labels on the axes, but so far they've all used only plain, unformatted text. Sometimes we might want to use a formula instead.

Incanter lets you add a formula to a chart using LaTeX's mathematical notation. **LaTeX** is a professional grade document typesetting system. We won't go into the details of its math notation, but instead we'll just see how to use it with Incanter.

In this recipe, we'll take the chart from the last recipe, *Creating function plots with Incanter*, and add the function as a subtitle.

## Getting ready

We'll use the same dependencies in our `project.clj` file as we did in the *Creating scatter plots with Incanter* recipe.

We'll use the following set of imports in our script or REPL:

```
(require '[incanter.core :as i]
         '[incanter.charts :as c]
         '[incanter.latex :as latex])
```

We'll also use the chart that we made in the *Creating function plots with Incanter* recipe. We'll still use the `f-plot` variable for it.

## How to do it...

The LaTeX string that we want to add is fairly simple, and it gives us a good taste of what the syntax for this notation is.

1. We bind the LaTeX string to the name `inv-log`.

    ```
    (def inv-log "f(x)=\\frac{1.0}{\\log x}")
    ```

2. We apply that to a chart using the function `incanter.latex/add-latex-subtitle`.

    ```
    (latex/add-latex-subtitle f-plot inv-log)
    ```

3. The chart reflects the change immediately, shown as follows:

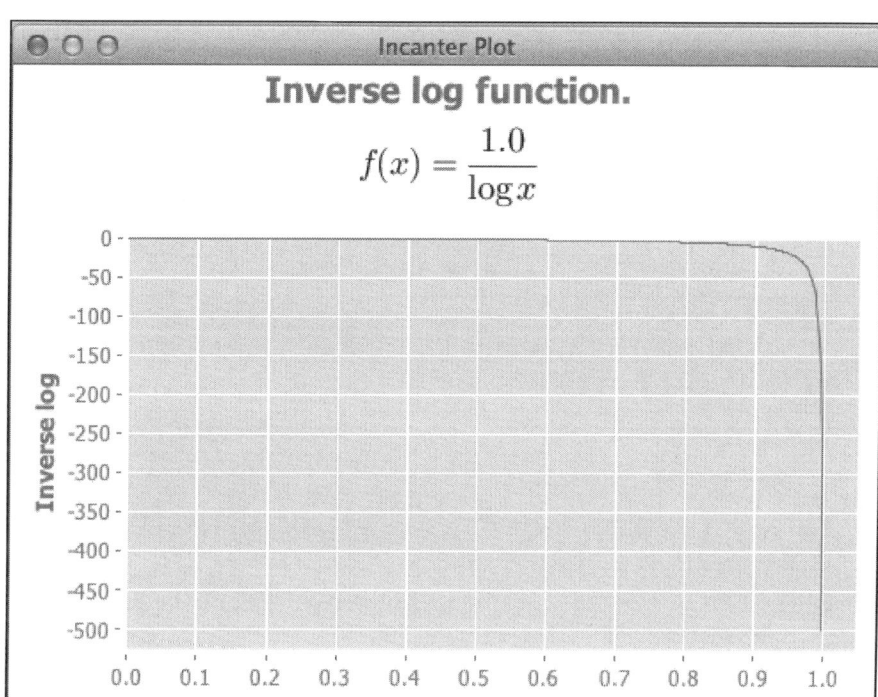

### There's more...

Full information about LaTeX and its math notation is beyond the scope of this recipe. The website for LaTeX is at http://www.latex-project.org/. The LaTeX wikibook has a good chapter on typesetting mathematical equations at http://en.wikibooks.org/wiki/LaTeX/Mathematics, and *The Not So Short Introduction to LaTeX 2ε* (http://tobi.oetiker.ch/lshort/lshort.pdf) is another good resource for learning LaTeX, including the math syntax.

## Adding lines to scatter charts

So far, all the recipes in this chapter have only created one type of chart. Incanter also lets us combine chart types. This allows us to layer on extra information and create a more useful, compelling chart. In fact, showing the interaction between the raw data and the output of a machine-learning algorithm is a common use for overlaying lines onto scatter plots.

In this recipe, we'll take the chart from the *Creating scatter plots with Incanter* recipe and add a line from a linear regression.

*Graphing in Incanter*

## Getting ready

We'll use the same dependencies in our project.clj file as we did in the *Creating scatter plots with Incanter* recipe with Incanter.

We'll use the following set of imports in our script or REPL:

```
(require '[incanter.core :as i]
         '[incanter.charts :as c]
         '[incanter.io :as iio]
         '[incanter.stats :as s])
```

We'll start with the chart we made in the *Creating scatter plots with Incanter* recipe. We'll keep it assigned to the `iris-petal-scatter` variable.

## How to do it...

For this recipe, we'll create the linear model and then add that to the existing chart from the previous recipe.

1. First, we have to create the linear model for the data. We'll do that using the `incanter.stats/linear-model` function.

   ```
   (def iris-petal-lm
     (s/linear-model
       (i/sel iris :cols :Petal.Length)
       (i/sel iris :cols :Petal.Width)
       :intercept false))
   ```

2. Next, we take the `:fitted` data from the model and add it to the chart using `incanter.charts/add-lines`.

   ```
   (c/add-lines
     iris-petal-scatter
     (i/sel iris :cols :Petal.Width)
     (:fitted iris-petal-lm)
     :series-label "Linear Relationship")
   ```

Once we've added that, our chart now looks like the following.

## How it works...

The fitted values for the linear regression is just a sequence of *y* values corresponding to the sequence of *x* values. When we add that line to the graph, Incanter pairs the *x* and *y* values together, and draws a line on the graph linking each point. Since the points describe a straight line, we end up with the line found by the linear regression.

## See also

- The *Modeling linear relationships* recipe in *Chapter 7, Preparing for and Performing Statistical Data Analysis with Incanter*

# Customizing charts with JFreeChart

Incanter's chart API is easy to use and provides a powerful wrapper around JFreeChart (http://www.jfree.org/jfreechart/); however, it doesn't expose JFreeChart's full variety of chart types or all of the options that JFreeChart provides. In order to access those, we have to dive from Incanter's API to the JFreeChart objects. Fortunately, that's quite easy to do. Let's see how.

## Getting ready

We'll use the same dependencies in our `project.clj` file as we did in the *Creating scatter plots with Incanter* recipe.

We'll use the following set of imports in our script or REPL:

```
(require '[incanter.core :as i]
         '[incanter.charts :as c]
         'incanter.datasets)
(import org.jfree.chart.renderer.category.LayeredBarRenderer
        org.jfree.util.SortOrder)
```

We'll use the Iris dataset again. Here's how to load it into Incanter.

```
(def iris (incanter.datasets/get-dataset :iris))
```

## How to do it...

For this recipe, we'll create a bar chart with multiple columns: one for each measurement column in the Iris dataset.

1. We'll first create the bar chart and add a category for each measurement.
   ```
   (def iris-dimensions
     (i/with-data
       iris
       (doto (c/bar-chart :Species :Petal.Width
                          :title "iris' dimensions"
                          :x-label "species"
                          :y-label "cm"
                          :series-label "petal width"
                          :legend true)
         (c/add-categories
           :Species :Sepal.Width
           :series-label "sepal width")
         (c/add-categories
           :Species :Petal.Length
   ```

```
                  :series-label "petal length")
        (c/add-categories
          :Species :Sepal.Length
          :series-label "sepal length"))))
```

2. The `iris-dimensions` object is the `JFreeChart` object for this chart. We can call its methods to change how the chart is created. In this case, we'll change the renderer to layer the bars on top of each other, and we'll change the rendering order so that we can see each bar in the stack.

   ```
   (doto (.getPlot iris-dimensions)
     (.setRenderer (doto (LayeredBarRenderer.)
                     (.setDrawBarOutline false)))
     (.setRowRenderingOrder SortOrder/DESCENDING))
   ```

3. Now, like the other charts, we display this one using `incanter.core/view`.

   ```
   (i/view iris-dimensions)
   ```

4. The results are something we can't get from Incanter's chart API alone. The resulting chart is as follows:

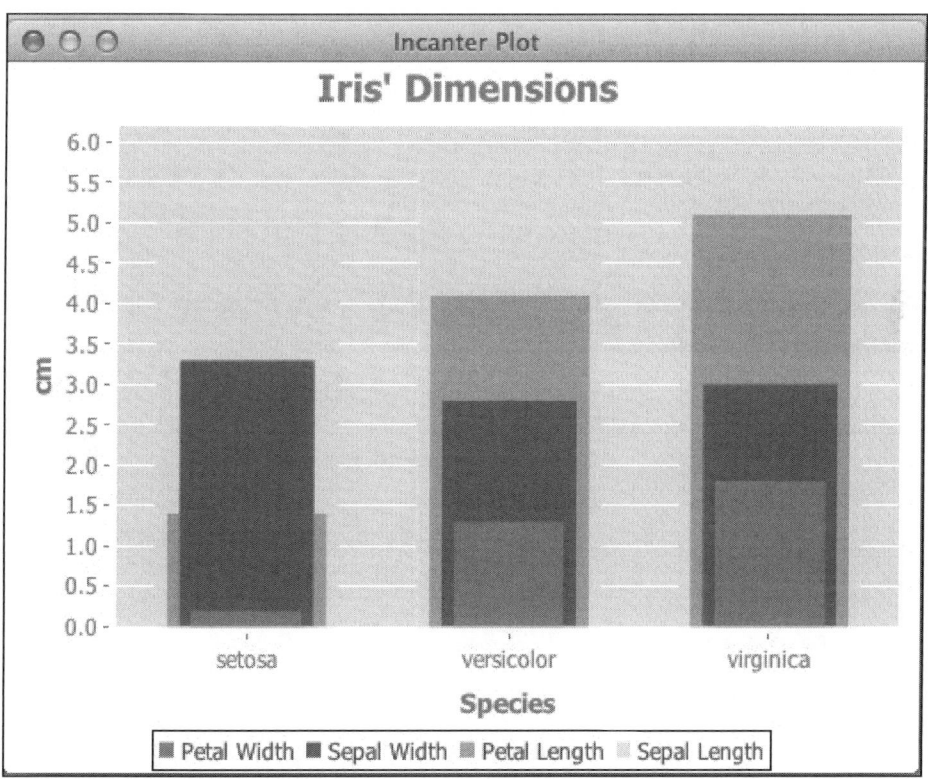

*Graphing in Incanter*

## How it works...

The object returned by the Incanter chart functions is the `JFreeChart` object. This is the builder class for all of the charts. From this object, we can access the plot objects, which provide interfaces for different types of charts, and from the plot objects we can access options like axes, annotations, colors, and renderers, which handle actually drawing the chart.

That's what we do in this recipe. The pertinent code snippet is as follows:

```
(doto (.getPlot iris-dimensions)
  (.setRenderer (doto (LayeredBarRenderer.)
                  (.setDrawBarOutline false)))
  (.setRowRenderingOrder SortOrder/DESCENDING))
```

In it, we get the plot, set the renderer to an instance of `LayeredBarRenderer`, and then we change the row rendering order. If we don't do that, then the shorter rows get rendered behind the taller ones, which isn't useful.

## See also

- The class hierarchy for this is quite complex and fully featured. To get a good feel for its breadth and for what the library is capable of, browse the Java docs for it at http://www.jfree.org/jfreechart/api/javadoc/org/jfree/chart/JFreeChart.html.

- If you plan on using JFreeChart much, the developer guide may be a good investment. You can find more information about it at http://www.jfree.org/jfreechart/devguide.html.

# Saving Incanter graphs to PNG

So far, we've been viewing the graphs we've created in a window on our computer. This is extremely handy, especially for quickly generating a graph and seeing what's on it. However, the chart would be more useful if we could save it. Then, we could embed it into Word documents or web pages, or wherever.

In this recipe, we'll save a graph of the Iris data that we created in the *Creating scatter plots with Incanter* recipe.

## Getting ready

We'll use the same dependencies in our `project.clj` file as we did in the *Creating scatter plots with Incanter* recipe.

We'll use the following set of imports in our script or REPL:

```
(require '[incanter.core :as i]
         '[incanter.charts :as c])
```

We'll also use the chart object that we created in the *Creating scatter plots with Incanter* recipe, and we'll keep using the variable name `iris-petal-scatter` for it.

## How to do it...

Since we already have the chart, saving it is simple. We just call `incanter.core/save` on it with the filename we want to save it to.

```
(i/save iris-petal-scatter "iris-petal-scatter.png")
```

## How it works...

Calling `incanter.core/save` on a chart saves it as a PNG. We can also include options to the `save` function to set the output image's dimensions using the `:height` and `:width` parameters.

There's also another way to save images. If we right-click on a chart after displaying it with `incanter.core/view`, it gives us the option to save the chart from there.

# Using PCA to graph multi-dimensional data

So far, we've been limiting ourselves to two-dimensional data. After all, the human mind has a lot of trouble dealing with more than three dimensions, and even two-dimensional visualizations of three-dimensional space can be difficult to comprehend.

But we can use **principal component analysis** (**PCA**) to project higher-dimensional data down into lower dimensions and still capture the most significant relationships in the data. It does this by re-projecting the data onto a lower dimension in a way that captures the maximum amount of variance in the data. This makes the data easier to visualize in three- or two-dimensional space, and it also provides a way to select the most relevant features in a dataset.

In this recipe, we'll take the US Census race data that we've worked with in previous chapters and create a two-dimensional scatter plot of it.

*Graphing in Incanter*

## Getting ready

We'll use the same dependencies in our `project.clj` file as we did in the *Creating scatter plots with Incanter* recipe.

We'll use the following set of imports in our script or REPL:

```
(require '[incanter.core :as i]
         '[incanter.charts :as c]
         '[incanter.io :as iio]
         '[incanter.stats :as s])
```

We'll use the aggregated census race data for all states. You can download this from `http://www.ericrochester.com/clj-data-analysis/data/all_160.P3.csv`. We'll assign it to the variable `race-data`.

```
(def race-data (iio/read-dataset "data/all_160.P3.csv"
                                 :header true))
```

## How to do it...

We'll first summarize the data to make it more manageable and easier to visualize. Then we'll use PCA to project it onto two-dimensional space. We'll graph this view of the data.

1. First, we need to summarize the columns that we're interested in, getting the sum population of each racial group by state.

   ```
   (def fields [:P003002 :P003003 :P003004 :P003005
                :P003006 :P003007 :P003008])
   (def race-by-state
     (reduce #(i/$join [:STATE :STATE] %1 %2)
             (map #(i/$rollup :sum % :STATE race-data)
                  fields)))
   ```

2. Next, we'll take the summary and create a matrix from it. From that matrix, we'll extract the columns that we're interested in analyzing and graphing.

   ```
   (def race-by-state-matrix (i/to-matrix race-by-state))
   (def x (i/sel race-by-state-matrix :cols (range 1 8)))
   ```

3. Now, we'll perform the principal component analysis.

   ```
   (def pca (s/principal-components x))
   ```

4. From the output of the PCA, we'll get the components for the first two dimensions and multiply all of the columns in the data matrix by each component.

   ```
   (def components (:rotation pca))
   (def pc1 (i/sel components :cols 0))
   (def pc2 (i/sel components :cols 1))
   (def x1 (i/mmult x pc1))
   (def x2 (i/mmult x pc2))
   ```

5. We can plot x1 and x2. We'll use them to create a two-dimensional scatter plot.

   ```
   (def pca-plot
     (c/scatter-plot
       x1 x2
       :x-label "PC1", :y-label "PC2"
       :title "Census Race Data by State"))
   ```

6. We can view that chart as we normally would.

   ```
   (i/view pca-plot)
   ```

7. This provides us with a graph expressing the most salient features of the dataset in two dimensions.

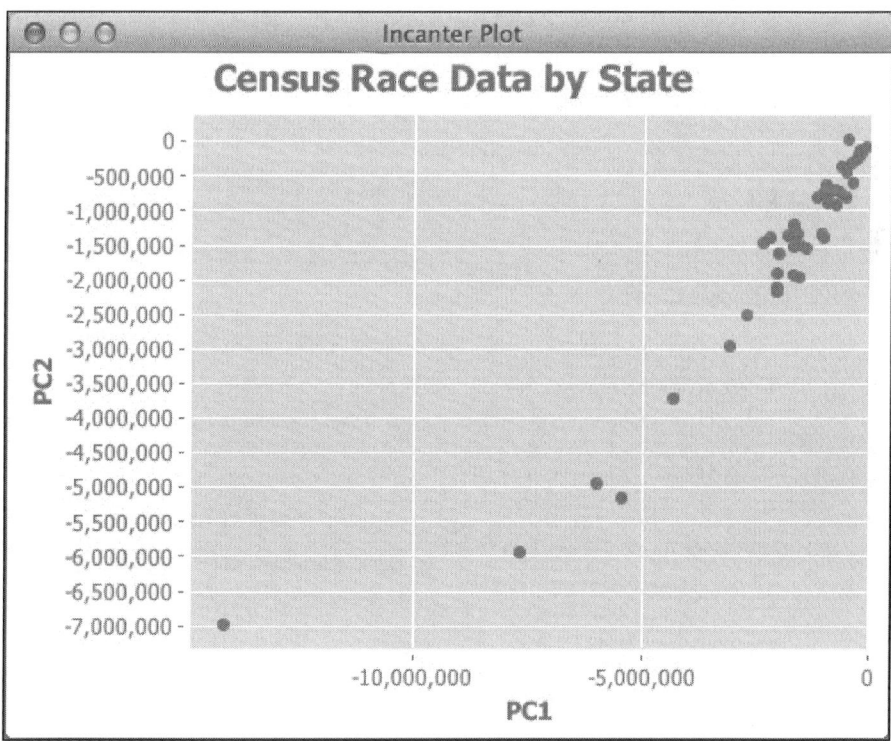

*Graphing in Incanter*

### How it works...

Conceptually, PCA projects the entire dataset into a lower-dimensional space and rotates to a view that captures the maximum variability that it can see from that dimension.

In the chart we just saw, we can see that most of the data clusters around the origin. A few points trail off into the higher numbers of the graph.

### There's more...

- For a easy, visual explanation of PCA, see the video *A layman's introduction to principle component analysis* at http://youtu.be/BfTMmoDFXyE
- For more detail, see *A Tutorial on Principle Component Analysis* by Jonathon Shlens at http://www.snl.salk.edu/~shlens/pca.pdf

## Creating dynamic charts with Incanter

Charts are a powerful tool to explore data, and dynamic charts—charts that react to user input—are even more useful.

In this recipe, we'll create a simple chart that graphs the quadratic equation, as well as lets us play with the parameters and see the results in real time.

### Getting ready

We'll use the same dependencies in our project.clj file as we did in the *Creating scatter plots with Incanter* recipe.

We'll use the following set of imports in our script or REPL:

```
(require '[incanter.core :as i]
         '[incanter.charts :as c])
```

### How to do it...

It seems like creating a dynamic chart would be difficult, but it's really not. We just define a dynamic-xy-plot with the variables and relationships that we want, and Incanter will do the rest.

```
(def d-plot
  (let [x (range -1 1 0.1)]
    (c/dynamic-xy-plot
      [a (range -1.0 1.0 0.1)
```

```
         b (range -1.0 1.0 0.1)
         c (range -1.0 1.0 0.1)]
       [x (i/plus (i/mult a x x) (i/mult b x) c)])))
(i/view d-plot)
```

This presents us with a slider for each dynamic variable. Here's the slider for *a*:

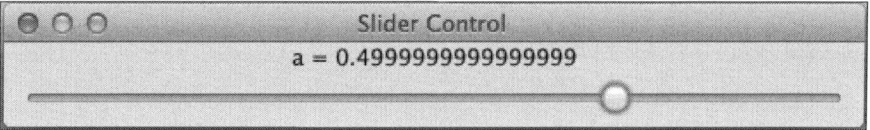

We can use these to control the values and the line in the graph. Here it is after I've played with it a little.

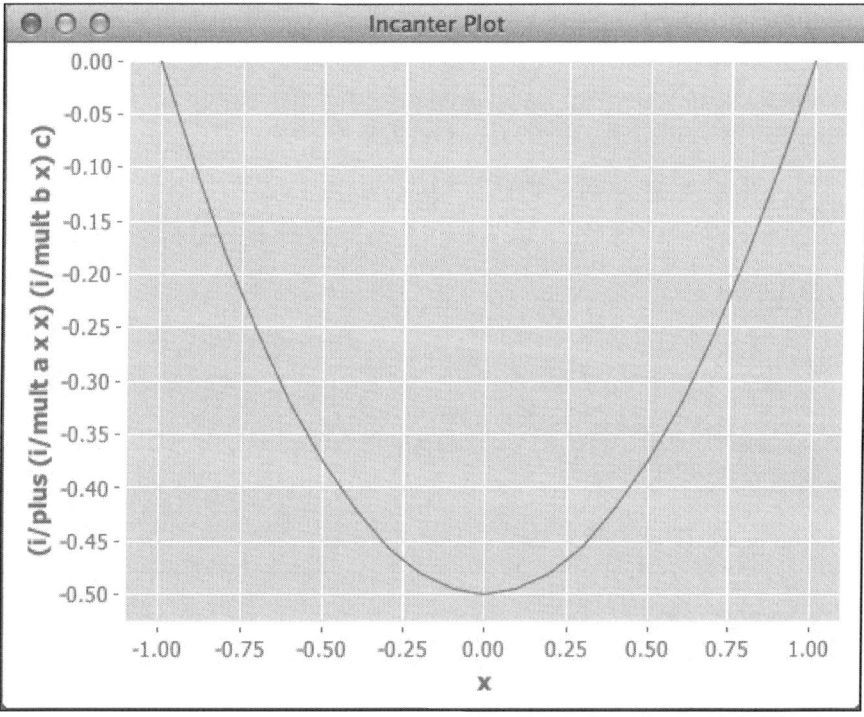

*Graphing in Incanter*

## How it works...

The magic in this recipe is in the call to `incanter.charts/dynamic-xy-plot`. This defines the domain of the chart, the range of the parameters, and the function. Let's look at a few lines from it in more detail.

```
(let [x (range -1 1 0.1)]
```

This defines the domain of the chart, that is, the extent of the x axis.

```
(c/dynamic-xy-plot
```

This is the macro call that creates the chart. The parameters passed into this define the parameters and function for the chart.

```
[a (range -1.0 1.0 0.1)
 b (range -1.0 1.0 0.1)
 c (range -1.0 1.0 0.1)]
```

The first parameter to `dynamic-xy-plot` defines the function parameters for the chart. This defines three variables that range from `-1` to `1`, incremented by `0.1`.

```
[x (i/plus (i/mult a x x) (i/mult b x) c)]))
```

This defines the function. It specifies the quadratic equation in terms of the range of the x axis, and using the current values of the parameters from the sliders. The dynamic plot charts the output of this equation and those parameters on the chart.

# 11
# Creating Charts for the Web

In this chapter, we will cover:

- Serving data with Ring and Compojure
- Creating HTML with Hiccup
- Setting up to use ClojureScript
- Creating scatter plots with NVD3
- Creating bar charts with NVD3
- Creating histograms with NVD3
- Visualizing graphs with force-directed layouts
- Creating interactive visualizations with D3

## Introduction

In the last chapter, we saw how to create graphs for publishing in print or online by creating PNGs. Of course, the Internet can do a lot more than publish static images. Much of the power of the Internet is that it's interactive. In this chapter, we'll see how to create a full web application using Clojure, including interactive graphs.

First, we'll set up a web application with Ring (https://github.com/ring-clojure/ring) and Compojure (http://compojure.org). **Ring** is an interface between web servers and web applications. **Compojure** is a small web framework that provides a convenient way to define and handle routes (the associations between URLs and functions to provide data for them).

Next, we'll see how to use **Hiccup** (https://github.com/weavejester/hiccup) to generate HTML from data structures.

We'll complete our web stack with the **ClojureScript** (https://github.com/clojure/clojurescript). This is just Clojure, but instead of compiling to the JVM, it compiles to JavaScript. We can load its output into our web pages and use it to create stunning graphs.

The rest of the chapter will involve seeing what we can create using this Clojure-dominated web stack. We'll use the **D3** (http://d3js.org/) and **NVD3** (http://nvd3.org/): JavaScript libraries to create visualizations from data. In the end, we'll wind up with some very nice graphs and a productive environment for publishing the results of our data analysis.

The stack from this chapter can be deployed easily to services such as **Heroku** (http://www.heroku.com/), which makes for a fast way to set up the server side of this system and to make our information available to the general public.

## Serving data with Ring and Compojure

While we could load compiled ClojureScript from static pages, often we'll want to combine the dynamic charts with dynamic pages. For instance, we may want to provide a search form to filter the data that's graphed.

In this recipe, we'll get started with a typical Clojure web stack. Even if we don't use ClojureScript, this system is useful for creating web applications. We'll use **Jetty** (http://jetty.codehaus.org/jetty/) to serve the requests, Ring (https://github.com/ring-clojure/ring) to connect the server to the different parts of our web application, and Compojure (http://compojure.org) to define the routes and handlers.

### Getting ready

We'll first need to include Jetty, Ring, and Compojure in our Leiningen `project.clj` file.

```
:dependencies [[org.clojure/clojure "1.4.0"]
               [ring/ring-core "1.1.7"]
               [ring/ring-jetty-adapter "1.1.7"]
               [compojure "1.1.3"]]
```

We'll also want to use Ring as a development plugin for this project, so let's include it in the `project.clj` file under the `:plugins` key.

```
:plugins [[lein-ring "0.8.3"]]
```

We'll also need to have data to serve. For this recipe, we'll serve the 2010 US census race data that we've been using throughout this book. I've converted it to JSON, though, so we can load it into D3 more easily. You can download this file from http://www.ericrochester.com/clj-data-analysis/data/census-race.json.

## How to do it...

Setting up a web application is relatively simple, but there are a number of steps. We'll create the namespace and configuration, then we'll set up the application, and finally we'll add resources.

### Configuring and setting up the web application

The code for the web application will need to be run again and again, so it won't be appropriate to use the REPL. Instead, let's create a namespace inside our Leiningen project for it. Right now, my Leiningen project is named `web-viz`, so I'll use that in this example, but you should replace it with whatever your project is named.

1. Inside of the project `src` directory, let's create a file named `web.clj`. It's full path will be `src/web_viz/web.clj`. This will contain the web application and the routes.

2. We'll use this namespace declaration at the top of `web.clj`. Note that you'll need to change the namespace to match your project.

   ```
   (ns web-viz.web
     (:require [compojure.route :as route]
               [compojure.handler :as handler]
               [clojure.string :as str])
     (:use compojure.core
           ring.adapter.jetty
           [ring.middleware.content-type :only
            (wrap-content-type)]
           [ring.middleware.file :only (wrap-file)]
           [ring.middleware.file-info :only
            (wrap-file-info)]
           [ring.middleware.stacktrace :only
            (wrap-stacktrace)]
           [ring.util.response :only (redirect)]))
   ```

3. Now that we have a namespace for it, we need to tell Ring where our web application is. In the `project.clj` file, include the following line:

   ```
   :ring {:handler web-viz.web/app}
   ```

### Serving data

For this recipe, we'll serve the JSON data file statically. By default, Ring serves static files out of the `/resources` directory of your project. In this case, create the directory `/resources/data` and put the data file that you downloaded from http://www.ericrochester.com/clj-data-analysis/data/census-race.json into it.

## Defining routes and handlers

1. Now we can connect the IBM dataset to the Internet.
2. Now, we'll define the routes using Compojure's `defroutes` macro.

   ```
   (defroutes
     site-routes
     (GET "/" [] (redirect "/data/census-race.json"))
     (route/resources "/")
     (route/not-found "Page not found"))
   ```

   This creates a `GET` request that redirects to our data file. It also defines routes to serve any static resources from the classpath—in this case to serve the resources directory—and a 404 (resource missing) page.

3. We use these routes as the basis of our web app.

   ```
   (def app
     (-> (handler/site site-routes)
       (wrap-file "resources")
       (wrap-file-info)
       (wrap-content-type)))
   ```

Along with serving the routes we defined, this function adds more functionality to our web app. We serve static files from the resources directory (`wrap-file`). We add content-type and other HTTP headers whenever we serve files (`wrap-file-info`). And we make sure to always include a content-type header, even if it's just "application/octet-stream" (`wrap-content-type`).

## Running the server

Starting the server for development is a Leiningen task handled by the Ring plugin.

```
$ lein ring server
2013-01-16 09:01:47.630:INFO:oejs.Server:jetty-7.6.1.v20120215
Started server on port 3000
2013-01-16 09:01:47.687:INFO:oejs.AbstractConnector:Started
SelectChannelConnector@0.0.0.0:3000
```

This starts the server on port 3000 and opens a web browser to the home page of the site at `http://localhost:8000/`. In this case, that just redirects to the census data, so your browser should look something like the following screenshot, unless your browser attempts to download the JSON and save it to your drive. (Your text editor should still be able to open it, however.)

```
[{"black":58,"geoid":100100,"white":129,"white_2000":null,"state":
banda
CDP","other_2000":null,"asian":0,"total_2000":null,"hu100_2000":nu
aiian":0,"asian_2000":null,"multiracial":3,"multiracial_2000":null
{"black":1113,"geoid":100124,"white":1463,"white_2000":1692,"state
me":"Abbeville
city","other_2000":85,"asian":26,"total_2000":2987,"hu100_2000":13
ian":0,"asian_2000":2,"multiracial":31,"multiracial_2000":15,"hawa
{"black":2030,"geoid":100460,"white":2366,"white_2000":3763,"state
me":"Adamsville
city","other_2000":8,"asian":14,"total_2000":4965,"hu100_2000":204
ian":1,"asian_2000":7,"multiracial":38,"multiracial_2000":33,"hawa
{"black":1,"geoid":100484,"white":751,"white_2000":719,"state":1,"
ison
town","other_2000":0,"asian":1,"total_2000":723,"hu100_2000":339,"
,"asian_2000":1,"multiracial":5,"multiracial_2000":1,"hawaiian_200
```

## How it works...

The first part of this system, and the foundation of it, is Ring. Ring is an abstraction over HTTP. It makes it easier to write web applications that will work in a variety of settings and run under a variety of servers. You can write the web application to work with the Ring specification, and you can connect Ring to the web server using an adapter. There are a number of central concepts in Ring.

- **Handlers** are the core of the web application. Handlers are Clojure functions that take a map with information about the request and return a map with the response. Each web application has one handler function.

- **Middleware** transforms incoming requests or outgoing responses. Generally middleware wraps an existing handler to provide extra functionality. For instance, authentication can be handled through middleware. The project *Friend* (https://github.com/cemerick/friend) does this. Middleware can also handle requests for static resources, cookies, and many other things.

- **Adapters** connect Ring to web servers. Ring has an adapter for the Jetty web server, and that's what we use in this recipe.

*Creating Charts for the Web*

Ring's good for connecting a web application to a web server, but it's a little too close to the metal. You wouldn't want to write your web application to talk to Ring directly. Compojure (https://github.com/weavejester/compojure/wiki) steps into the gap. It provides a simple DSL for defining routes and response functions and composing them into a single Ring application handler function. It allows you to define which type of HTTP request each route function can accept (GET, POST, and so on.) and what parameters each expects.

Here's how the earlier example breaks down into the components we just discussed:

- `site-routes` is the composed Compojure route, which act as the Ring handler
- `app` composes the Ring handler function with some middleware

In our `project.clj` file, we define connect Ring to our handler function with the following line:

```
:ring {:handler web-viz.web/app}
```

## There's more...

- The Ring wiki at https://github.com/ring-clojure/ring/wiki has a lot of useful information for getting started and working with Ring.
- Ring's API documentation at http://ring-clojure.github.com/ring/ is also very helpful. However, if you want to get the complete information, you should look at the Ring specification at https://github.com/ring-clojure/ring/blob/master/SPEC. It's really quite readable.
- The Compojure wiki at https://github.com/weavejester/compojure/wiki has information on many aspects of using Compojure.
- The Compojure API documentation available at http://weavejester.github.com/compojure/ is also helpful.

# Creating HTML with Hiccup

For the last recipe, we set up a server and returned some data. However, most people want to view HTML, not JSON. In this recipe, we'll look at Hiccup (https://github.com/weavejester/hiccup). This is a library that allows us to build web pages from Clojure expressions and data structures. It takes vectors, maps, keywords, and strings—or functions that return those—and turns them into HTML. This makes a good solution for generating HTML from within Clojure web applications.

This recipe will build on the *Serving data with Ring and Compojure* recipe. I'll point out where we need to change or add things from that recipe, highlighting them as necessary. By the end of this recipe, we'll be serving a simple index page along with the census dataset.

*Chapter 11*

## Getting ready

First, we'll use the same dependencies in our `project.clj` file as we did in the last recipe, plus one more. Here's the full list:

```
:dependencies [[org.clojure/clojure "1.5.0-RC1"]
               [ring/ring-core "1.1.7"]
               [ring/ring-jetty-adapter "1.1.7"]
               [compojure "1.1.3"]
               [hiccup "1.0.2"]]
```

We'll also add Hiccup to the namespace declaration as follows:

```
(ns web-viz.tmp-web
  (:require [compojure.route :as route]
            [compojure.handler :as handler]
            [clojure.string :as str])
  (:use compojure.core
        ring.adapter.jetty
        [ring.middleware.content-type :only (wrap-content-type)]
        [ring.middleware.file :only (wrap-file)]
        [ring.middleware.file-info :only (wrap-file-info)]
        [ring.middleware.stacktrace :only (wrap-stacktrace)]
        [ring.util.response :only (redirect)]
        [hiccup core element page]
        [hiccup.middleware :only (wrap-base-url)]))
```

## How to do it...

In Hiccup, HTML is represented as vectors with keyword tag names and attribute maps.

1. We'll define a function that builds a simple web page with a link to the data set.

   ```
   (defn index-page []
     (html5
       [:head
        [:title "Web Charts"]]
       [:body
        [:h1 {:id "web-charts"} "Web Charts"]
        [:ol
         [:li [:a {:href "/data/census-race.json"}
               "2010 Census Race Data"]]]]))
   ```

2. Now, instead of having the root URL redirect, we'll have it serve that function.

   ```
   (defroutes
     site-routes
     (GET "/" [] (index-page))
     (route/resources "/")
     (route/not-found "Page not found"))
   ```

3. Now, when we run the server and visit the home page at `http://localhost:3000/`, we'll get something much different.

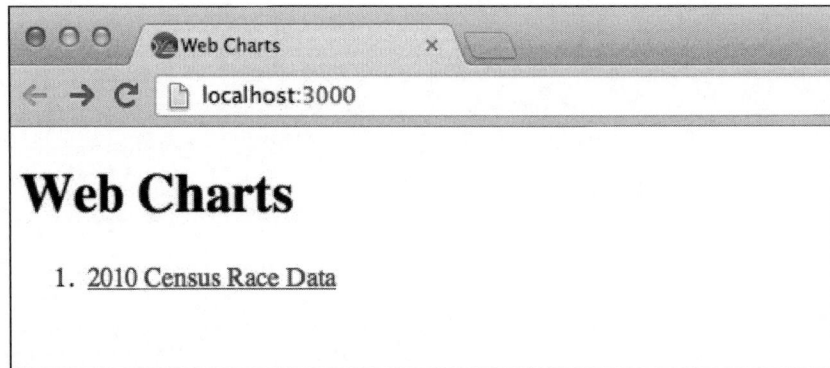

## How it works...

The Hiccup DSL is quite simple, and we can see examples of almost all of its syntax in this recipe.

1. We have an HTML tag with some text content.

   ```
   [:title "Web Charts"]
   ```

2. We have nested elements.

   ```
   [:head
     [:title "Web Charts"]]
   ```

3. We can include attributes as a hash map after the tag-name keyword.

   ```
   [:h1 {:id "web-charts"} "Web Charts"]
   ```

4. Whatever the structure is, we eventually pass it to one of the rendering functions. In this case, we're displaying it as HTML5, so we use that builder function.

   ```
   (html5
   ```

Hiccup also has a number of functions for inserting links to CSS files and script elements. We'll see examples of these in the *Creating scatter plots with NVD3* recipe.

## There's more...

- The Hiccup site and wiki at `https://github.com/weavejester/hiccup` are a good starting point for using Hiccup
- For actually writing HTML pages using Hiccup, the page on its syntax at `https://github.com/weavejester/hiccup/wiki/Syntax` will be particularly useful

# Setting up to use ClojureScript

The only thing that's missing is JavaScript. We can generate that also with ClojureScript (https://github.com/clojure/clojurescript). This is an implementation of Clojure that compiles to JavaScript.

Why would we want to write JavaScript in Clojure? First, it simplifies our project when both the client and the server are written in the same language. It also allows us to share code between the two sides of our application, which can cut down on the complexity of our code, as well as the lines of the code.

For the rest of this chapter, we'll be creating charts and graphs using ClojureScript. These recipes will show us how to install it and get it working. We'll take the web application we started in the *Serving data with Ring and Compojure* recipe and the *Creating HTML with Hiccup* recipe and add an alert to the index page. This isn't anything more than a *hello world* application, but it will prove that ClojureScript is working in our application.

## Getting ready

To add ClojureScript to our project, we'll add the `lein-cljsbuild` plugin to our Leiningen `project.clj` file. Now, our `:plugins` should look like this:

```
:plugins [[lein-ring "0.7.5"]
          [lein-cljsbuild "0.2.10"]]
```

## How to do it...

To set up ClojureScript, most of what we need to do is configuration. We have to tell the ClojureScript compiler where to find the input and where to put the output. We'll go into detail on this in a minute.

1. First, we'll just add this key-value pair to our `project.clj` file.

    ```
    :cljsbuild {:crossovers [web-viz.x-over],
                :builds
                [{:source-paths ["src-cljs"],
                  :crossover-path "xover-cljs",
                  :compiler
                  {:pretty-print true,
                   :output-to "resources/js/script.js",
                   :optimizations :whitespace}}]}
    ```

2. Now, let's go to the command prompt and create the directories we'll use.

    ```
    $ mkdir -p src-cljs/webviz
    $ mkdir -p resources/js
    ```

## Creating Charts for the Web

3. Create the file `src-cljs/webviz/core.cljs`. This is going to look a lot like a regular Clojure file.

   ```
   (ns webviz.core)
   (defn ^:export hello [world]
     (js/alert (str "Hello, " world)))
   ```

4. From the command line, enter this command. It will start the ClojureScript compiler watching all the ClojureScript files and automatically compiling them whenever we save one.

   ```
   $ lein cljsbuild auto
   Compiling ClojureScript.
   Compiling "resources/js/scripts.js" from "src-cljs"...
   Successfully compiled "resources/js/script.js" in 4.707129 seconds.
   ```

5. Next, we'll add our compiled ClojureScript file to our Hiccup template. Let's open `src/web_viz/web.clj` again and change the `index-page` function to look like this:

   ```
   (defn index-page []
     (html5
       [:head
        [:title "Web Charts"]]
       [:body
        [:h1 {:id "web-charts"} "Web Charts"]
        [:ol
         [:li [:a {:href "/data/census-race.json"}
               "2010 Census Race Data"]]]
        (include-js "js/script.js")
        (javascript-tag
          "webviz.core.hello('from ClojureScript!');")]))
   ```

Now, when we start the Ring server and look at the main page, we should see something like the following screenshot:

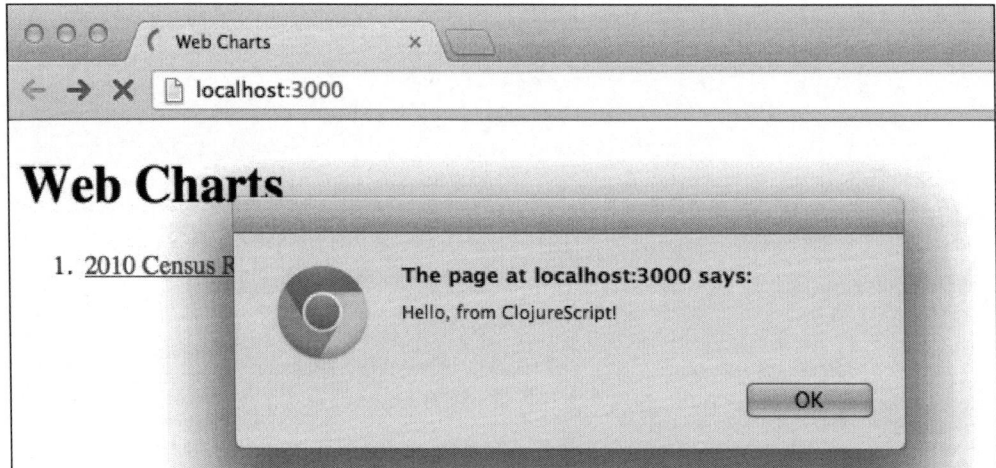

## How it works...

A lot happened in this recipe, and there's a lot that we need to talk about.

First, ClojureScript. If we open up the generated file, `resources/js/script.js`, we'll see a lot that's not our code. Why is so much else in there?

The explanation is pretty simple. ClojureScript doesn't just target JavaScript as a compilation platform. It targets `Google-Closure-compiler-advanced-mode` JavaScript. Because of this, it includes much of the Google Closure libraries, so we have those immediately available, and we'll use them in the coming recipes. Also, we can run our output through the Closure compilers by changing the `:optimizations` parameter in the `:cljsbuild` options, and it will shake out the parts of the code that we don't use. This includes not only our code, but also the parts of the Clojure libraries and the Google Closure libraries we don't use. In the end, this is a huge win. Unfortunately, not all libraries can be used with the Closure compiler's advanced mode: D3, for example, requires a file listing all the functions it exports. The *d3-externs* project (https://github.com/shripadk/d3-externs) is one attempt to provide this interface file for the Closure compiler.

Notice too that the `hello` function is annotated with `^:export` metadata. This signals the ClojureScript compiler that it needs to make that function available to the outside world. This is a nice, lightweight way of enforcing scoping according to JavaScript best practices.

Also, inside the `hello` function, the `alert` function is called from the `js` namespace (`js/alert`). This represents the global JavaScript context. Whenever we call a JavaScript object from the global context (when working in the browser, `window`), we have to prefix it with the `js` namespace in ClojureScript.

Next, we should look at the `:cljsbuild` configuration in the `project.clj` file. It has three main pieces of information. First, it defines which namespaces from your Clojure files will contain crossover code. This is the code that's available to both Clojure and ClojureScript.

This configuration section also defines the build information. In this case, we tell it to copy the crossover namespaces into `xover-cljs/` and to compile everything in that directory and `src-cljs/` to `js/script.js`.

Finally, I should make a note here too about workflow. If you're keeping count, you probably have at least three terminal or console windows open. One for the Ring server, one for the ClojureScript compiler, and one or more for the REPL or shell to work in. That's what I have going right now. If you can use a terminal multiplexer such as tmux (http://tmux.sourceforge.net/) or screen (http://www.gnu.org/software/screen/) this can simplify things. You can set the Ring server and ClojureScript compiler running in a background window and just check them for errors periodically.

## There's more...

- ClojureScript ships with the Google Closure library. It's a fully featured library and it's there, so you might as well use it. You can learn more about it at `https://developers.google.com/closure/`.

- For more information about the configuration options available, visit `https://github.com/emezeske/lein-cljsbuild/blob/master/sample.project.clj`.

- The home page for screen is (`http://www.gnu.org/software/screen/`). The best tutorial I've found for it is at `http://www.kuro5hin.org/story/2004/3/9/16838/14935`.

- If you're interested in using tmux, the best tutorial I've found is `http://blog.hawkhost.com/2010/06/28/tmux-the-terminal-multiplexer/`. Another good tutorial is at `http://lukaszwrobel.pl/blog/tmux-tutorial-split-terminal-windows-easily`.

# Creating scatter plots with NVD3

If you've been following along with the previous recipes in this chapter, you'll now have a complete web application stack ready, and we can use it to create charts and graphs for the Web.

For this recipe, we'll create a scatter plot of the US census Race Data that we saw in the *Grouping Data with $group-by* recipe in *Chapter 6, Working with Incanter Datasets*. In fact, this will be the same as we saw in the *Creating scatter plots with Incanter* recipe in *Chapter 10, Graphing in Incanter*, only this time we'll be creating a web page.

To do this, we'll use the D3 JavaScript library (`http://d3js.org/`). **D3** stands for **Data-Driven Documents**, and this library makes it easy to load data and create HTML and SVG structures from data. You can use it to transform data into tables or charts. It is pretty low-level, though. With D3, we'd be creating many of the actual elements. We'll do this in a later recipe, but for now we'll use the NVD3 library (`http://nvd3.org/`), which is a collection of pre-built charts. We can set a few parameters, pass them our data, and immediately get a great looking chart back out.

Another option for visualizing data on the web that's gaining traction is Kevin Lynagh's C2 project (`http://keminglabs.com/c2/`). This is similar to D3, except it's in ClojureScript. It uses a more declarative approach to building data-centric documents, and it works by transforming Clojure data structures into HTML and SVG elements and document structures, just like in Hiccup (see the *Creating HTML with Hiccup* recipe).

## Getting ready

We'll again build on the previous recipes in this chapter, so make sure you have the environment and web application described in the *Setting up to use ClojureScript* recipe running.

We can use the same namespace declaration that we did in the *Creating HTML with Hiccup* recipe.

I've transformed the CSV data into JSON, so we can serve it statically. You can download this from `http://www.ericrochester.com/clj-data-analysis/data/census-race.json` and put it into the `resources/data/` directory in your project.

## How to do it...

There are a number of steps to adding a resource to a web application given as follows:

1. Before we get started, we need to download the NVD3 stylesheet from `https://raw.github.com/novus/nvd3/master/src/nv.d3.css` and save it into `resources/css`.

2. Now, let's add a Hiccup template function to the file `src/web_viz/web.clj`. We can pass it a title and some content, and it will fill in the rest of the page around it.

```
(defn d3-page
  [title js body & {:keys [extra-js] :or {extra-js []}}]
  (html5
    [:head
     [:title title]
     (include-css "/css/nv.d3.css")
     (include-css "/css/style.css")]
    [:body
     (concat
       [body]
       [(include-js "http://d3js.org/d3.v3.min.js")
        (include-js (str "https://raw.github.com"
                         "/novus/nvd3"
                         "/master/nv.d3.min.js"))]
       (map include-js extra-js)
       [(include-js "/js/script.js")
        (javascript-tag js)])]))
```

3. Let's also add some ClojureScript infrastructure. This function will abstract out the boilerplate of creating NVD3 and D3 charts.

   ```
   ;;; A group of values. Each group has a key/label and
   ;;; a JS array of point values.
   (deftype Group [key values])
   ;;; A point. Each point has a location (x, y) and a
   ;;; size.
   (deftype Point [x y size])
   ```

4. We'll also define some functions to help build the chart.

   ```
   ;;; This sets an axis' label if not nil.
   (defn add-label
     [chart axis label]
     (if-not (nil? label)
       (.axisLabel (aget chart axis) label)))
   ;;; Add axes' labels to the chart.
   (defn add-axes-labels [chart x-label y-label]
     (doto chart
       (add-label "xAxis" x-label)
       (add-label "yAxis" y-label)))
   ;;; This builds the chart from the selector.
   (defn populate-node
     [selector chart groups transition continuation]
     (-> (.select js/d3 selector)
       (.datum groups)
       (.transition)
       (.duration (if transition 500 0))
       (.call chart)
       (.call continuation)))
   ```

5. We'll also create some data structures for representing points and groups of points. This is how NVD3 wants the input data represented. Let's open `src-cljs/webviz/core.cljs` and add this to the file.

   ```
   ;;; Create a chart with the data's URL, a selector,
   ;;; and functions to create the chart and transform
   ;;; the data.
   (defn create-chart
     [data-url selector make-chart json->groups &
       {:keys [transition continuation x-label y-label]
        :or {transition false, continuation (fn [_]),
             x-label nil, y-label nil}}]
     (.json
       js/d3 data-url
       (fn [error data]
   ```

```
            (when data            (.addGraph
                js/nv
                (fn []
                   (let [chart (make-chart)]
                      (add-axes-labels chart x-label y-label)
                      (populate-node selector chart
                                     (json->groups data)
                                     transition continuation)
                      (.windowResize js/nv.utils
                                     #(.update chart)))))))))
```

With those bits of infrastructure, we can create the plot.

1. We'll define a handler for the page itself, in the `src/web_viz/web.clj` file, using the `d3-page` function. This will embed the JavaScript to create the chart and create an SVG element to contain it.

   ```
   (defn scatter-charts []
     (d3-page "Scatter Chart"
              "webviz.scatter.scatter_plot();"
              [:div#scatter.chart [:svg]]))
   ```

2. Next we'll define the routes for it. You can add the highlighted routes to the current set.

   ```
   (defroutes
     site-routes
     (GET "/scatter" [] (scatter-charts))
     (GET "/scatter/data.json" []
       (redirect "/data/census-race.json"))
     (route/resources "/")
     (route/not-found "Page not found"))
   ```

3. Let's add a little style for the chart. Create `resources/css/style.css` and add the following:

   ```
   div.chart {
       height: 450px;
       width: 650px;
   }
   body {
       font-family: Helvetica, Arial, sans-serif;
       font-size: smaller;
   }
   ```

4. Now, let's create a new file named `src-cljs/webviz/scatter.cljs`. The namespace declaration for it is as follows:

   ```
   (ns webviz.scatter
     (:require [webviz.core :as webviz]))
   ```

*Creating Charts for the Web*

5. We'll need to summarize the data to get the totals for white and African-American populations by state. These functions will take care of that.

```clojure
;;; This maps the values in a collection across a
;;; function and sums the results.
(defn sum-by [key-fn coll]
  (reduce + 0 (map key-fn coll)))
;;; This takes a function and a map associating a
;;; label with a sequence of values. It replaces those
;;; values with their sums after passing them through
;;; the function.
(defn sum-values [key-fn coll]
  (reduce
    (fn [m [k vs]] (assoc m k (sum-by key-fn vs)))
    {}
    coll))
;;; This generates by-state sums for different groups.
(defn sum-data-fields [json]
  (let [by-state (group-by #(.-state_name %) json)
        white-by-state
          (sum-values #(.-white %) by-state)
        afam-by-state
          (sum-values #(.-black %) by-state)
        total-by-state
          (sum-values #(.-total %) by-state)]
    (map #(hash-map :state %
                    :white (white-by-state %)
                    :black (afam-by-state %)
                    :total (total-by-state %))
         (keys by-state))))
```

6. NVD3 expects the data to be in points and groups. We'll use the types we defined in `webviz.core`. These functions will convert the summarized data into the objects that NVD3 expects.

```clojure
(defn ->nv [item]
  (let [{:keys [white black]} item]
    (webviz/Point. (/ white 1000) (/ black 1000) 1)))
(defn ->nv-data [key-name data]
  (->> data
    sum-data-fields
    (map ->nv)
    (apply array)
    (webviz/Group. key-name)
    (array)))
```

7. This function will actually create the chart and set the options and formatting for it.

```clojure
(defn make-chart []
  (let [c (-> (.scatterChart js/nv.models)
              (.showDistX true)
```

```
                    (.showDistY true)
                    (.useVoronoi false)
                    (.color (.. js/d3 -scale category10 range)))]
        (.tickFormat (.-xAxis c) (.format js/d3 "d"))
        (.tickFormat (.-yAxis c) (.format js/d3 "d"))
        c))
```

8. Actually pulling all of this together is pretty simple.

```
(defn ^:export scatter-plot []
  (webviz/create-chart
    "/scatter/data.json"
    "#scatter svg"
    make-chart
    (partial ->nv-data "Racial Data")
    :x-label "Population, whites, by thousands"
    :y-label (str "Population, African-Americans, "
                  "by thousands")
    :transition true))
```

When we visit `http://localhost:3000/scatter` now, we get a nice-looking chart as follows:

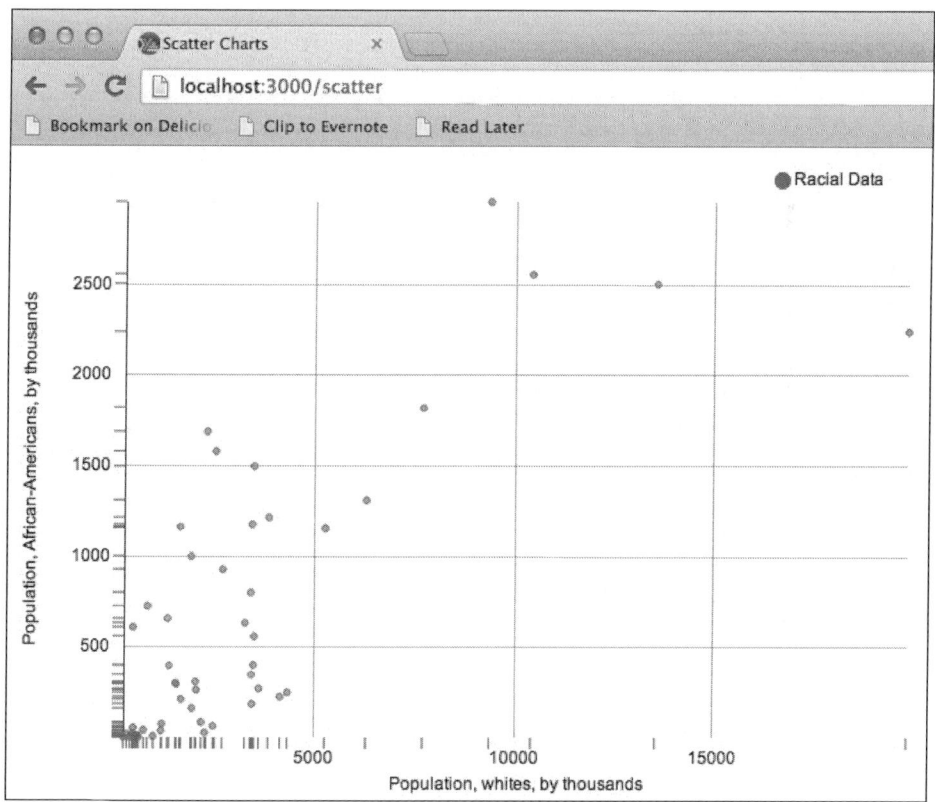

## How it works...

NVD3 expects the data to be in a specific format. We create an `adapter` function for the data and a function to create and configure the specific plot we want. With those, we call `webviz/create-chart` to actually populate the HTML elements and display the chart.

The function `create-chart` takes a URL to load the data, the path to select the element to create the chart in, a function to create the chart, and a function to convert the data into points and groups. The function `create-chart` uses those parameters to request the data, create the chart, and associate the data with it. These steps are common to any chart built with NVD3, so abstracting them out will save us in the long run.

## There's more...

- The page for D3 is at `http://d3js.org/`. The gallery there is a good place to start looking, to get inspiration, and to learn what the library is capable of.
- The page for NVD3 is at `http://nvd3.org/`.
- An alternative to D3 and NVD3 is Kevin Lynagh's C2 (`http://keminglabs.com/c2/`). This allows a more declarative approach to creating HTML and SVG structures, to using Hiccup-style data structures in the browser.

# Creating bar charts with NVD3

Bar charts are good for comparing the sums or counts of categories of data in a dataset. For example, in this recipe, we'll create a chart comparing the weight of chicks being fed one of four diets.

Like most of the recipes in this chapter, this one builds on the previous ones. It will take the foundation from the *Setting up to use ClojureScript* recipe, along with the infrastructure added in the *Creating scatter plots with NVD3* recipe, and build the bar chart on it.

Let's get started.

## Getting ready

We'll use the same dependencies and plugins in our `project.clj` file as we did in the *Creating scatter plots with NVD3* recipe. We'll also use the `sum-by` function from that recipe.

We'll also use the chick weight dataset that we've seen before. I've transformed it into JSON, and you can download it from `http://www.ericrochester.com/clj-data-analysis/data/chick-weight.json`. Save it into the `resources/data/` directory of your project.

## How to do it...

We'll follow the same workflow as we did in the last recipe: write a handler, add a route, and write the client-side ClojureScript.

1. The handler will return a D3 page, complete with code to create DIV and SVG elements, and to call the ClojureScript function we'll define in a minute.

   ```
   (defn bar-chart []
     (d3-page "Bar Chart"
              "webviz.barchart.bar_chart();"
              [:div#barchart.chart [:svg]]))
   ```

2. Next, we'll add the routes for this chart.

   ```
   (defroutes
     site-routes
     (GET "/barchart" [] (bar-chart))
     (GET "/barchart/data.json" []
          (redirect "/data/chick-weight.json"))
     (route/resources "/")
     (route/not-found "Page not found"))
   ```

3. Now we'll create the ClojureScript. Create a file `src-cljs/webviz/barchart.cljs` and add the following namespace declaration:

   ```
   (ns webviz.barchart
     (:require [webviz.core :as webviz]))
   ```

4. We'll convert the data into two categories of the Group and Point data structures that NVD3 expects. For the first category, `get-diet-counts` expects a hash table associating a diet code with the items from the dataset that have that diet code. The *y* value for the point is the count of those items.

   ```
   (defn count-point [pair]
     (let [[diet items] pair]
       (webviz/Point. diet (count items) 1)))
   (defn get-diet-counts [diet-groups]
     (apply array (map count-point diet-groups)))
   ```

5. We'll now add a pair of functions for the other category. The *y* value for these points will be the sum of the weights.

   ```
   (defn weight-point [pair]
     (let [[diet items] pair
           weight-total (sum-by #(.-weight %) items)]
       (webviz/Point. diet weight-total 1)))
   (defn get-diet-weights [diet-groups]
     (apply array (map weight-point diet-groups)))
   ```

## Creating Charts for the Web

6. Here's the function that will transform the JSON input into JavaScript objects for NVD3.

   ```
   (defn json->nv-groups [json]
     (let [diet-groups (group-by #(.-diet %) json)]
       (array (webviz/Group.
                "Chick Counts"
                (get-diet-counts diet-groups))
              (webviz/Group.
                "Chick Weights"
                (get-diet-weights diet-groups)))))
   ```

7. Finally, here's the function that ties it all together and creates the chart (with the help of `create-chart`).

   ```
   (defn ^:export bar-chart []
     (webviz/create-chart "/barchart/data.json"
                          "#barchart svg"
                          #(.multiBarChart js/nv.models)
                          json->nv-groups))
   ```

When we visit `http://localhost:3000/barchart`, here's what we get:

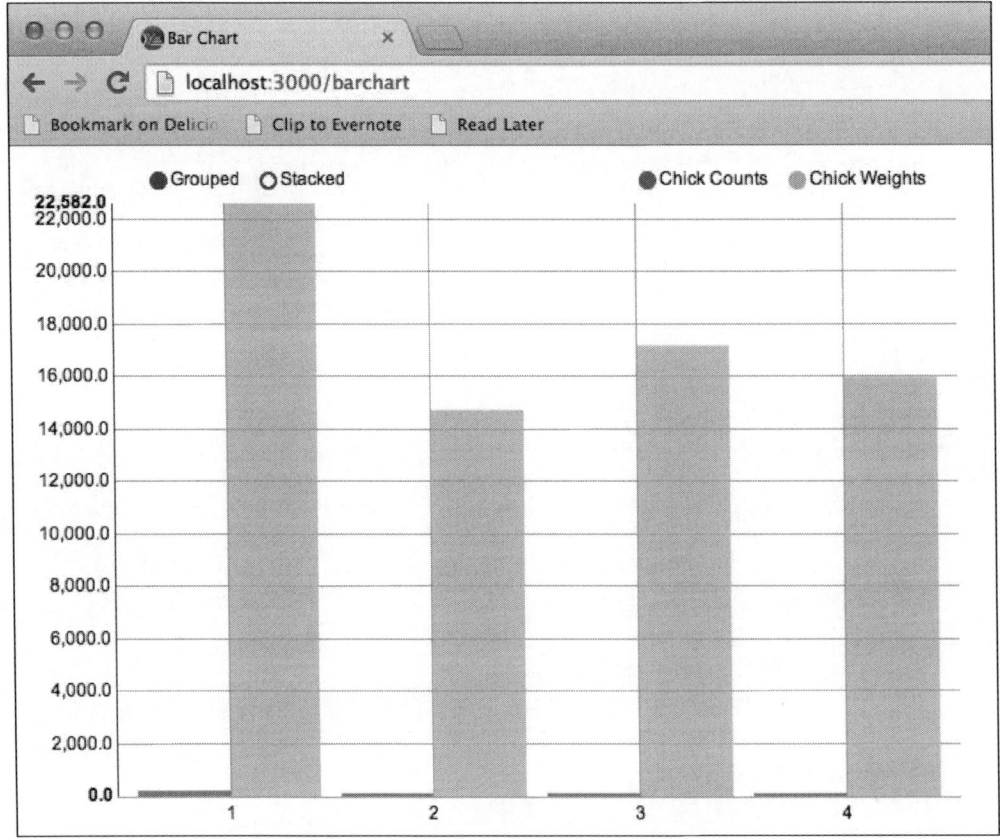

## How it works...

At this point, we see some payoff for all of the work and code we put into the *Creating scatter plot with NVD3* recipe. Because we could leverage the `create-chart` function, we avoided a lot of the boilerplate involved in creating graphs.

However, setting up a web resource like this still involves a number of standard steps:

1. Define the resource on the server (bar-chart).
2. Define the routes to access that resource.
3. Create the ClojureScript file.
4. In ClojureScript, write functions to transform the data.
5. In ClojureScript, create the chart.

# Creating histograms with NVD3

To show the distribution of our data, generally we'll use a histogram. In this recipe, we'll use one to display the distribution of lengths in the abalone dataset.

## Getting ready

We'll use the same dependencies and plugins in our `project.clj` file as we did in the *Creating scatter plots with NVD3* recipe. We'll also use the framework we've created in the recipes in this chapter up to the *Creating scatter plots with NVD3* recipe.

For the data, we'll use the abalone dataset from the *Creating histograms with Incanter* recipe in *Chapter 10*, *Graphing in Incanter*. I've transformed the data to JSON, and you can download it from `http://www.ericrochester.com/clj-data-analysis/data/abalone.json`. Save it to the `resources/data/` directory in your web application.

## How to do it...

We'll create the handler and the routes, and then we'll spend most of this recipe adding the ClojureScript to create the graph.

1. For the handler, we'll pass the options for this chart to the `d3-page` function.

    ```
    (defn hist-plot []
      (d3-page "Histogram"
               "webviz.histogram.histogram();"
               [:div#histogram.chart [:svg]]))
    ```

Creating Charts for the Web

2. And we'll add that and the data URL to the routes.

   ```
   (defroutes
     site-routes
     (GET "/histogram" [] (hist-plot))
     (GET "/histogram/data.json" []
          (redirect "/data/abalone.json"))
     (route/resources "/")
     (route/not-found "Page not found"))
   ```

3. Now for the ClojureScript file, we'll open `src-cljs/webviz/histogram.cljs` and add the following namespace declaration:

   ```
   (ns webviz.histogram
     (:require [webviz.core :as webviz]))
   ```

4. We'll need a function to group the data into buckets.

   ```
   (defn get-bucket-number [mn size x]
     (Math/round (/ (- x mn) size)))
   (defn inc-bucket [mn size buckets x]
     (let [b (get-bucket-number mn size x)]
       (assoc buckets b (inc (buckets b)))))
   (defn get-buckets [coll n]
     (let [mn (reduce min coll)
           mx (reduce max coll)
           bucket-size (/ (- mx mn) n)
           first-center (+ mn (/ bucket-size 2.0))
           centers (map #(* (inc %) first-center)
                        (range n))
           initial (reduce #(assoc %1 %2 0) {}
                           (range n))]
       (->> coll
            (reduce (partial inc-bucket mn bucket-size)
                    initial)
            seq
            (sort-by first)
            (map second)
            (map vector centers))))
   ```

5. Here are two functions to take the JSON, put it into buckets, and convert it to points and groups:

   ```
   (defn ->point [pair]
     (let [[bucket count] pair]
       (webviz/Point. (inc bucket) count 1)))
   (defn data->nv-groups [data]
     (let [lengths (map #(.-length %) data)
           buckets (apply array
                          (map ->point
   ```

```
                           (get-buckets
                              lengths 10)))]
     (array (webviz/Group. "Abalone Lengths" buckets))))
```

6. Initializing the chart is simple. We just want a standard multi-bar chart.

   ```
   (defn make-chart [] (.multiBarChart (.-models js/nv)))
   ```

7. Creating the chart just involves tying these together with `create-chart`.

   ```
   (defn ^:export histogram []
     (webviz/create-chart
       "/histogram/data.json"
       "#histogram svg"
       make-chart
       data->nv-groups
       :transition true))
   ```

Now, when we visit `http://localhost:3000/histogram`, we can see our histogram:

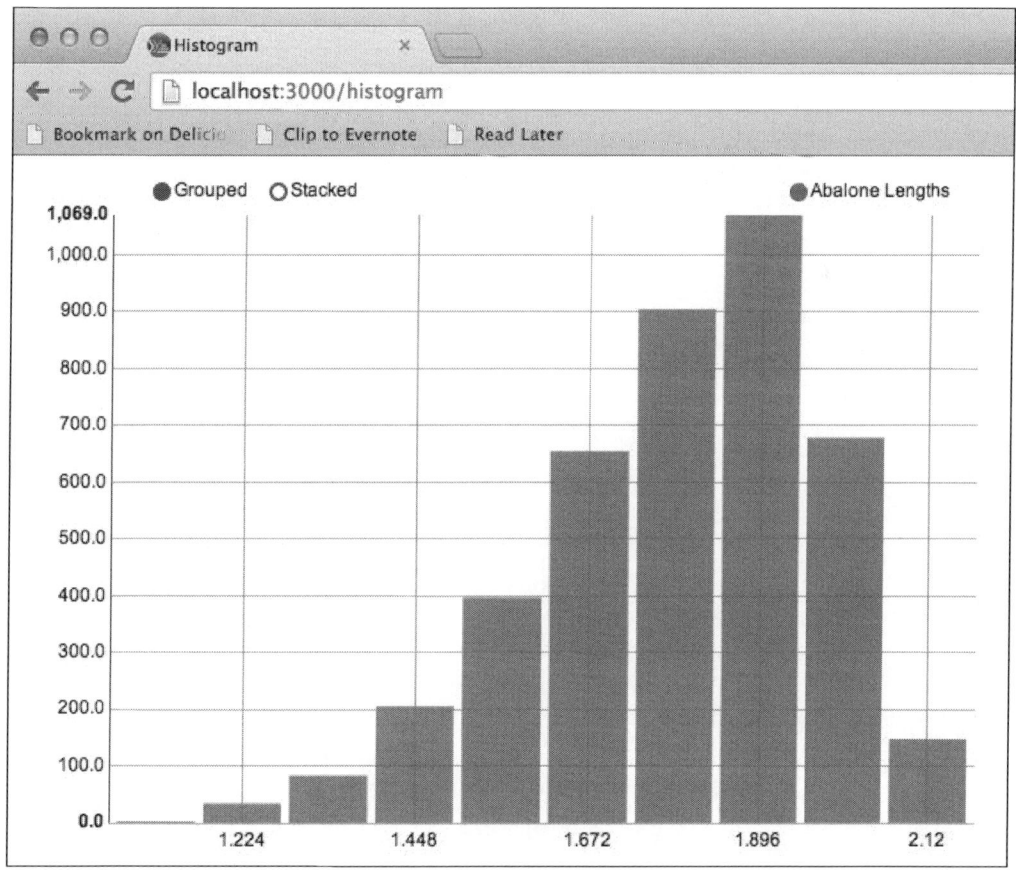

## How it works...

For the most part, this recipe is very similar to the preceding ones. The interesting difference involves partitioning the data into buckets.

To do this, we get the minimum and maximum values in the bucket and divide the difference between them by the number of buckets. This gives us the width of each bucket in the data. We use this to determine which bucket each data point goes into, and we count those.

We also get the center value for each bucket, and we use this to label the columns in the graph.

# Visualizing graphs with force-directed layouts

One popular way of visualizing graphs of data is to use a force-directed layout. This employs a physical simulation of charged particles and springs to create an aesthetically pleasing visualization. It minimizes crossed lines, while keeping all edges more or less the same length. This makes the relationships in the graph immediately clear, at the expense of expressing the distances between nodes. For example, consider the following diagram. On the left, we have a graph randomly laid out. On the right, it's laid out using a force-directed layout. Each of the edges is approximately as long as the others, and each node is as far away from its neighbors as it can get.

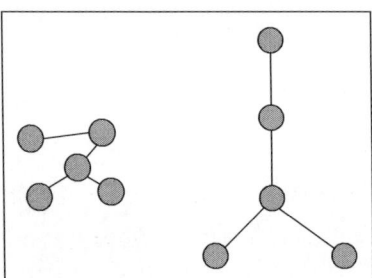

In this recipe, we'll create a force-directed graph visualization for a K-means cluster of the US Census Race Data, aggregated by state.

## Getting ready

We'll use the same dependencies and plugins in our `project.clj` file as we did in the *Creating scatter plots with NVD3* recipe.

As I just mentioned, we'll use a graph of clusters of US Census Race Data by state. I've already compiled this, and you can download it from `http://www.ericrochester.com/clj-data-analysis/data/clusters.json`. Place it into the `resources/data/` directory of your project, and you should be ready.

## How to do it...

This recipe will follow the same pattern we've seen in the last few recipes. We'll define a handler, routes, and then the ClojureScript.

1. The handler is similar to what we've seen so far, and it uses the d3-page function also.

   ```
   (defn force-layout-plot []
     (d3-page "Force-Directed Layout"
              "webviz.force.force_layout();"
              [:div#force.chart [:svg]]))
   ```

2. The routes are also as we'd expect.

   ```
   (defroutes
     site-routes
     (GET "/force" [] (force-layout-plot))
     (GET "/force/data.json" []
          (redirect "/data/clusters.json"))
     (route/resources "/")
     (route/not-found "Page not found"))
   ```

3. We'll also need some style. Open `resources/css/style.css` and add these lines:

   ```
   #force { width: 650px; height: 500px; }
   #force .node { stroke: #fff; stroke-width: 1.5px; }
   #force .link { stroke: #999; stroke-opacity: 1; }
   ```

4. Now, let's create the ClojureScript file. Open `src-cljs/webviz/force.cljs` and add the following for the namespace declaration.

   ```
   (ns webviz.force)
   ```

5. First, we'll create the force diagram.

    ```
    (defn create-force [width height]
      (-> js/d3 .-layout
        (.force)
        (.charge -120)
        (.linkDistance 30)
        (.size (array width height))))
    ```

6. Now, we'll create the SVG element to contain it.

    ```
    (defn create-svg [width height]
      (-> js/d3
        (.select "#force svg")
        (.attr "width" width)
        (.attr "height" height)))
    ```

7. With the force diagram, we need to set the nodes and edges and start the animation.

    ```
    (defn start-force [force graph]
      (-> force
        (.nodes (aget graph "nodes"))
        (.links (aget graph "links"))
        .start))
    ```

8. We also need to create the lines for the edges and the circles for the nodes.

    ```
    (defn create-links [svg graph]
      (-> svg
        (.selectAll "line.link")
        (.data (aget graph "links"))
        (.enter)
        (.append "line")
        (.attr "class" "link")
        (.style "stroke-width"
                #(.sqrt js/Math (inc (aget % "value"))))))
    (defn create-nodes [svg force color graph]
      (-> svg
        (.selectAll "circle.node")
        (.data (aget graph "nodes"))
        (.enter)
        (.append "circle")
        (.attr "class" "node")
        (.attr "r" 5)
        (.attr "data-n" #(aget % "n"))
        (.style "fill" #(color (aget % "group")))
        (.call (aget force "drag"))))
    ```

9. The `tick` handler transfers the animation from the force chart's objects to the SVG elements displaying them.

```clojure
(defn on-tick-handler [link node]
  (fn []
    (-> link
      (.attr "x1" #(-> % .-source .-x))
      (.attr "y1" #(-> % .-source .-y))
      (.attr "x2" #(-> % .-target .-x))
      (.attr "y2" #(-> % .-target .-y)))
    (-> node
      (.attr "cx" #(aget % "x"))
      (.attr "cy" #(aget % "y")))))
```

10. We'll add a `title` element to the nodes for a tooltip.

```clojure
(defn set-title [node]
  (-> node
    (.append "title")
    (.text #(aget % "name"))))
```

11. Now, we use all of these to render the graph. We'll also save the input graph that we are visualizing. We'll query this to make the visualization interactive in the next recipe, *Creating interactive visualizations with D3*. If you don't care about that, you can remove the call to `swap!`.

```clojure
(def census-graph (atom nil))
(defn render-graph [color force svg graph]
  (swap! census-graph (fn [] graph))
  (start-force force graph)
  (let [link (create-links svg graph)
        node (create-nodes svg force color graph)]
    (set-title node)
    (.on force "tick" (on-tick-handler link node))))
```

12. Here's the function that we'll export. It makes the AJAX call to download the JSON, creates the base objects, and calls `render-graph`.

```clojure
(defn ^:export force-layout []
  (let [width 650, height 500]
    (.json js/d3 "force/data.json"
           (partial
             render-graph
             (.category20c (aget js/d3 "scale"))
             (create-force width height)
             (create-svg width height)))))
```

*Creating Charts for the Web*

When we visit `http://localhost:3000/force`, we get this nice visualization:

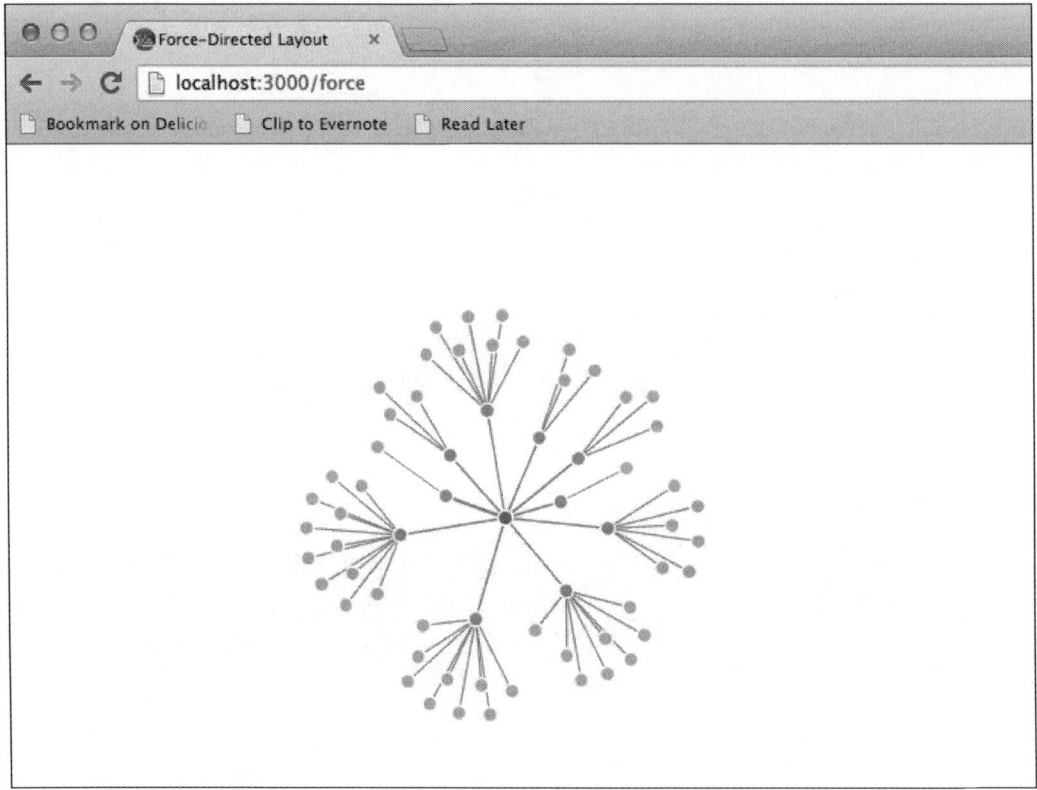

## How it works...

This is a good example of a pure D3 visualization, without NVD3. We've broken the task up into functions to make them easier to understand, but let's look at the typical D3 visualization process and see how the functions in this recipe fit into it.

1. **Create the chart**: The `create-force` function takes care of creating the controller for the chart.
2. **Call select on the container**: The `create-svg` function selects the SVG elements for rendering the graph.
3. **Call selectAll on the element we want created to contain each data point**: Two functions, `create-links` and `create-nodes`, start by calling `selectAll` on line nodes and circle nodes.
4. **Associate the data with the chart**: This happens in three places. The functions `create-links` and `create-nodes` associate the edges and nodes with their elements, and `start-force` pass a copy of both to the `force` object.

5. **Enter each data point and create the HTML using append and attr**: Again, `create-links` and `create-nodes` do this for their respective data types.

All of these work together to create the graph. Additionally, since the force-directed layout is animated, we also create a `tick` handler to update the browser with the latest positions of the objects.

## There's more...

For more about D3, see it's website at http://d3js.org/.

# Creating interactive visualizations with D3

One of the great things about working on the Web is how easy it is to make things interactive. Since D3 exposes the underlying HTML elements—it often forces you to work in them, in fact—making a D3 graph interactive is pretty straightforward: we just use standard HTML events.

For this recipe, we'll take the force-directed layout visualization of the US Census Race Data that we did in the last recipe, *Visualizing graphs with force-directed layout*, and make it interactive. We'll add a data pane to the right of the graph, and whenever the user hovers over a node, the page will display the census data from that node in the data pane.

## Getting ready

We'll start with the visualization from the last recipe, *Visualizing graphs with force-directed layout*, and add to it.

## How to do it...

Even though we're adding to an existing graph, we'll do it on a new URL, so we'll need to add a handler, route, and ClojureScript for it also.

1. Here's the handler. It also includes the HTML for the data pane.

    ```
    (defn interactive-force-plot []
      (d3-page "Interactive Force-Directive Layout"
            (str "webviz"
                 ".int_force"
                 ".interactive_force_layout();")
            [:div
             [:div#force.chart [:svg]]
             [:div#datapane]]))
    ```

2. And the route.

```
(defroutes
  site-routes
  (GET "/int-force" [] (interactive-force-plot))
  (GET "/int-force/data.json" []
       (redirect "/data/clusters.json"))
  (route/resources "/")
  (route/not-found "Page not found"))
```

3. We'll need extra style for the data panel. Open up `resources/css/style.css` and add these lines.

```
#datapane { float: right; width: 250px; }
#datapane dt { font-weight: bold; }
```

4. Now for this graph, let's open `src-cljs/webviz/int_force.cljs` and add the following namespace declaration:

```
(ns webviz.int-force
  (:require [clojure.browser.dom :as dom]
            [webviz.force :as force]
            [goog.events :as gevents]))
```

5. In the data pane, for each census item, we'll add a DT/DD element combination. We'll encapsulate that into a function since we'll define a number of these.

```
(defn dl-item [title data key]
  (let [val2000 (aget data (str key "-2000"))]
    (str "<dt>" title "</dt>"
         "<dd>" (.round js/Math (aget data key))
         " <em>(2000: "
         (.round js/Math val2000)
         ")</em>"
         "</dd>")))
```

6. Our most complicated function builds the HTML to populate the data pane.

```
(defn update-data [node]
  (let [data (aget node "data")
        content
        (str "<h2>" (aget node "name") "</h2>"
             "<dl>"
             (dl-item "Total" data "race-total")
             (dl-item "White" data "race-white")
             (dl-item "African-American" data
                      "race-black")
             (dl-item "Native American" data
                      "race-indian")
             (dl-item "Asian" data "race-asian")
             (dl-item "Hawaiian" data "race-hawaiian")
             (dl-item "Other" data "race-other")
```

```
              (dl-item "Multi-racial" data
                       "race-two-more")
              "</dl>")]
    (dom/remove-children :datapane)
    (dom/append
      (dom/get-element :datapane)
      (dom/html->dom content))))
```

7. Our `mouseover` event, which will get called whenever the user hovers over a node, pulls the `circle` element out of the event, gets the index of the node from the element, and pulls the data item out of the graph.

```
(defn on-mouseover [ev]
  (let [target (.-target ev)]
    (if (= (.-nodeName target) "circle")
      (let [n (+ (.getAttribute target "data-n"))]
        (update-data
          (aget (.-nodes @force/census-graph) n))))))
```

8. Now we create the chart using the `force-layout` function from the last recipe, and then we add an event handler to the chart's parent.

```
(defn ^:export interactive-force-layout []
  (force/force-layout)
  (gevents/listen (dom/get-element "force")
                  (.-MOUSEOVER gevents/EventType)
                  on-mouseover))
```

When we visit `http://localhost:3000/int-force` and hover over one of the circles, we get this:

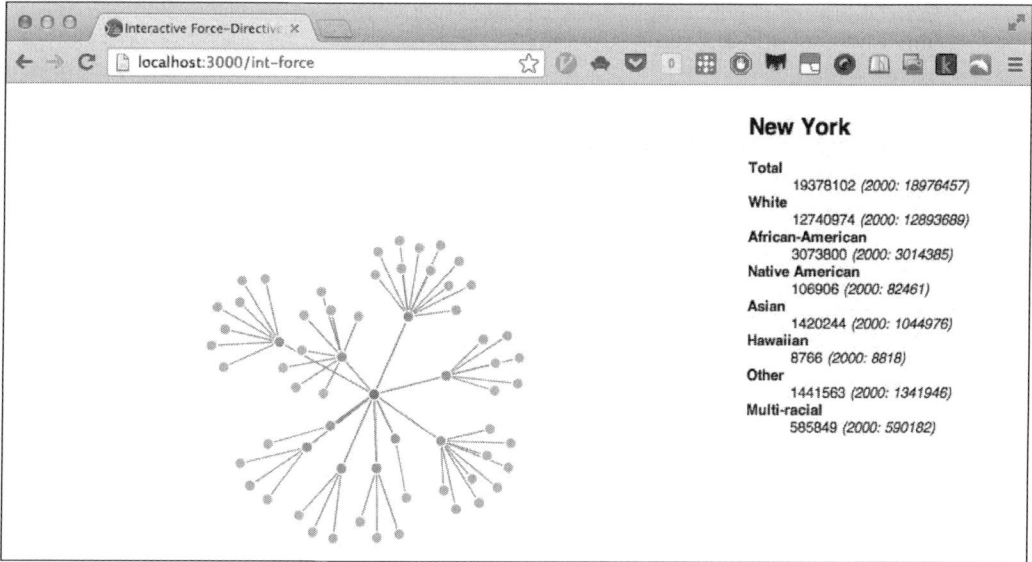

## How it works...

This recipe works the same way that interaction works on any web page. We listen to events that the user generates on certain HTML tags. In this case, we pay attention to whenever the mouse moves over a node on the graph. We bind our event handler to that event in Step 7.

When the event is triggered, the event handler is called. In our example, the event handler function, `on-mouseover`, is defined in Step 6.

The event handler retrieves the data for the node that the user moved their mouse cursor over, and it calls `update-data` and `dl-item` to build the HTML structure to display the data about that node.

We've mentioned before that the Google Closure library comes with ClojureScript. In this recipe, we use its events module (http://docs.closure-library.googlecode.com/git/namespace_goog_events.html) to bind `on-mouseover` to the appropriate event.

We also use the ClojureScript `clojure.browser.dom` namespace to delete and create HTML elements on the fly. This namespace is a thin, Clojure-friendly wrapper around the Closure library for manipulating the DOM, goog.dom (http://docs.closure-library.googlecode.com/git/namespace_goog_dom.html).

Finally, we also interface a few times with JavaScript itself. We do that by prefixing the name of the JavaScript object or module with `js`: js/Math, for example.

## There's more...

- Google's Closure library is bundled with ClojureScript and provides a lot of functionality for manipulating the DOM and other common tasks for writing in-browser web apps. You can learn more about this library at https://developers.google.com/closure/library/.
- The standard ClojureScript namespace `clojure.browser.dom` provides a Clojure-like wrapper over some of the Closure library's DOM manipulation functionality. You can see what's in this library by browsing it at https://github.com/clojure/clojurescript/blob/master/src/cljs/clojure/browser/dom.cljs.
- A good resource for working with HTML, CSS, and JavaScript is the Mozilla Developer Network. You can find it at https://developer.mozilla.org/.

# Index

## Symbols

$cljsbuild option  295
$continue option  92
:$eq (equal) option  173
$fail option  92
$ function  169
$group-by function
  about  174
  used, for grouping data  174
:$gte (greater than or equal)  173
:$gt (greater than)  173
$join
  multple datasets, projecting from  177-179
:$lte (less than or equal)  173
:$lt (less than)  173
:$ne (not equal)  173
$optimizations parameter  295
$rollup
  summary statistics, generating with  182-184
$where
  datasets, filtering with  171-173
\D{0,2}, regular expressions  43
(\d{3}), regular expressions  43
(\d{4}), regular expressions  43
(\d{3}) flag  43
<| function  63
->options function  235
(?x) flag  43
Ø, sine wave function  204
ω, sine wave function  204

## A

accum-counts function  115
accum-hash function  31
acid-code function  63
acid-code parser  64
adapters  289
agent function  73
agent-ints function  86
agents
  and STM, combining  77-79
  errors, recovering from  91
  program complexity, managing with  73-75
aggregate operators
  creating  145
alert function  295
Alexandru Nedelcu
  URL  255
Amazon Web Services (AWS)  153
AMDs tutorial
  URL  120
Ant
  URL  213
Apache Ant
  URL  216
Apache HDFS. *See also* HDFS
Apache HDFS
  data, distributing with  134-137
app  290
Apriori algorithm
  data associations, finding with  258, 260
  URL  260
Apriori class  259
ARFF file
  loading, into Weka  234-236
ARFF format  236
A, sine wave function  204
atom  82
Attribute-Relation File Format. *See* ARFF format

**Avro**
  URL 139

# B

**bar charts**
  creating, with Incanter 266
  creating, with NVD3 302-305
  non-numeric data, graphing 266-268
**benchmarking**
  with Criterium 123-125
**Benford's law**
  about 207
  testing, URL for 209
  used, for finding data errors 208, 209
  wikipedia, URL 209
  working 209
**benford-test function 209**
**body mass index (BMI) 197**
**bootstrapping**
  about 194
  used, for validating sample statistics 195, 196
**Brown Corpus 79**
**buffer operators**
  creating 145

# C

**C2 project**
  URL 296
**Calx**
  GPU, harnessing with 116-118
  URL 116
**Cascading**
  URL 128
**Cascalog**
  complex queries, with 139-141
  CSV files, parsing with 137-139
  data, aggregating with 142, 143
  data, querying with 132-134
  data, transforming with 151
  distributed processing with 129-132
  operators, defining 143
  queries, composing 146-149
  URL 128
**Cascalog workflows**
  errors, handling in 149, 150

**census data file**
  URL, for downloading 146
**charts**
  customizing, with JFreeChart 276
**Clojars**
  URL 9
**Clojuratica**
  Mathematica functions, calling from 218
  Mathematica scripts, evaluating from 220, 221
  Mathematica setting up, for Linux 212-215
  Mathematica setting up, for Mac OS X 212-215
  Mathematica setting up, for Windows 216, 217
  matrices, sending to Mathematica 219, 220
  URL 216
**Clojure**
  about 12
  R files, evaluating from 228-230
  R functions, calling from 226
  R, plotting in 230, 232
  R, setting up 224, 225
  talking to, by setting up R 224
  URL 216
**Clojure data structures**
  loading, into datasets 161-163
**Clojure documentation**
  Agents and Asynchronous Actions, URL 93
  URL 75
**Clojure library**
  URL 26
**ClojureScript**
  setting up 293-296
  URL 286, 293
**clojure.string library 42, 48**
**Cloud**
  Cascalog queries executing, with Pallet 152-157
**columns**
  selecting, with Incanter macro $ 168, 169
**columns, Weka datasets**
  hiding 238, 239
  removing 238
  renaming 237
**comma-separated values.** *See* **CSV**

**commute**
  used, for getting better performance  76
**companions**
  URL  130
**Compojure**
  about  285
  data, serving with  286
  URL  285, 290
**Compojure API documentation**
  URL  290
**Compojure wiki**
  URL  290
**compute-file function  82**
**compute-frequencies  82**
**compute-report function  82**
**concurrent processing  95**
**concurrent programs**
  about  68
  debugging, with watchers  90, 91
**configuration options**
  URL  296
**correct function  60**
**Coursera**
  about  182
  URL  182
**create-force function  312**
**create-svg function  312**
**Criterium**
  benchmarking with  123-125
  documentation, URL  125
  URL  123
**CSV**
  data, reading into Incanter datasets  9, 10
  data, saving as  176
  datasets, saving to  175, 176
**CSV file**
  loading, into Weka  234-236
  parsing, with Cascalog  137-139
**CSV format**
  URL  169
**currency data**
  loading  37, 38

# D

**D3**
  about  296
  URL  286, 302
  used, for creating interactive
      visualizations  313-316
**d3-externs project**
  URL  295
**d3-page function  299**
**data**
  aggregating, from different formats  34, 35
  aggregating, with Cascalog  142, 143
  associations, finding with Apriori
      algorithm  258, 260
  classifying, Naive Bayesian classifier
      used  253, 254
  classifying, with decision trees  250, 252
  classifying, with SVMs  255, 257
  cleaning, with regular expressions  42
  consistency, maintaining with synonym
      maps  44, 45
  distributing, with Apache HDFS  134-137
  grouping, $group-by used  174
  pre-processing  80, 81
  querying, with Cascalog  132-134
  reading from Excel, with Incanter  12, 13
  reading from JDBC databases  13, 15
  saving, as CSV  176
  saving, as JSON  176
  scraping, from tables in web pages  19-22
  server, running  288, 289
  serving  287
  serving, with Compojure  286
  serving, with Ring  286
  transforming, with Cascalog  151
  validating, with Valip  64, 65
  web application, configuring  287
  web application, setting up  287
**database, Incanter**
  loading  160, 161
**Data-Driven Documents.** *See* **D3**
**data errors**
  finding, with Benfords law  207
**data formats**
  custom data formats, parsing  61-64

**datasets**
  Clojure data structures, loading  161-163
  converting, to matrices  164-166
  filtering, with $where  171-173
  large data sets, lazily processing  54, 55
  large data sets, sampling from  56
  multiple datasets, projecting from,
    with $join  177-179
  saving, to CSV  175, 176
  saving, to JSON  175, 176
  viewing, view used  163, 164
  web page, URL  266
**dates and times**
  normalizing  51, 53
**David Blei**
  URL  248
**David Cabana**
  URL  216
**David Liebkes talk**
  URL  99
**DBPedia**
  URL  29
**decision trees**
  data, classifying with  250, 252
**defanalysis macro  246, 251**
**delete-char  60**
**deref function  69**
**distributed processing**
  with Cascalog  129-132
  with Hadoop  129-132
**domain-specific language (DSL)  19**
**dosync block  72**
**DRY-up (Don't Repeat Yourself)  242**
**duplicate data**
  identifying  45-48
  removing  45-48
**dynamic charts**
  creating, with Incanter  283, 284

# E

**Enlive library**
  URL  19
**equations**
  adding, to Incanter charts  272, 273

**errors**
  continuing on  92
  custom error handler, using  92, 93
  falling on  92
  handling, in Cascalog workflows  149, 150
  recovering from, in agents  91
**EuroClojure 2012**
  URL  113
**exact count**
  sampling for  56, 57
**Excel**
  data reading from, with Incanter  12, 13
**exchange rates**
  scraping  35-37

# F

**FASTA data**
  URL  61
**filter operators**
  creating  144
**fix-headers function  27**
**force-directed layouts**
  used, for visualizing graphs  308-313
**formats**
  data aggregating from  34, 35
  triple store, creating  35
**function plots**
  creating, with Incanter  270, 271
**functions**
  creating, from Mathematica  221, 222
**future-call  70**
**fuzzy-dist function  47**
**fuzzy string matching function  47**

# G

**get-dataset function  161**
**getting-data.core namespace  8**
**Giorgio Ingargiola of Temple University**
  URL  253
**Git**
  URL  42
**Glenn Murray**
  URL  152
**Google Closure library**
  URL  316

**Google Finance**
  URL 189
**GPU**
  code, writing in C 119
  harnessing, with Calx 116-118
  harnessing, with OpenCL 116-118
**graphs**
  visualizing, with force-directed layouts 308-313

## H

**Hadoop**
  distributed processing with 129-132
  URL 128
  URL, for downloading and installing 134
**hadoop command 136**
**Hadoop Distributed File System.** *See* **HDFS**
**handlers 289**
**Harvard**
  URL 182
**HDFS 129**
**header-keyword function 27**
**Heroku**
  URL 286
**hfs-tap function 139**
**Hiccup**
  HTML, creating with 290-292
  site and wiki, URL 292
  URL 286
**Hiccup DSL 292**
**HierarchicalClusterer class 245, 248**
**hierarchical clusters**
  finding, in Weka 245-248
  wikipedia, URL 248
**histograms**
  creating, with Incanter 268-270
  creating, with NVD3 305-308
**home page**
  for screen, URL 296
**How to Write a Spelling Corrector**
  URL 57
**HTML**
  creating, with Hiccup 290-292

## I

**immutable 68**

**Incanter**
  about 8
  bar charts, creating with 266
  charts, equations adding to 272, 273
  data, reading from Excel 12, 13
  datasets, XML data reading into 16-18
  documentation, URL 12
  function plots, creating with 270, 271
  histograms, creating with 268-270
  infix formulas, using 166-168
  parallelizing processing with 100-102
  sample database, loading 160, 161
  SOMs, clustering with 248, 249
  URL 159
  used, for creating dynamic charts 283, 284
  zoo, used, for working with time series data 189-191
**Incanter API documentation**
  URL 161, 264
**Incanter charts**
  equations, adding to 272, 273
**incanter.charts/function-plot function 271**
**incanter datasets**
  CSV data, reading into 9, 10
  JSON data, reading into 11, 12
**Incanter macro $**
  columns, selecting with 168, 169
  rows, selecting with 170, 171
**incanter.stats/bootstrap function 195**
**Incanter wiki**
  on Github, URL 264
**Incanter zoo**
  used, for working with time series data 189-191
**incanter.zoo/roll-mean function 191**
**index-page function 294**
**infix formulas**
  using, in Incater 166-168
**input**
  managing, with sized queues 93, 94
**insert-split 60**
**interactive visualizations**
  creating, with D3 313-316
**Investigative Reporters and Editors' US census site**
  URL 70

**ionosphere dataset**
  information, URL  258
  URL, for downloading  256
**IRE download page**
  for census data, URL  169
**Iris dataset**
  URL  246

## J

**Java Development Kit**
  URL  216
**JavaDocs**
  for pattern class, URL  44
**JavaScript Object Notation.** *See* **JSON data**
**JDBC databases**
  data, reading from  13, 15
**Jetty**
  URL  286
**JFreeChart**
  library, URL  262
  used, for customizing charts  276
**jobtracker node  155**
**Joda Java library**
  URL  51
**JSON**
  and XML, comparing  19
  data, reading into Incanter datasets  11, 12
  data, saving as  176
  datasets, saving to  175, 176

## K

**Kevin Lyanghs C2**
  URL  262
**K-means clustering**
  about  239, 243
  macros, building  244, 245
  results, analyzing  244
  URL  245
  used, for discovering data groups  240-243

## L

**LaTeX string**
  about  272
  URL  273
**lazy-read-csv  55**

**least squares linear regression  199**
**lein-cljsbuild plugin  293**
**Leiningen**
  URL  8
**lein new command  8**
**LibSVM class**
  URL  258
**linear regression**
  about  197
  least squares linear regression used  199
**linear relationships**
  modeling  197-199
**lines**
  adding, to scatter charts  273-275
**Linux**
  Mathematica setting up, to talk to
    Clojuratica  212-215
**load-arff function**
  URL  246

## M

**Mac OS X**
  Mathematica setting up, to talk to
    Clojuratica  212-215
**macros**
  building  244, 245
**Mandelbrot  96**
**map concatenation operations**
  creating  144
**map operators  144**
**MapReduce**
  URL  128
**Mathematica**
  about  212
  functions, calling from Clojuratica  218
  functions, creating from  221, 222
  functions, processing in parallel  222, 223
  matrices sending, from Clojuratica  219, 220
  scripts, evaluating from Clojuratica  220, 221
  setting up, to talk to Clojuratica for
    Linux  212-215
  setting up, to talk to Clojuratica for Mac
    OS X  212-215
  setting up, to talk to Clojuratica for
    Windows  216, 217
  URL  212, 216
**math macro  223**

**matrices**
  datasets, converting to 164-166
  sending to Mathematica, from
        Clojuratica 219, 220
**Maven**
  URL 213, 224
**middleware 289**
**Monte Carlo simulations**
  estimating with 105
  partitioning, for improving pmap
        performance 102-105
  URL 105
**mouseover event 315**
**Mozilla Developer Network**
  URL 316
**multimodal Bayesian distributions**
  about 204
  modeling 205-207
**mushroom dataset**
  URL 253

# N

**Naive Bayesian classifier**
  used, for classifying data 253, 254
**National Highway Traffic Safety**
       **Administration**
  URL 200
**noise**
  decreasing, by smoothing variables 192, 194
**non-linear relationships**
  modeling 200
  modeling, steps 201-203
**non-numeric data**
  in bar charts, graphing 266-268
**numbers**
  normalizing 48, 49
**NVD3**
  histograms, creating with 305-308
  URL 286, 296, 302
  used, for creating bar charts 302-305
  used, for creating scatter plots 296-300
  working 302

# O

**object 28**

**online summary statistics**
  generating, with reducers 114-116
**on-mouseover 316**
**OpenCL**
  GPU, harnessing with 116-118
  URL 116
**operators, Cascalog**
  about 143
  aggregate operators, creating 145
  buffer operators, creating 145
  filter operators, creating 144
  map concatenation operations, creating 144
  map operators, creating 144
  parallel aggregate operators, creating 145
**optimal partition size**
  finding, with simulated annealing 106-110
**optimization algorithms 110**
**Oracle**
  tutorial, URL 16
**output-points 97**

# P

**Pallet**
  Cascalog queries, executing in
        Cloud 152-157
  URL 128, 152
**pallet-hadoop-example namespace 154**
**Pallet-Hadoop library**
  URL 157
**Pallet Hadoop project**
  URL 152
  URL, for downloading 152
**parallel aggregate operators**
  creating 145, 146
**Parallel Colt Java library**
  URL 100
**parallelism 68**
**parallelizing**
  reducers 110-113
**parallelizing processing**
  with Incanter 100-102
  with pmap 96-99
**parallel programming 96**
**parse-ez library**
  URL 61

**PCA**
  about 262
  using, to graph multi-dimensional data 279-282
**percentage**
  sampling by 56
**pipeline**
  processing 18
**pmap**
  data, chunking 106
  parallelizing processing with 96-99
**pmap performance**
  improving, by partitioning Monte Carlo simulations 102-105
**PNG**
  intergraphs, saving to 278, 279
**predicate 28**
**Principal Component Analysis.** *See* **PCA**
**processing**
  tracking, watchers used 87-89
**program complexity**
  managing, with agents 73-75
  managing, with STM 69-73
**project**
  creating 8, 9
**Project Gutenberg**
  URL 192
**Prolog**
  URL 134

## Q

**queries, Cascalog**
  complex queries 139-141
  composing 146-149
  executing in Cloud, with Pallet 152-157

## R

**R**
  about 212
  Clojure, setting up 225
  configuring, to talk to Clojure 224, 225
  files, evaluating from Clojure 228-230
  functions, calling from Clojure 226
  plotting in, from Clojure 230, 232
  URL 212
  vectors, passing 227, 228

**R. Berwick**
  SVMs, URL 258
**RDF data**
  about 26, 27
  reading, with SPARQL 29-33
**read-eval-print-loop.** *See* **REPL**
**reducers**
  online summary statistics, generating 114-116
  parallelizing with 110-113
**ref function 69**
**RegexPlant**
  online tester, URL 44
**regular expressions**
  \D? 43
  \D{0,2} 43
  (\d{3}) 43
  (\d{3}) flag 43
  (\d{4}) 43
  (?x) flag 43
  data, cleaning with 42
  Java tutorial, URL 44
  resources, URL 44
**REPL 8**
**replace-split 60**
**rescale-by-group function 51**
**Resource Description Format.** *See* **RDF data**
**R gallery**
  URL 232
**Rich Hickeys blog spot**
  URL 113
**Ring**
  about 285
  data, serving with 286
  URL 285, 286
**Ring API documentation**
  URL 290
**Ring wiki**
  URL 290
**routes**
  using 288
**rows**
  selecting, with Incanter macro $ 170, 171
**R qr function**
  about 227
  URL 227
**Rserve package 226**

## S

**sampling**
   by exact count 56
   by percentage 56
**Sam Ritchie**
   URL 152
**scatter charts**
   lines, adding 273-275
**scatter plots**
   creating, with NVD3 296-300
**sequence files**
   URL 139
**Sesame**
   URL 26
**SimpleKMeans class**
   URL 245
**simulated annealing**
   optimal partition size, finding with 106-110
**sine wave function**
   A 204
   t 204
   Ø 204
   ω 204
**site-routes** 290
**sized queues**
   input, managing with 93, 94
**Software Transactional Memory.** *See* **STM**
**SOMs**
   about 248, 249
   algorithm, using in core library 249
**som/som-batch-train function** 250
**source tap, Cascalog**
   URL 139
**SPARQL**
   RDF data, reading with 29-33
**species attribute** 250
**spelling errors**
   fixing 57-61
**StackExchange**
   URL 215
**Stat Trek**
   URL 199
**STM**
   about 68
   and agents, combining 77-79
   program complexity, managing 69-73
   safe side effects 82-84
**subject** 28
**summary statistics**
   generating, with $rollup 182, 184
**Support vector machines.** *See* **SVMs**
**SVMs**
   about 255
   data, classifying with 255, 257
**synonym maps**
   used, for maintaining data consistency 44, 45

## T

**tap sink** 132
**term frequency-inverse document frequency.** *See* **tf-idf**
**TextDelimited scheme object** 139
**textual data**
   scraping, from web pages 23-25
**tf-idf** 50
**thread starvation** 82
**thunk function**
   URL 72
**times.** *See* **dates and times**
**time series data**
   working with, Incanter zoo used 189-191
**tmux**
   URL 296
**to-dataset function** 163
**to-matrix function** 166
**Tom Germano**
   URL 250
**transpose-char** 60
**trap** 149
**triple store**
   creating 35
**t, sine wave function** 204
**type hints** 120, 121, 122

## U

**upper-case function** 44

## V

**validators**
   used, for maintaining data consistency 84-87
**Valip**
   URL 64
   used, for validating data 64, 65
**values**
   rescaling 50, 51
**variable binding 134**
**variables**
   differencing, to show changes 185, 186
   scaling 186
   scaling, ways for 187, 188
   smotthing, to decrese noise 192, 194
**vectors**
   passing, into R 227, 228
**view**
   used, for viewing datasets 163, 164
**Virginia census data**
   URl, for downloading 185

## W

**watchers**
   concurrent programs, debugging with 90, 91
   used, for tracking processing 87-89
**web application**
   configuring 287
   setting up 287
**web pages**
   data, scraping from tables 19-22
   textual data, scraping 23-25

**Weka**
   about 234
   ARFF file, loading 234-236
   CSV file, loading 234-236
   documentation, URL 260
   hierarchical clusters, finding 245, 247
   machine learning and data mining library URL 234
   wiki, URL 240
**weka.clusters.SimpleKMeans class 240**
**Weka datasets**
   columns, hiding 238, 239
   columns, removing 238
   columns, renaming 237
**Wikipedia page**
   URL 114
**Windows**
   Mathematica setting up, to talk to Clojuratica 216, 217
**within-cluster sum of squared errors (WCSS) 244**

## X

**XML**
   and JSON, comparing 19
   data, reading into Incanter databases 16
**X-Rates**
   URL 34

## Z

**zipper**
   about 18
   structure, navigating with 18

# Thank you for buying
# Clojure Data Analysis Cookbook

## About Packt Publishing

Packt, pronounced 'packed', published its first book "*Mastering phpMyAdmin for Effective MySQL Management*" in April 2004 and subsequently continued to specialize in publishing highly focused books on specific technologies and solutions.

Our books and publications share the experiences of your fellow IT professionals in adapting and customizing today's systems, applications, and frameworks. Our solution based books give you the knowledge and power to customize the software and technologies you're using to get the job done. Packt books are more specific and less general than the IT books you have seen in the past. Our unique business model allows us to bring you more focused information, giving you more of what you need to know, and less of what you don't.

Packt is a modern, yet unique publishing company, which focuses on producing quality, cutting-edge books for communities of developers, administrators, and newbies alike. For more information, please visit our website: www.packtpub.com.

## About Packt Open Source

In 2010, Packt launched two new brands, Packt Open Source and Packt Enterprise, in order to continue its focus on specialization. This book is part of the Packt Open Source brand, home to books published on software built around Open Source licences, and offering information to anybody from advanced developers to budding web designers. The Open Source brand also runs Packt's Open Source Royalty Scheme, by which Packt gives a royalty to each Open Source project about whose software a book is sold.

## Writing for Packt

We welcome all inquiries from people who are interested in authoring. Book proposals should be sent to author@packtpub.com. If your book idea is still at an early stage and you would like to discuss it first before writing a formal book proposal, contact us; one of our commissioning editors will get in touch with you.

We're not just looking for published authors; if you have strong technical skills but no writing experience, our experienced editors can help you develop a writing career, or simply get some additional reward for your expertise.

## Statistical Analysis with R Beginner's Guide

ISBN: 978-1-84951-208-4  Paperback: 300 pages

Take control of your data and produce superior statistical analyses with R

1. An easy introduction for people who are new to R, with plenty of strong examples for you to work through
2. This book will take you on a journey to learn R as the strategist for an ancient Chinese kingdom!
3. A step by step guide to understand R, its benefits, and how to use it to maximize the impact of your data analysis
4. A practical guide to conduct and communicate your data analysis with R in the most effective manner

## Hadoop MapReduce Cookbook

ISBN: 978-1-84951-728-7  Paperback: 300 pages

Recipes for analyzing large and complex datasets with Hadoop MapReduce

1. Learn to process large and complex data sets, starting simply, then diving in deep
2. Solve complex big data problems such as classifications, finding relationships, online marketing and recommendations
3. More than 50 Hadoop MapReduce recipes, presented in a simple and straightforward manner, with step-by-step instructions and real world examples

Please check www.PacktPub.com for information on our titles

## Hadoop Real-World Solutions Cookbook

ISBN: 978-1-84951-912-0    Paperback: 316 pages

Realistic, simple code examples to solve problems at scale with Hadoop and related technologies

1. Solutions to common problems when working in the Hadoop environment
2. Recipes for (un)loading data, analytics, and troubleshooting
3. In depth code examples demonstrating various analytic models, analytic solutions, and common best practices

## Hadoop Beginner's Guide

ISBN: 978-1-84951-730-0    Paperback: 398 pages

Learn how to crunch big data to extract meaning from the data avalanche

1. Learn tools and techniques that let you approach big data with relish and not fear
2. Shows how to build a complete infrastructure to handle your needs as your data grows
3. Hands-on examples in each chapter give the big picture while also giving direct experience

Please check **www.PacktPub.com** for information on our titles

Printed in Great Britain
by Amazon.co.uk, Ltd.,
Marston Gate.